Arline Niles

Febr. 21 - 1899.

"I stood in Venice, on the Bridge of Sighs;
A palace and a prison on each hand."

Page 177.

CHILDE HAROLD'S PILGRIMAGE.

A Romaunt.

BY

LORD BYRON.

A New Edition, with all the Notes,

EDITED BY

THOMAS MOORE.

NEW YORK:
THOMAS Y. CROWELL & CO.

L'univers est une espèce de livre, dont on n'a lu que la première page quand on n'a vu que son pays. J'en ai feuilleté un assez grand nombre, que j'ai trouvé également mauvaises. Cet examen ne m'a point été infructueux. Je haïssais ma patrie. Toutes les impertinences des peuples divers, parmi lesquels j'ai vécu, m'ont reconcilié avec elle. Quand je n'aurais tiré d'autre bénéfice de mes voyages que celui-là, je n'en regretterais ni les frais ni les fatigues.

LE COSMOPOLITE.*

---

* [Par M. de Montborn Paris, 1798. Lord Byron somewhere calls it "an amusing little volume, full of French flippancy." — E.]

PREFACE

[TO THE FIRST AND SECOND CANTOS.]

THE following poem was written, for the most part, amidst the scenes which it attempts to describe. I was begun in Albania; and the parts relative to Spain and Portugal were composed from the author's ob servations in those countries. Thus much it may be necessary to state for the correctness of the descriptions. The scenes attempted to be sketched are in Spain, Portugal, Epirus, Acarnania, and Greece. There, for the present, the poem stops: its reception will determine whether the author may venture to conduct his readers to the capital of the East, through Ionia and Phrygia: these two cantos are merely experimental.

A fictitious character is introduced for the sake of giving some connection to the piece; which, however, makes no pretension to regularity. It has been suggested to me by friends, on whose opinions I set a high value, that in this fictitious character, "Childe Harold," I may incur the suspicion of having intended some real personage; this I beg leave, once for all, to disclaim—Harold is the child of imagination, for the purpose I have stated. In some very trivial particulars, and those merely local, there might be grounds for such a notion; but in the main points, I should hope, none whatever.

It is almost superfluous to mention that the appellation "Childe," as "Childe Waters," "Childe Childers," &c., is used as more consonant with the old structure of versification which I have adopted. The "Good Night," in the beginning of the first canto, was suggested by "Lord Maxwell's Good Night," in the Border Minstrelsy, edited by Mr. Scott.[1]

With the different poems which have been published on Spanish subjects, there may be found some slight coincidence in the first part, which treats of the Peninsula, but it can only be casual; as, with the exception of a few concluding stanzas, the whole of this poem was written in the Levant.

The stanza of Spenser, according to one of our most successful poets, admits of every variety. Dr. Beattie makes the following observation;—"Not long ago, I began a poem in the style and stanza of Spenser, in which I propose to give full scope to my inclination, and be either droll or pathetic, descriptive or sentimental, tender or satirical, as the humour strikes me; for, if I mistake not, the measure which I have adopted admits equally of all these kinds of composition."[2]—Strengthened in my opinion by such authority, and by the example of some in the highest order of Italian poets, I shall make no apology for attempts at similar variations in the following composition; satisfied that if they are unsuccessful, their failure must be in the execution, rather than in the design sanctioned by the practice of Ariosto, Thomson, and Beattie.

London, February, 1812.

[1] [See Sir Walter Scott's Poetical Works, vol. ii. p. 141, ed. 1834.]

[2] Beattie's Letters.

ADDITION TO THE PREFACE

I HAVE now waited till almost all our periodical journals have distributed their usual portion of criticism. To the justice of the generality of their criticisms I have nothing to object: it would ill become me to quarrel with their very slight degree of censure, when, perhaps, if they had been less kind they had been more candid. Returning, therefore, to all and each my best thanks for their liberality, on one point alone shall I venture an observation. Amongst the many objections justly urged to the very indifferent character of the "vagrant Childe," (whom, notwithstanding many hints to the contrary, I still maintain to be a fictitious personage,) it has been stated, that, besides the anachronism, he is very *unknightly*, as the times of the knights were times of love, honour, and so forth. Now, it so happens that the good old times, when "l'amour du bon vieux tems, l'amour antique" flourished, were the most profligate of all possible centuries. Those who have any doubt on this subject may consult Sainte-Palaye, *passim*, and more particularly vol. ii. p. 69.[1] The vows of chivalry were no better kept than any other vows whatsoever;

[1] ["Qu'on lise dans l'Auteur du roman de Gérard de Roussillon, en Provençal, les détails très-circonstanciés dans lesquels il entre sur la réception faite par le Comte Gérard à l'ambassadeur du roi Charles; on y verra des particularités singulières, qui donnent une étrange idee des mœurs et de la politesse de ces siècles aussi corrompus qu'ignorans."—*Mémoires sur l'Ancienne Chevalerie*, par M. de la Curne de Sainte-Palaye, Paris, 1781.]

and the songs of the troubadours were not more decent, and certainly were much less refined, than those of Ovid. The "Cours d'amour, parlemens d'amour, ou de courtesie et de gentilesse" had much more of love than of courtesy or gentleness. See Roland on the same subject with Sainte-Palaye. Whatever other objection may be urged to that most unamiable personage, Childe Harold, he was so far perfectly knightly in his attributes—"No waiter, but a knight templar."[1] By-the-by, I fear that Sir Tristram and Sir Lancelot were no better than they should be, although very poetical personages and true knights "sans peur," though not "sans reproche." If the story of the institution of the "Garter" be not a fable, the knights of that order have for several centuries borne the badge of a Countess of Salisbury, of indifferent memory. So much for chivalry. Burke need not have regretted that its days are over, though Marie-Antoinette was quite as chaste as most of those in whose honours lances were shivered, and knights unhorsed.

Before the days of Bayard, and down to those of Sir Joseph Banks, (the most chaste and celebrated of ancient and modern times,) few exceptions will be found to this statement; and I fear a little investigation will teach us not to regret these monstrous mummeries of the middle ages.

I now leave "Childe Harold" to live his day, such as he is; it had been more agreeable, and certainly more easy, to have drawn an amiable character. It had been easy to varnish over his faults, to make him do more and express less; but he never was intended as an example, further than to show, that early

[1] The Rovers, or the Double Arrangement.—[By Messrs. Canning and Frere; first published in the Anti-jacobin, or Weekly Examiner.]

perversion of mind and morals leads to satiety of past pleasures and disappointment in new ones, and that even the beauties of nature, and the stimulus of travel (except ambition, the most powerful of all excitements) are lost on a soul so constituted, or rather misdirected. Had I proceeded with the poem, this character would have deepened as he drew to the close; for the outline which I once meant to fill up for him was, with some exceptions, the sketch of a modern Timon,[1] perhaps a poetical Zeluco.[2]

London, 1813.

[1] [In one of his early poems—"Childish Recollections," Lord Byron compares himself to the Athenian misanthrope, of whose bitter apophthegms many are upon record, though no authentic particulars of his life have come down to us:—

> "Weary of love, of life, devoured with spleen,
> I rest a perfect Timon, not nineteen," &c.]

[2] [It was Dr Moore's object, in this powerful romance, (now unjustly neglected,) to trace the fatal effects resulting from a fond mother's unconditional compliance with the humours and passions of an only child. With high advantages of person, birth, fortune, and ability, Zeluco is represented as miserable, through every scene of life, owing to the spirit of unbridled self-indulgence thus pampered in infancy.]

TO IANTHE.[1]

Not in those climes where I have late been straying,
Though beauty long hath there been matchless deem'd;
Not in those visions to the heart displaying
Forms which it sighs but to have only dream'd,
Hath aught like thee in truth or fancy seem'd;
Nor, having seen thee, shall I vainly seek
To paint those charms which varied as they beam'd—
To such as see thee not my words were weak;
To those who gaze on thee what language could they speak?

Ah! mayst thou ever be what now thou art,
Nor unbeseem the promise of thy spring,
As fair in form, as warm yet pure in heart,
Love's image upon earth without his wing,
And guileless beyond Hope's imagining!
And surely she who now so fondly rears
Thy youth, in thee thus hourly brightening,
Beholds the rainbow of her future years,
Before whose heavenly hues all sorrow disappears.

[1] [The Lady Charlotte Harley, second daughter of Edward, fifth Earl of Oxford, (now Lady Charlotte Bacon,) in the autumn of 1812, when these lines were addressed to her, had not completed her eleventh year. Mr. Westall's portrait of the juvenile beauty, painted at Lord Byron's request, is engraved in "Finden's Illustrations of the Life and Works of Lord Byron."]

Young Peri[1] of the west!—'tis well for me
My years already doubly number thine;
My loveless eye unmoved may gaze on thee,
And safely view thy ripening beauties shine;
Happy, I ne'er shall see them in decline;
Happier, that while all younger hearts shall bleed,
Mine shall escape the doom thine eyes assign
To those whose admiration shall succeed,
But mix'd with pangs to Love's even loveliest hours decreed.

Oh! let that eye, which, wild as the gazelle's,[2]
Now brightly bold or beautifully shy,
Wins as it wanders, dazzles where it dwells,
Glance o'er this page, nor to my verse deny
That smile for which my breast might vainly sigh
Could I to thee be ever more than friend:
This much, dear maid, accord; nor question why
To one so young my strain I would commend,
But bid me with my wreath one matchless lily blend.

Such is thy name with this my verse entwined;
And long as kinder eyes a look shall cast
On Harold's page, Ianthe's here enshrined
Shall thus be first beheld, forgotten last:
My days once number'd, should this homage past
Attract thy fairy fingers near the lyre
Of him who hail'd thee, loveliest as thou wast,
Such is the most my memory may desire;
Though more than Hope can claim, could Friendship less require?

[1] [*Peri*, the Persian term for a beautiful intermediate order of beings, is generally supposed to be another form of our own word *Fairy*.]

[2] [A species of the antelope. "You have the eyes of a gazelle," is considered all over the East as the greatest compliment that can be paid to a woman.]

CHILDE HAROLD'S PILGRIMAGE

CANTO THE FIRST.

CHILDE HAROLD'S PILGRIMAGE

CANTO THE FIRST.

I.

Oh, thou! in Hellas deem'd of heavenly birth,
Muse! form'd or fabled at the minstrel's will!
Since shamed full oft by later lyres on earth,
Mine dares not call thee from thy sacred hill:
Yet there I've wander'd by thy vaunted rill;
Yes! sigh'd o'er Delphi's long deserted shrine,[1]
Where, save that feeble fountain, all is still;
Nor mote my shell awake the weary Nine
To grace so plain a tale—this lowly lay of mine.[2]

[1] The little village of Castri stands partly on the site of Delphi. Along the path of the mountain, from Chrysso, are the remains of sepulchres hewn in and from the rock. "One," said the guide, "of a king who broke his neck hunting." His majesty had certainly chosen the fittest spot for such an achievement. A little above Castri is a cave, supposed the Pythian, of immense depth; the upper part of it is paved, and now a cow-house. On the other side of Castri stands a Greek monastery; some way above which is the cleft in the rock, with a range of caverns difficult of ascent, and apparently leading to the interior of the mountain; probably to the Corycian Cavern mentioned by Pausanias. From this part descend the fountain and the "Dews of Castalie."—["We were sprinkled," says Mr. Hobhouse, "with the spray of the immortal rill, and here, if anywhere, should have felt the poetic inspiration: we drank deep, too, of the spring; but—(I can answer for myself) —without feeling sensible of any extraordinary effect."—E.]

[2] [This stanza is not in the original MS.]

II.

Whilome in Albion's isle there dwelt a youth,
Who ne in virtue's ways did take delight;
But spent his days in riot most uncouth,
And vex'd with mirth the drowsy ear of Night.
Ah me! in sooth he was a shameless wight,
Sore given to revel and ungodly glee;
Few earthly things found favour in his sight[1]
Save concubines and carnal companie,
And flaunting wassailers of high and low degree

III.

Childe Harold[2] was he hight:—but whence his name
And lineage long, it suits me not to say;
Suffice it, that perchance they were of fame,
And had been glorious in another day:
But one sad losel soils a name for aye,
However mighty in the olden time;
Nor all that heralds rake from coffin'd clay,
Nor florid prose, nor honied lies of rhyme,
Can blazon evil deeds, or consecrate a crime

IV.

Childe Harold bask'd him in the noontide sun,
Disporting there like any other fly;
Nor deem'd before his little day was done
One blast might chill him into misery.
But long ere scarce a third of his pass'd by,
Worse than adversity the Childe befell,
He felt the fulness of satiety:
Then loathed he in his native land to dwell,
Which seem'd to him more lone than eremite's sad cell.

[1] ["He cheer'd the bad and did the good affright;
With concubines," &c.—MS.]

[2] ["Childe Buron."—MS.]

V.

For he through Sin's long labyrinth had run,
Nor made atonement when he did amiss,
Had sigh'd to many, though he loved but one,[1]
And that loved one, alas! could ne'er be his.
Ah, happy she! to 'scape from him whose kiss
Had been pollution unto aught so chaste;
Who soon had left her charms for vulgar bliss,
And spoil'd her goodly lands to gild his waste,
Nor calm domestic peace had ever deign'd to taste

VI.

And now Childe Harold was sore sick at heart,
And from his fellow bacchanals would flee;
'Tis said, at times the sullen tear would start,
But Pride congeal'd the drop within his ee:
Apart he stalk'd in joyless revery,[2]
And from his native land resolved to go,
And visit scorching climes beyond the sea;
With pleasure drugg'd, he almost long'd for woe
And e'en for change of scene would seek the shades below [3]

[1] [See Stanzas written to a Lady, on leaving England: Works, vol. vii. p. 302;—

["And I must from this land be gone,
Because I cannot love but one."]

[2] ["And straight he fell into a revery."—MS.]

[3] In these stanzas, and indeed throughout his works, we must not accept too literally Lord Byron's testimony against himself—he took a morbid pleasure in darkening every shadow of his self-portraiture. His interior at Newstead had, no doubt, been, in some points, loose and irregular enough; but it certainly never exhibited any thing of the profuse and Satanic luxury which the language in the text might seem to indicate. In fact, the narrowness of his means at the time the verses refer to would alone have precluded this. His household economy, while he remained at the Abbey, is known to have been conducted on a very moderate scale; and, besides, his usual companions, though far from being averse to convivial indulgences, were not only, as Mr. Moore

VII.

The Childe departed from his father's hall·
It was a vast and venerable pile;
So old, it seemed only not to fall,
Yet strength was pillar'd in each massy aisle.
Monastic dome! condemn'd to uses vile!
Where Superstition once had made her den,
Now Paphian girls were known to sing and smile;
And monks might deem their time was come agen,
If ancient tales say true, nor wrong these holy men.

VIII.

Yet oft-times in his maddest mirthful mood
Strange pangs would flash along Childe Harold's
brow,
As if the memory of some deadly feud
Or disappointed passion lurk'd below:
But this none knew, nor haply cared to know;
For his was not that open, artless soul
That feels relief by bidding sorrow flow,
Nor sought he friend to counsel or condole,
Whate'er the grief mote be, which he could not control.

IX.

And none did love him—though to hall and bower
He gather'd revellers from far and near,
He knew them flatterers of the festal hour;
The heartless parasites of present cheer.
Yea! none did love him—nor his lemans dear—
But pomp and power alone are woman's care,
And where these are light Eros finds a feere;
Maidens, like moths, are ever caught by glare,
And Mammon wins his way where seraphs might
despair.

says, "of habits and tastes too intellectual for mere vulgar debauchery," but, assuredly, quite incapable of playing the parts of flatterers and parasites.]

X.

Childe Harold had a mother—not forgot,
Though parting from that mother he did shun;
A sister whom he loved, but saw her not
Before his weary pilgrimage begun:
If friends he had, he bade adieu to none.
Yet deem not thence his breast a breast of steel:[1]
Ye, who have known what 'tis to dote upon
A few dear objects, will in sadness feel
Such partings break the heart they fondly hope to heal.

XI.

His house, his home, his heritage, his lands,
The laughing dames in whom he did delight,[2]
Whose large blue eyes, fair locks, and snowy hands
Might shake the saintship of an anchorite,
And long had fed his youthful appetite:
His goblets brimm'd with every costly wine,
And all that mote to luxury invite,
Without a sigh he left, to cross the brine,
And traverse Paynim shores, and pass earth's central line.[3]

XII.

The sails were fill'd, and fair the light winds blew
As glad to waft him from his native home;
And fast the white rocks faded from his view,
And soon were lost in circumambient foam:
And then, it may be, of his wish to roam
Repented he, but in his bosom slept
The silent thought, nor from his lips did come
One word of wail, whilst others sate and wept,
And to the reckless gales unmanly moaning kept.

[1] ["Yet deem him not from this with breast of steel."—MS.]

[2] ["His house, his home, his vassals and his lands,
The Dalilahs," &c.—MS.]

[3] [Lord Byron originally intended to visit India.]

XIII.

But when the sun was sinking in the sea,
He seized his harp, which he at times could string
And strike, albeit with untaught melody,
When deem'd he no strange ear was listening:
And now his fingers o'er it he did fling,
And tuned his farewell in the dim twilight.
While flew the vessel on her snowy wing,
And fleeting shores receded from his sight,
Thus to the elements he pour'd his last "Good-night."

1.

"ADIEU, adieu! my native shore
Fades o'er the waters blue;
The night-winds sigh, the breakers roar,
And shrieks the wild sea-mew.
Yon sun that sets upon the sea
We follow in his flight;
Farewell a while to him and thee,
My native Land—Good-night!

2.

"A few short hours and he will rise
To give the morrow birth;
And I shall hail the main and skies,
But not my mother earth.
Deserted is my own good hall,
Its hearth is desolate;
Wild weeds are gathering on the wall;
My dog howls at the gate.

3.

"Come hither, hither, my little page![2]
Why dost thou weep and wail?

[1] [See Lord Maxwell's "Good Night," in Scott's Minstrelsy of the Scottish Border: Poetical Works, vol. ii. p. 141, ed. 1834—"Adieu, madame, my mother dear," &c.]

[2] [This "little page" was Robert Rushton, the son of one o

Or dost thou dread the billow's rage,
  Or tremble at the gale?
But dash the tear-drop from thine eye,
  Our ship is swift and strong:
Our fleetest falcon scarce can fly
  More merrily along."[1]

4.

'Let winds be shrill, let waves roll high,
  I fear not wave nor wind:[2]
Yet marvel not, Sir Childe, that I
  Am sorrowful in mind;[3]
For I have from my father gone,
  A mother whom I love,
And have no friend, save thee alone,
  But thee—and One above.

5.

'My father bless'd me fervently,
  Yet did not much complain;

Lord Byron's tenants. "Robert I take with me," says the poet, in a letter to his mother; "I like him, because, like myself, he seems a friendless animal: tell his father he is well and doing well."

[1] ["Our best goshawk can hardly fly
  So merrily along."—MS.]

[2] ["Oh master dear! I do not cry
  From fear of wave or wind."—MS.]

[3] Seeing that the boy was "sorrowful" at the separation from his parents, Lord Byron, on reaching Gibraltar, sent him back to England under the care of his old servant Joe Murray. "Pray," he says to his mother, "show the lad every kindness, as he is my great favourite." He also wrote a letter to the father of the boy, which leaves a most favourable impression of his thoughtfulness and kindliness. "I have," he says, "sent Robert home, because the country which I am about to travel through is in a state which renders it unsafe, particularly for one so young. I allow you to deduct from your rent five-and-twenty pounds a year for his education, for three years, provided I do not return before that time, and I desire he may be considered as in my service. He has behaved extremely well."]

But sorely will my mother sigh
  Till I come back again.'—
"Enough, enough, my little lad!
  Such tears become thine eye;
If I thy guileless bosom had,
  Mine own would not be dry.[1]

6.

"Come hither, hither, my staunch yeoman,[2]
  Why dost thou look so pale?
Or dost thou dread a French foeman?
  Or shiver at the gale?"—
'Deem'st thou I tremble for my life?
  Sir Childe, I'm not so weak;
But thinking on an absent wife
  Will blanch a faithful cheek.

[1] [Here follows in the original MS:—
'My mother is a high-born dame,
  And much misliketh me;
She saith my riot bringeth shame
  On all my ancestry:
I had a sister once, I ween,
  Whose tears perhaps will flow:
But her fair face I have not seen
  For three long years and moe.']

[2] [William Fletcher, the faithful valet; who, after a service of twenty years, ("during which," he says, "his Lord was more to him than a father,") received the *Pilgrim's* last words at Missolonghi, and did not quit his remains, until he had seen them deposited in the family vault at Hucknall. This unsophisticated "yeoman" was a constant source of pleasantry to his master:—*e. g.* "Fletcher," he says in a letter to his mother, "is not valiant; he requires comforts that I can dispense with, and sighs for beer, and beef, and tea, and his wife, and the devil knows what besides. We were one night lost in a thunder-storm, and since, nearly wrecked. In both cases he was sorely bewildered; from apprehensions of famine and banditti in the first, and drowning in the second instance. His eyes were a little hurt by the lightning, or

7.

'My spouse and boys dwell near thy hall,
Along the bordering lake,
And when they on their father call,
What answer shall she make?'—
"Enough, enough, my yeoman good,
Thy grief let none gainsay;
But I, who am of lighter mood,
Will laugh to flee away.[1]

8.

"For who would trust the seeming sighs
Of wife or paramour?
Fresh feres will dry the bright blue eyes
We late saw streaming o'er.[2]
For pleasures past I do not grieve,
Nor perils gathering near;
My greatest grief is that I leave
No thing that claims a tear.[3]

crying I don't know which. I did what I could to console him, but found him incorrigible. He sends six sighs to Sally. I shall settle him in a farm; for he has served me faithfully, and Sally is a good woman." After all his adventures by flood and field, short commons included, this humble Achates of the poet has now established himself as the keeper of an Italian warehouse, in Charles Street, Berkeley Square, where, if he does not thrive, every one who knows any thing of his character will say he deserves to do so.]

[1] ["Enough, enough, my yeoman good,
All this is well to say;
But if I in thy sandals stood,
I'd laugh to get away."—MS.]

[2] ["For who would trust a paramour,
Or e'en a wedded freere,
Though her blue eyes were streaming o'er,
And torn her yellow hair?"—MS.]

[3] ["I leave England without regret—I shall return to it without pleasure. I am like Adam, the first convict sentenced to transportation; but I have no Eve, and have eaten no apple but what was as sour as a crab."—*Lord B. to Mr. Hodgson.*]

9.

"And now I'm in the world alone,
Upon the wide, wide sea:
But why should I for others groan,
When none will sigh for me?
Perchance my dog[1] will whine in vain,
Till fed by stranger hands;
But long ere I come back again
He'd tear me where he stands.[2]

10.

"With thee, my bark, I'll swiftly go
Athwart the foaming brine;
Nor care what land thou bear'st me to,
So not again to mine,
Welcome, welcome, ye dark-blue waves!
And when you fail my sight,
Welcome, ye deserts, and ye caves!
My native land—Good-night!"[3]

[1] [From the following passage in a letter to Mr. Dallas, it would appear that that gentleman had recommended the suppression or alteration of this stanza;—"I do not mean to exchange the ninth verse of the 'Good Night.' I have no reason to suppose my dog better than his brother brutes, mankind; and Argus we know to be a fable."]

[2] [Here follows in the original MS.—

"Methinks it would my bosom glad
To change my proud estate,
And be again a laughing lad
With one beloved playmate,
Since youth I scarce have passed an hour
Without disgust or pain,
Except sometimes in lady's bower,
Or when the bowl I drain."]

[3] [Originally, the "little page" and the "yeoman" were introduced in the following stanzas:—

"And of his train there was a henchman page,
A peasant boy, who served his master well;
And often would his pranksome prate engage
Childe Harold's ear, when his proud heart did swell

XIV.

On, on the vessel flies, the land is gone,
And winds are rude in Biscay's sleepless bay.
Four days are sped, but with the fifth, anon,
New shores descried make every bosom gay;
And Cintra's mountain greets them on their way,
And Tagus dashing onward to the deep,
His fabled golden tribute bent to pay;
And soon on board the Lusian pilots leap, [reap.
And steer 'twixt fertile shores where yet few rustics

XV.

Oh, Christ! it is a goodly sight to see
What Heaven hath done for this delicious land!
What fruits of fragrance blush on every tree!
What goodly prospects o'er the hills expand!
But man would mar them with an impious hand:
And when the Almighty lifts his fiercest scourge
'Gainst those who most transgress his high command,
With treble vengeance will his hot shafts urge
Gaul's locust host, and earth from fellest foeman purge.[1]

With sable thoughts that he disdain'd to tell;
Then would he smile on him, and Alwin smiled,
When aught that from his young lips archly fell
The gloomy film from Harold's eye beguiled;
And pleased for a glimpse appear'd the woeful Childe.

"Him and one yeoman only did he take
To travel eastward to a far countrie;
And, though the boy was grieved to leave the lake
On whose fair banks he grew from infancy,
Eftsoons his little heart beat merrily
With hope of foreign nations to behold,
And many things right marvellous to see,
Of which our vaunting voyagers oft have told,
In many a tome as true as Mandeville's of old."]

[1] ["These Lusian brutes, and earth from worst of wretches purge."—MS.]

XVI.

What beauties doth Lisboa[1] first unfold!
Her image floating on that noble tide,
Which poets vainly pave with sands of gold,[2]
But now whereon a thousand keels did ride
Of mighty strength, since Albion was allied,
And to the Lusians did her aid afford:
A nation swoln with ignorance and pride,
Who lick yet loathe the hand that waves the sword
To save them from the wrath of Gaul's unsparing lord.[3]

XVII.

But whoso entereth within this town,
That, sheening far, celestial seems to be,
Disconsolate will wander up and down,
Mid many things unsightly to strange ee;[4]
For hut and palace show like filthily:
The dingy denizens are rear'd in dirt;
No personage of high or mean degree
Doth care for cleanness of surtout or shirt,
Though shent with Egypt's plague, unkempt, unwash'd; unhurt.

[1] ["A friend advises *Ulissipont*; but *Lisboa* is the Portuguese word, consequently the best. Ulissipont is pedantic; and as I had lugged in *Hellas* and *Eros* not long before, there would have been something like an affectation of Greek terms, which I wished to avoid. On the submission of *Lusitania* to the Moors, they changed the name of the capital, which till then had been Ulisipo, or Lispo; because, in the Arabic alphabet, the letter *p* is not used. Hence, I believe, Lisboa; whence, again, the French Lisbonne, and our Lisbon,—God knows which the earlier corruption!"—*Byron*, MS.]

[2] ["Which poets, prone to lie, have paved with gold."—MS.]

[3] [By comparing this and the thirteen following stanzas with the account of his progress which Lord Byron sent home to his mother, the reader will see that they are the exact echoes of the thoughts which occurred to his mind as he went over the spots described.—MOORE.]

[4] ["Mid many things that grieve both nose and ee."—MS.]

XVIII.

Poor, paltry slaves! yet born 'midst noblest scenes—
Why, Nature, waste thy wonders on such men?
Lo! Cintra's[1] glorious Eden intervenes
In variegated maze of mount and glen.
Ah, me! what hand can pencil guide, or pen,
To follow half on which the eye dilates
Through views more dazzling unto mortal ken
Than those whereof such things the bard relates,
Who to the awe-struck world unlock'd Elysium's
gates?

XIX.

The horrid crags, by toppling convent crown'd,
The cork-trees hoar that clothe the shaggy steep,
The mountain-moss by scorching skies imbrown'd,
The sunken glen, whose sunless shrubs must weep
The tender azure of the unruffled deep,
The orange tints that gild the greenest bough,
The torrents that from cliff to valley leap,
The vine on high, the willow branch below,
Mix'd in one mighty scene, with varied beauty glow.

XX.

Then slowly climb the many-winding way,
And frequent turn to linger as you go,

[1] ["To make amends for the filthiness of Lisbon, and its still filthier inhabitants, the village of Cintra, about fifteen miles from the capital, is, perhaps, in every respect, the most delightful in Europe. It contains beauties of every description, natural and artificial: palaces and gardens rising in the midst of rocks, cataracts, and precipices; convents on stupendous heights; a distant view of the sea and the Tagus; and, besides, (though that is a secondary consideration,) is remarkable as the scene of Sir Hew Dalrymple's convention. It unites in itself all the wildness of the western Highlands with the verdure of the south of France."
—*Lord B. to Mrs. Byron*, 1809.]

From loftier rocks new loveliness survey
And rest ye at "Our Lady's house of woe;"[1]
Where frugal monks their little relics show,
And sundry legends to the stranger tell:
Here impious men have punish'd been, and, lo!
Deep in yon cave Honorius long did dwell,
In hope to merit Heaven by making earth a Hell.

XXI.

And here and there, as up the crags you spring,
Mark many rude-carved crosses near the path:
Yet deem not these devotion's offering—
These are memorials frail of murderous wrath:
For wheresoe'er the shrieking victim hath
Pour'd forth his blood beneath the assassin's knife,
Some hand erects a cross of mouldering lath;
And grove and glen with thousand such are rife
Throughout this purple land, where law secures not life.[2]

[1] The convent of "Our Lady of Punishment," *Nossa Señora de Pena*, on the summit of the rock. Below, at some distance, is the Cork Convent, where St. Honorius dug his den, over which is his epitaph. From the hills, the sea adds to the beauty of the view.—*Note to 1st Edition.*—Since the publication of this poem, I have been informed of the misapprehension of the term *Nossa Señora de Pena.* It was owing to the want of the *tilde* or mark over the *ñ*, which alters the signification of the word: with it, *Peña*, signifies a rock; without it, *Pena* has the sense I adopted. *I* do not think it necessary to alter the passage; as, though the common acceptation affixed to it is "Our Lady of the Rock," I may well assume the other sense from the severities practised there.—*Note to 2d Edition.*

[2] It is a well known fact, that in the year 1809, the assassinations in the streets of Lisbon and its vicinity were not confined by the Portuguese to their countrymen; but that Englishmen were daily butchered: and so far from redress being obtained, we were requested not to interfere if we perceived any compatriot defending himself against his allies. I was once stopped in the

XXII.

On sloping mounds, or in the vale beneath,
Are domes where whilome kings did make repair:
But now the wild flowers round them only breathe;
Yet ruin'd splendour still is lingering there.
And yonder towers the prince's palace fair:
There thou too, Vathek![1] England's wealthiest son,
Once form'd thy Paradise, as not aware

way to the theatre at eight o'clock in the evening, when the streets were not more empty than they generally are at that hour, opposite to an open shop, and in a carriage with a friend: had we not fortunately been armed, I have not the least doubt that we should have "adorned a tale" instead of telling one. The crime of assassination is not confined to Portugal: in Sicily and Malta we are knocked on the head at a handsome average nightly, and not a Sicilian or Maltese is ever punished!

[1] ["Vathek" (says Lord Byron, in one of his diaries) "was one of the tales I had a very early admiration of. For correctness of costume, beauty of description, and power of imagination, it far surpasses all European imitations; and bears such marks of originality, that those who have visited the East will find some difficulty in believing it to be more than a translation. As an eastern tale, even Rasselas must bow before it; his 'happy valley' will not bear a comparison with the 'Hall of Eblis.'"—William Beckford, Esq., son of the once-celebrated alderman, and heir to his enormous wealth, published, at the early age of eighteen, "Memoirs of extraordinary Painters;" and in the year after, the romance thus eulogized. After sitting for Hindon in several parliaments, this gifted person was induced to fix, for a time, his residence in Portugal, where the memory of his magnificence was fresh at the period of Lord Byron's pilgrimage. Returning to England, he realized all the outward shows of Gothic grandeur in his unsubstantial pageant of Fonthill Abbey; and has more recently been indulging his fancy with another, probably not more lasting, monument of architectural caprice, in the vicinity of Bath. It is much to be regretted, that, after a lapse of fifty years, Mr. Beckford's literary reputation should continue to rest on his juvenile performances. It is said, however, that he has prepared several works for posthumous publication]

When wanton Wealth her mightiest deeds hath done,
Meek Peace voluptuous lures was ever wont to shun.[1]

XXIII.

Here didst thou dwell, here schemes of pleasure plan,
Beneath yon mountain's ever beauteous brow:
But now, as if a thing unbless'd by man,
Thy fairy dwelling is as lone as thou!
Here giant weeds a passage scarce allow
To halls deserted, portals gaping wide:
Fresh lessons to the thinking bosom, how
Vain are the pleasaunces on earth supplied;
Swept into wrecks anon by Time's ungentle tide!

XXIV.

Behold the hall where chiefs were late convened![2]
Oh! dome displeasing unto British eye!
With diadem hight foolscap, lo! a fiend,
A little fiend that scoffs incessantly,
There sits in parchment robe array'd and by
His side is hung a seal and sable scroll,
Where blazon'd glare names known to chivalry,
And sundry signatures adorn the roll,
Whereat the urchin points and laughs with all his soul.[3]

[1] ["When Wealth and Taste their worst and best have done,
Meek Peace pollution's lure voluptuous still must shun."
—MS.]

[2] The Convention of Cintra was signed in the palace of the Marchese Marialva.—["The armistice, the negotiations, the convention itself, and the execution of its provisions, were all commenced, conducted, and concluded, at the distance of thirty miles from Cintra, with which place they had not the slightest connection, political, military, or local; yet Lord Byron has gravely asserted, in prose and verse, that the convention was signed at the Marquis of Marialva's house at Cintra; and the author of 'The Diary of an Invalid,' improving upon the poet's discovery, detected the stains of the ink spilt by Junot upon the occasion." —*Napier's History of the Peninsular War.*]

[3] The passage stood differently in the original MS. Some

XXV.

Convention is the dwarfish demon styled
That foil'd the knights in Marialva's dome:
Of brains (if brains they had) he them beguiled,
And turn'd a nation's shallow joy to gloom.
Here Folly dash'd to earth the victor's plume,
And policy regained what arms had lost:
For chiefs like ours in vain may laurels bloom!

verses which the poet omitted at the entreaty of his friends **can** *now* offend no one, and may perhaps amuse many:—

In golden characters right well design'd,
First on the list appeareth one "Junot;"
Then certain other glorious names we find,
Which rhyme compelleth me to place below!
Dull victors! baffled by a vanquish'd foe,
Wheedled by conynge tongues of laurels due,
Stand, worthy of each other, in a row—
Sir Arthur, Harry, and the dizzard Hew
Dalrymple, seely wight, sore dupe of t'other tew.

Convention is the dwarfish demon styled
That foil'd the knights in Marialva's dome:
Of brains (if brains they had) he them beguiled
And turn'd a nation's shallow joy to gloom.
For well I wot, when first the news did come,
That Vimiera's field by Gaul was lost,
For paragraph ne paper scarce had room,
Such pæans teem'd for our triumphant host,
In Courier, Chronicle, and eke in Morning Post:

But when convention sent his handy-work,
Pens, tongues, feet, hands, combined in wild uproar;
Mayor, alderman, laid down the uplifted fork,
The Bench of Bishops half forgot to snore;
Stern Cobbett, who for one whole week forbore
To question aught, once more with transport leapt,
And bit his devilish quill agen, and swore
With foe such treaty never should be kept, [slept!
Then burst the blatant* beast, and roar'd, and raged, and—

* "Blatant beast"—a figure for the mob, I think first used by Smollett in his 'Adventures of an Atom." Horace has the "bellua multorum capitum:" in England, fortunately enough, the illustrious mobility have not even one.

Woe to the conquering, not the conquer'd host,
Since baffled Triumph droops on Lusitania's coast!

XXVI.

And ever since that martial synod met,
Britannia sickens, Cintra! at thy name;
And folks in office at the mention fret,
And fain would blush, if blush they could, for shame
How will posterity the deed proclaim!
Will not our own and fellow-nations sneer
To view these champions cheated of their fame,
By foes in fight o'erthrown, yet victors here, [year?
Where Scorn her finger points through many a coming

XXVII.

So deem'd the Childe as o'er the mountains he
Did take his way in solitary guise:
Sweet was the scene, yet soon he thought to flee,
More restless than the swallow in the skies:
Though here a while he learn'd to moralize,
For Meditation fix'd at times on him;
And conscious Reason whisper'd to despise
His early youth, misspent in maddest whim;
But as he gazed on truth his aching eyes grew dim.

Thus unto Heaven appeal'd the people: Heaven,
Which loves the lieges of our gracious king,
Decreed that, ere our generals were forgiven,
Inquiry should be held about the thing.
But Mercy cloak'd the babes beneath her wing;
And as they spared our foes, so spared we them;
(Where was the pity of our sires for Byng?*)
Yet knaves, not idiots, should the law condemn;
Then live, ye gallant knights! and bless your judges' phlegm!

---

* By this query it is not meant that our foolish generals should have been shot, but that Byng might have been spared, though the one suffered and the others escaped, probably for Candide's reason, "pour encourager les autres." [See Croker's "Boswell," vol. i. p. 298; and the Quarterly Review, vol. xxvii p. 207, where the question, whether the admiral was or was not a politica martyr, is treated at large.]

XXVIII.

To horse! to horse![1] he quits, forever quits
A scene of peace, though soothing to his soul:
Again he rouses from his moping fits,
But seeks not now the harlot and the bowl.
Onward he flies, nor fix'd as yet the goal
Where he shall rest him on his pilgrimage;
And o'er him many changing scenes must roll
Ere toil his thirst for travel can assuage,
Or he shall calm his breast, or learn experience sage.

XXIX.

Yet Mafra shall one moment claim delay,
Where dwelt of yore the Lusians' luckless queen;[2]
And church and court did mingle their array,
And mass and revel were alternate seen;
Lordlings and freres—ill-sorted fry, I ween!
But here the Babylonian whore hath built[3]
A dome, where flaunts she in such glorious sheen,
That men forget the blood which she hath spilt,
And bow the knee to pomp, that loves to varnish guilt.

[1] ["After remaining ten days in Lisbon, we sent our baggage and part of our servants by sea to Gibraltar, and travelled on horseback to Seville; a distance of nearly four hundred miles. The horses are excellent: we rode seventy miles a-day. Eggs and wine, and hard beds, are all the accommodation we found, and, in such torrid weather, quite enough."—*B. Letters*, 1809.]

[2] "Her luckless majesty went subsequently mad; and Dr Willis, who so dexterously cudgelled kingly pericraniums, could make nothing of hers."—*Byron MS.* [The queen laboured under a melancholy kind of derangement, from which she never recovered. She died at the Brazils, in 1816.]

[3] The extent of Mafra is prodigious: it contains a palace, convent, and most superb church. The six organs are the most beautiful I ever beheld, in point of decoration: we did not hear them, but were told that their tones were correspondent to their splendour. Mafra is termed the Escurial of Portugal. ["About ten miles to the right of Cintra," says Lord Byron, in a letter to

XXX

O'er vales that teem with fruits, romantic hills,
(Oh, that such hills upheld a freeborn race!)
Whereon to gaze the eye with joyaunce fills,
Childe Harold wends through many a pleasant place.
Though sluggards deem it but a foolish chase,
And marvel men should quit their easy chair,
The toilsome way, and long, long league to trace,
Oh! there is sweetness in the mountain air,
And life, that bloated Ease can never hope to share.

XXXI.

More bleak to view the hills at length recede,
And, less luxuriant, smoother vales extend;
Immense horizon-bounded plains succeed!
Far as the eye discerns, withouten end,
Spain's realms appear, whereon her shepherds tend
Flocks, whose rich fleece right well the trader knows—
Now must the pastor's arm his lambs defend:
For Spain is compassed by unyielding foes,
And all must shield their all, or share Subjection's woes.

his mother, "is the palace of Mafra, the boast of Portugal, as it might be of any country, in point of magnificence, without elegance. There is a convent annexed: the monks, who possess large revenues, are courteous enough, and understand Latin; so that we had a long conversation. They have a large library, and asked me if the English had *any books* in their country."—Mafra was erected by John V., in pursuance of a vow, made in a dangerous fit of illness, to found a convent for the use of the poorest friary in the kingdom. Upon inquiry, this poorest was found at Mafra; where twelve Franciscans lived together in a hut. There is a magnificent view of the existing edifice in Finden's Illustrations."]

XXXII.

Where Lusitania and her sister meet,
Deem ye what bounds the rival realms divide?
Or ere the jealous queens of nations greet,
Doth Tayo interpose his mighty tide?
Or dark Sierras rise in craggy pride?
Or fence of art, like China's vasty wall?—[1]
Ne barrier wall, ne river deep and wide,
Ne horrid crags, nor mountains dark and tall,
Rise like the rocks that part Hispania's land from
Gaul·

XXXIII.

But these between a silver streamlet glides,
And scarce a name distinguisheth the brook,
Though rival kingdoms press its verdant sides.
Here leans the idle shepherd on his crook,
And vacant on the rippling waves doth look,
That peaceful still 'twixt bitterest foemen flow;
For proud each peasant as the noblest duke:
Well doth the Spanish hind the difference know
'Twixt him and Lusian slave, the lowest of the low.[2]

XXXIV.

But ere the mingling bounds have far been pass'd,
Dark Guadiana rolls his power along[3]

[1] [Or art's vain fence, like China's vasty wall?—MS.]

[2] As I found the Portuguese, so I have characterized them. That they are since improved, at least in courage, is evident. The late exploits of Lord Wellington have effaced the follies of Cintra. He has, indeed, done wonders: he has, perhaps, changed the character of a nation, reconciled rival superstitions and baffled an enemy who never retreated before his predecessors.—1812.

[3] ["But ere the bounds of Spain have far been pass'd,
Forever famed in many a noted song."—MS.]

In sullen billows, murmuring and vast,
So noted ancient roundelays among.[1]
Whilome upon his banks did legions throng
Of Moor and knight, in mailed splendour drest:
Here ceased the swift their race, here sunk the strong;
The Paynim turban and the Christian crest
Mix'd on the bleeding stream, by floating hosts oppress'd.

XXXV.

Oh, lovely Spain! renown'd romantic land!
Where is that standard which Pelagio bore,
When Cava's traitor-sire first call'd the band
That dyed thy mountain streams with Gothic gore?[2]
Where are those bloody banners which of yore
Waved o'er thy sons, victorious to the gale,
And drove at last the spoilers to their shore?
Red gleam'd the cross, and waned the crescent pale,
While Afric's echoes thrill'd with Moorish matrons' wail.

[1] [Lord Byron seems to have thus early acquired enough of Spanish to understand and appreciate the grand body of ancient popular poetry,—unequalled in Europe,—which must ever form the pride of that magnificent language. See his beautiful version of one of the best of the ballads of the Grenada war—the "Romance muy doloroso del sitio y toma de Alhama." Vol. ii. p. 354.]

[2] Count Julian's daughter, the Helen of Spain. Pelagius preserved his independence in the fastnesses of the Asturias, and the descendants of his followers, after some centuries, completed their struggle by the conquest of Grenada.—["Almost all the Spanish historians, as well as the voice of tradition, ascribe the invasion of the Moors to the forcible violation by Roderick of Florinda, called by the Moors Caba, or Cava. She was the daughter of Count Julian, one of the Gothic monarch's principal lieutenants, who, when the crime was perpetrated, was engaged in the defence of Ceuta against the Moors. In his indignation at the ingratitude of his sovereign, and the dishonour of his daughter,

XXXVI.

Teems not each ditty with the glorious tale?
Ah! such, alas! the hero's amplest fate!
When granite moulders and when records fail,
A peasant's plaint prolongs his dubious date.
Pride! bend thine eye from heaven to thine estate,
See how the mighty shrink into a song!
Can volume, pillar, pile, preserve thee great?
Or must thou trust Tradition's simple tongue,
When Flattery sleeps with thee, and History does
thee wrong?

XXXVII.

Awake, ye sons of Spain! awake! advance!
Lo! Chivalry, your ancient goddess, cries;
But wields not, as of old, her thirsty lance,
Nor shakes her crimson plumage in the skies:
Nor in the smoke of blazing bolts she flies,
And speaks in thunder through yon engine's roar
In every peal she calls—"Awake! arise!"
Say, is her voice more feeble than of yore,
When her war-song was heard on Andalusia's shore.

XXXVIII.

Hark! heard you not those hoofs of dreadful note?
Sounds not the clang of conflict on the heath?

Count Julian forgot the duties of a Christian and a patriot, and, forming an alliance with Musa, then the Caliph's lieutenant in Africa, he countenanced the invasion of Spain by a body of Saracens and Africans, commanded by the celebrated Tarik; the issue of which was the defeat and death of Roderick, and the occupation of almost the whole peninsula by the Moors. The Spaniards, in detestation of Florinda's memory, are said, by Cervantes, never to bestow that name upon any human female, reserving it for their dogs."—SIR WALTER SCOTT, Poetical Works, vol. ix. p 375.]

Saw ye not whom the reeking sabre smote;
Nor saved your brethren ere they sank beneath
Tyrants and tyrants' slaves?—the fires of death,
The bale-fires flash on high;—from rock to rock
Each volley tells that thousands cease to breathe,
Death rides upon the sulphury siroc,[1]
Red Battle stamps his foot, and nations feel the shock

XXXIX.

Lo! where the Giant on the mountain stands,
His blood-red tresses deepening in the sun,
With death-shot glowing in his fiery hands,
And eye that scorcheth all it glares upon;
Restless it rolls, now fix'd, and now anon
Flashing afar,—and at his iron feet
Destruction cowers, to mark what deeds are done;
For on this morn three potent nations meet,
To shed before his shrine the blood he deems most
sweet.[2]

XL.

By Heaven! it is a splendid sight to see
(For one who hath no friend, no brother there)
Their rival scarfs of mix'd embroidery,
Their various arms that glitter in the air!

1 [——— "from rock to rock
Blue columns soar aloft in sulphurous wreath,
Fragments on fragments in confusion knock."—MS.]

2 ["A bolder prosopopœia," says a nameless critic, "or one better imagined or expressed, cannot easily be found in the whole range of ancient and modern poetry. Unlike the 'plume of Horror,' or the 'eagle-winged Victory,' described by our great epic poet, this gigantic figure is a distinct object, perfect in lineaments, tremendous in operation, and vested with all the attributes calculated to excite terror and admiration."]

What gallant war-hounds rouse them from their lair,
And gnash their fangs, loud yelling for the prey!
All join the chase, but few the triumph share;
The grave shall bear the chiefest prize away,
And Havoc scarce for joy can number their array.

XLI.

Three hosts combine to offer sacrifice;
Three tongues prefer strange orisons on high;
Three gaudy standards flout the pale blue skies;
The shouts are France, Spain, Albion, Victory!
The foe, the victim, and the fond ally
That fights for all, but ever fights in vain,
Are met—as if at home they could not die—
To feed the crow on Talavera's plain,
And fertilize the field that each pretends to gain[1]

[1] [We think it right to restore here a note which Lord Byron himself suppressed with reluctance, at the urgent request of a friend. It alludes, *inter alia*, to the then recent publication of Sir Walter Scott's "Vision of Don Roderick," of which work the profits had been handsomely given to the cause of Portuguese patriotism:—"We have heard wonders of the Portuguese lately, and their gallantry. Pray Heaven it continue; yet 'would it were bedtime, Hal, and all were well!' They must fight a great many hours, by 'Shrewsbury clock,' before the number of their slain equals that of our own countrymen butchered by these kind creatures, now metamorphosed into 'caçadores,' and what not. I merely state a fact, not confined to Portugal; for in Sicily and Malta we are knocked on the head at a handsome average nightly, and not a Sicilian and Maltese is ever punished! The neglect of protection is disgraceful to our government and governors; for the murders are as notorious as the moon that shines upon them, and the apathy that overlooks them. The Portuguese, it is to be hoped, are complimented with the 'Forlorn Hope,'—if the cowards are become brave, (like the rest of their kind, in a corner,) pray let them display it. But there is a subscription for these 'θρασυ-δειλοι,' (they need not be ashamed of the epithet once applied to the Spartans;) and all the charitable patronymics, from ostentatious A. to diffident Z., and 1*l.* 1*s.* 0*d.* from 'An Admirer of Valour,' are in requisition for the lists at Lloyd's, and the honour of British

XLII.

There shall they rot—Ambition's honour'd fools![1]
Yes, Honour decks the turf that wraps their clay!
Vain Sophistry! in these behold the tools,
The broken tools that tyrants cast away

benevolence. Well! we have fought, and subscribed, and bestowed peerages, and buried the killed by our friends and foes; and, lo! all this is to be done over again! Like Lien Chi, (in Goldsmith's Citizen of the World,) as we 'grow older, we grow never the better.' It would be pleasant to learn who will subscribe for us, in or about the year 1815, and what nation will send fifty thousand men, first to be decimated in the capital, and then decimated again (in the Irish fashion, *nine* out of *ten*) in the 'bed of honour;' which, as Sergeant Kite says, is considerably larger and more commodious than 'the bed of Ware.' Then they must have a poet to write the 'Vision of Don Perceval,' and generously bestow the profits of the well and widely printed quarto, to rebuild the 'Backwynd' and the 'Canongate,' or furnish new kilts for the half-roasted Highlanders. Lord Wellington, however, has enacted marvels; and so did his oriental brother, whom I saw chariot-eering over the French flag, and heard clipping bad Spanish, after listening to the speech of a patriotic cobbler of Cadiz, on the event of his own entry into that city, and the exit of some five thousand bold Britons out of this 'best of all possible worlds.' Sorely were we puzzled how to dispose of that same victory of Talavera; and a victory it surely was somewhere, for everybody claimed it. The Spanish despatch and mob called it Cuesta's, and made no great mention of the viscount; the French called it theirs, (to my great discomfiture,—for a French consul stopped my mouth in Greece with a pestilent Paris gazette, just as I had killed Sebastiani 'in buckram,' and King Joseph 'in Kendal green,')—and we have not yet determined *what* to call it, or *whose*; for, certes, it was none of our own. Howbeit, Massena's retreat is a great comfort; and as we have not been in the habit of pursuing for some years past, no wonder we are a little awkward at first. No doubt we shall improve; or, if not, we have only to take to our old way of retrograding, and there we are at home."]

[1] [There let them rot—while rhymers tell the fools
How honour decks the turf that wraps their clay!
Liars, avaunt!"—MS.]

By myriads, when they dare to pave their way
With human hearts—to what?—a dream alone.
Can despots compass aught that hails their sway?
Or call with truth one span of earth their own,
Save that wherein at last they crumble bone by bone.

XLIII.

Oh, Albuera, glorious field of grief!
As o'er thy plain the Pilgrim prick'd his steed,
Who could foresee thee, in a space so brief,
A scene where mingling foes should boast and bleed.
Peace to the perish'd! may the warrior's meed
And tears of triumph their reward prolong!
Till others fall where other chieftains lead,
Thy name shall circle round the gaping throng,
And shine in worthless lays, the theme of transient song.[1]

XLIV.

Enough of Battle's minions! let them play
Their game of lives, and barter breath for fame:
Fame that will scarce reanimate their clay,
Though thousands fall to deck some single name.
In sooth 'twere sad to thwart their noble aim,
Who strike, blest hirelings! for their country's good,
And die, that living might have proved her shame;
Perish'd, perchance, in some domestic feud,
Or in a narrower sphere wild Rapine's path pursued.

[1] [This stanza is not in the original MS. It was written at Newstead, in August, 1811, shortly after the battle of Albuera, which took place on the 16th of May.]

XLV.

Full swiftly Harold wends his lonely way
Where proud Sevilla[1] triumphs unsubdued:
Yet is she free—the spoiler's wish'd-for prey!
Soon, soon shall Conquest's fiery foot intrude,
Blackening her lovely domes with traces rude.
Inevitable hour! 'Gainst fate to strive
Where desolation plants her famish'd brood
Is vain, or Ilion, Tyre might yet survive,
And Virtue vanquish all, and murder cease to thrive.

XLVI.

But all unconscious of the coming doom,
The feast, the song, the revel here abounds;
Strange modes of merriment the hours consume,
Nor bleed these patriots with their country's wounds;
Nor here War's clarion, but Love's rebeck[2] sounds;
Here Folly still his votaries inthralls;
And young-eyed Lewdness walks her midnight
rounds:
Girt with the silent crimes of capitals,
Still to the last kind vice clings to the tottering walls.

[1] [" At Seville, we lodged in the house of two Spanish unmarried ladies, women of character, the eldest a fine woman, the youngest pretty. The freedom of manner, which is general here, astonished me not a little; and, in the course of further observation, I find that reserve is not the characteristic of Spanish belles. The eldest honoured your unworthy son with very particular attention, embracing him with great tenderness at parting, (I was there but three days,) after cutting off a lock of his hair, and presenting him with one of her own, about three feet in length, which I send, and beg you will retain till my return. Her last words were, 'Adios, tu hermoso! me gusto mucho.' 'Adieu, you pretty fellow! you please me much.' "—*Lord B. to his Mother*, Aug. 1809.]

[2] [A kind of fiddle, with only two strings, played on by a bow said to have been brought by the Moors into Spain.]

XLVII.

Not so the rustic—with his trembling mate
He lurks, nor casts his heavy eye afar,
Lest he should view his vineyard desolate,
Blasted below the dun hot breath of war.
No more beneath soft Eve's consenting star
Fandango twirls his jocund castanet:
Ah, monarchs! could ye taste the mirth ye mar,
Not in the toils of Glory would ye fret;
The hoarse dull drum would sleep, and Man be happy
yet!

XLVIII.

How carols now the lusty muleteer?
Of love, romance, devotion is his lay,
As whilome he was wont the leagues to cheer,
His quick bells wildly jingling on the way?
No! as he speeds, he chants "Vivā el Rey!"[1]
And checks his song to execrate Godoy,
The royal wittol Charles, and curse the day
When first Spain's queen beheld the black-eyed boy
And gore-faced treason sprung from her adulterate
joy.

1 "Vivā el Rey Fernando!" Long live King Ferdinand! is the chorus of most of the Spanish patriotic songs. They are chiefly in dispraise of the old king Charles, the queen, and the Prince of Peace. I have heard many of them: some of the airs are beautiful. Don Manuel Godoy, the *Principe de la Paz*, of an ancient but decayed family, was born at Badajoz, on the frontiers of Portugal, and was originally in the ranks of the Spanish guards; till his person attracted the queen's eyes, and raised him to the dukedom of Alcudia, &c. &c. It is to this man that the Spaniards universally impute the ruin of their country.—[See for ample particulars concerning the flagitious court of Charles IV., Southey's History of the Peninsular War, vol. i.]

XLIX.

On yon long, level plain, at distance crown'd
With crags, whereon those Moorish turrets rest,
Wide scatter'd hoof-marks dint the wounded ground,
And, scathed by fire, the greensward's darken'd vest.
Tells that the foe was Andalusia's guest:
Here was the camp, the watch-flame, and the host,
Here the bold peasant storm'd the dragon's nest;
Still does he mark it with triumphant boast,
And points to yonder cliffs, which oft were won and lost.

L.

And whomsoe'er along the path you meet
Bears in his cap the badge of crimson hue,
Which tells you whom to shun and whom to greet:[1]
Woe to the man that walks in public view,
Without of loyalty this token true:
Sharp is the knife, and sudden is the stroke;
And sorely would the Gallic foeman rue,
If subtle poniards, wrap'd beneath the cloak,
Could blunt the sabre's edge, or clear the cannon's smoke.

LI.

At every turn Morena's dusky height
Sustains aloft the battery's iron load;
And, far as mortal eye can compass sight,
The mountain-howitzer, the broken road,
The bristling palisade, the fosse o'erflow'd,
The stationed bands, the never-vacant watch,
The magazine in rocky durance stow'd,
The holster'd steed beneath the shed of thatch,
The ball-piled pyramid,[2] the ever blazing match,

[1] The red cockade, with "Fernando Septimo," in the centre

[2] All who have seen a battery will recollect the pyramidal form in which shot and shells are piled. The Sierra Morena was

LII.

Portend the deeds to come:—but he whose nod
Has tumbled feebler despots from their sway,
A moment pauseth ere he lifts the rod;
A little moment deigneth to delay:
Soon will his legions sweep through these their way;
The West must own the scourger of the world.
Ah! Spain! how sad will be thy reckoning-day
When soars Gaul's vulture, with his wings unfurl'd,
And thou shalt view thy sons in crowds to Hades hurl'd.

LIII.

And must they fall? the young, the proud, the brave,
To swell one bloated chief's unwholesome reign?
No step between submission and a grave?
The rise of rapine and the fall of Spain?
And doth the power that man adores ordain
Their doom, nor heed the suppliant's appeal?
Is all that desperate Valour acts in vain?
And Counsel sage, and patriotic Zeal,
The Veteran's skill, Youth's fire, and Manhood's heart [of steel?

LIV.

Is it for this the Spanish maid, aroused,
Hangs on the willow her unstrung guitar,
And, all unsex'd, the anlace hath espoused,
Sung the loud song, and dared the deed of war?
And she, whom once the semblance of a scar
Appall'd, an owlet's larum chill'd with dread,
Now views the column-scattering bayonet jar,
The falchion flash, and o'er the yet warm dead
Stalks with Minerva's step where Mars might quake to tread.

fortified in every defile through which I passed in my way to Seville.

LV.

Ye who shall marvel when you hear her tale,
Oh! had you known her in her softer hour,
Mark'd her black eye that mocks her coal-black veil,
Heard her light, lively tones in lady's bower,
Seen her long locks that foil the painter's power,
Her fairy form, with more than female grace,
Scarce would you deem that Saragoza's tower
Beheld her smile in Danger's Gorgon face,
Thin the closed ranks, and lead in Glory's fearful chase.

LVI.

Her lover sinks—she sheds no ill-timed tear;
Her chief is slain—she fills his fatal post;
Her fellows flee—she checks their base career;
The foe retires—she heads the sallying host:
Who can appease like her a lover's ghost?
Who can avenge so well a leader's fall?
What maid retrieve when man's flush'd hope is lost?
Who hang so fiercely on the flying Gaul,
Foil'd by a woman's hand, before a batter'd wall?[1]

[1] Such were the exploits of the maid of Saragoza, who by her valour elevated herself to the highest rank of heroines. When the author was at Seville, she walked daily on the Prado, decorated with medals and orders, by command of the Junta.—[The exploits of Augustina, the famous heroine of both the sieges of Saragoza, are recorded at length in one of the most splendid chapters of Southey's History of the Peninsular War. At the time when she first attracted notice, by mounting a battery where her lover had fallen, and working a gun in his room, she was in her twenty-second year, exceedingly pretty, and in a soft feminine style of beauty. She has further had the honour to be painted by Wilkie, and alluded to in Wordsworth's Dissertation on the Convention (misnamed) of Cintra; where a noble passage concludes in these words:—"Saragoza has exemplified a melancholy, yea a dismal truth,—yet consolatory and full of joy,—that when a

LVII.

Yet are Spain's maids no race of Amazons,
But form'd for all the witching arts of love:
Though thus in arms they emulate her sons,
And in the horrid phalanx dare to move,
'Tis but the tender fierceness of the dove,
Pecking the hand that hovers o'er her mate:
In softness as in firmness far above
Remoter females, famed for sickening prate;
Her mind is nobler sure, her charms perchance as great.

LVIII.

The seal Love's dimpling finger hath impress'd
Denotes how soft that chin which bears his touch:[1]
Her lips, whose kisses pout to leave their nest,
Bid man be valiant ere he merit such:
Her glance how wildly beautiful! how much
Hath Phœbus woo'd in vain to spoil her cheek,
Which glows yet smoother from his amorous clutch!
Who round the North for paler dames would seek?
How poor their forms appear! how languid, wan, and weak!

people are called suddenly to fight for their liberty, and are sorely pressed upon, their best field of battle is the floors upon which their children have played; the chambers where the family of each man has slept; upon or under the roofs by which they have been sheltered; in the gardens of their recreation; in the street, or in the market-place; before the altars of their temples, and among their congregated dwellings, blazing or uprooted."]

[1] "Sigilla in mento impressa Amoris digitulo
Vestigio demonstrant mollitudinem."—AUL. GEL.

LIX.

Match me, ye climes! which poets love to laud;
Match me, ye harems of the land! where now[1]
I strike my strain, far distant, to applaud
Beauties that even a cynic must avow;[2]
Match me those Houries, whom ye scarce allow
To taste the gale, lest Love should ride the wind,
With Spain's dark-glancing daughters[3]—deign tc
know,
There your wise Prophet's paradise we find,
His black-eyed maids of heaven, angelically kind.

LX.

Oh, thou Parnassus![4] whom I now survey,
Not in the frenzy of a dreamer's eye,
Not in the fabled landscape of a lay,
But soaring snow-clad through thy native sky,
In the wild pomp of mountain-majesty!
What marvel if I thus essay to sing?
The humblest of thy pilgrims passing by
Would gladly woo thine Echoes with his string,
Though from thy heights no more one Muse will
wave her wing.

[1] This stanza was written in Turkey.

[2] ["Beauties that need not fear a broken vow."—MS.]

[3] ["Long black hair, dark languishing eyes, clear olive complexions, and forms more graceful in motion than can be conceived by an Englishman, used to the drowsy, listless air of his countrywomen, added to the most becoming dress, and, at the same time, the most decent in the world, render a Spanish beauty irresistible."—*Lord Byron to his Mother*, Aug. 1809.]

[4] These stanzas were written in Castri, (Delphos,) at the foot of Parnassus, now called Λιακυρα, (Liakura,) Dec. 1809.

LXI.

Oft have I dream'd of Thee! whose glorious name
Who knows not, knows not man's divinest lore:
And now I view thee, 'tis, alas! with shame
That I in feeblest accents must adore.
When I recount thy worshippers of yore,
I tremble and can only bend the knee;
Nor raise my voice, nor vainly dare to soar,
But gaze beneath thy cloudy canopy
In silent joy to think at last I look on thee![1]

LXII.

Happier in this than mightiest bards have been,
Whose fate to distant homes confined their lot,
Shall I unmoved behold the hallow'd scene,
Which others rave of, though they know it not?
Though here no more Apollo haunts his grot,
And thou, the Muses' seat, art now their grave,[2]
Some gentle spirit still pervades the spot,
Sighs in the gale, keeps silence in the cave,
And glides with glassy foot o'er yon melodious wave.

[1] ["Upon Parnassus, going to the fountain of Delphi, (Castri,) in 1809, I saw a flight of twelve eagles, (Hobhouse says they were vultures—at least in conversation,) and I seized the omen. On the day before, I composed the lines to Parnassus, (in Childe Harold,) and on beholding the birds, had a hope that Apollo had accepted my homage. I have at least had the name and fame of a poet, during the poetical period of life; (from twenty to thirty;) whether it will last is another matter: but I have been a votary of the deity and the place, and am grateful for what he has done in my behalf, leaving the future in his hands, as I left the past."—*B. Diary*, 1821.]

[2] ["Casting the eye over the site of ancient Delphi, one cannot possibly imagine what has become of the walls of the numerous buildings which are mentioned in the history of its former magnificence,—buildings which covered two miles of ground. With the exception of the few terraces or supporting walls, nothing now appears. The various robberies of Scylla, Nero, and Constantine, are inconsiderable; for the removal of the statues

LXIII.

Of thee hereafter.—Even amidst my strain
I turn'd aside to pay my homage here;
Forgot the land, the sons, the maids of Spain;
Her fate, to every freeborn bosom dear;
And hail'd thee, not perchance without a tear.
Now to my theme—but from thy holy haunt
Let me some remnant, some memorial bear;
Yield me one leaf of Daphne's deathless plant,[1]
Nor let thy votary's hope be deem'd an idle vaunt.

LXIV.

But ne'er didst thou, fair mount! when Greece was young,
See round thy giant base a brighter choir,
Nor e'er did Delphi, when her priestess sung
The Pythian hymn with more than mortal fire,
Behold a train more fitting to inspire
The song of love than Andalusia's maids,
Nursed in the glowing lap of soft desire:
Ah! that to these were given such peaceful shades
As Greece can still bestow, though Glory fly her glades.

of bronze, and marble, and ivory, could not greatly affect the general appearance of the city. The acclivity of the hill, and the foundations being placed on rock, without cement, would no doubt render them comparatively easy to be removed or hurled down into the vale below; but the vale exhibits no appearance of accumulation of hewn stones; and the modern village could have consumed but few. In the course of so many centuries, the débris from the mountain must have covered up a great deal, and even the rubbish itself may have acquired a soil sufficient to conceal many noble remains from the light of day. Yet we see no swellings or risings in the ground, indicating the graves of the temples. All therefore is mystery, and the Greeks may truly say, 'Where stood the walls of our fathers?' scarce their mossy tombs remain!" *H. W. Williams's Travels in Greece*, vol. ii. p. 254.]

[1] ["Some glorious thought to my petition grant."—MS.]

LXV.

Fair is proud Seville; let her country boast
Her strength, her wealth, her site of ancient days;[1]
But Cadiz, rising on the distant coast,
Calls forth a sweeter though ignoble praise.
Ah, Vice! how soft are thy voluptuous ways!
While boyish blood is mantling, who can 'scape
The fascination of thy magic gaze?[2]
A Cherub-hydra round us dost thou gape,
And mould to every taste thy dear delusive shape.

LXVI.

When Paphos fell by time—accursed time!
The queen who conquers all must yield to thee—
The Pleasures fled, but sought as warm a clime;
And Venus, constant to her native sea,
To naught else constant, hither deign'd to flee;
And fix'd her shrine within these walls of white;
Though not to one dome circumscribeth she
Her worship, but, devoted to her rite,
A thousand altars rise, forever blazing bright.[3]

LXVII.

From morn till night, from night till startled morn
Peeps blushing on the revel's laughing crew,
The song is heard, the rosy garland worn;
Devices quaint, and frolics ever new,

[1] Seville was the Hispalis of the Romans.

[2] ["The lurking lures of thy enchanting gaze."—MS.]

[3] ["Cadiz, sweet Cadiz!—it is the first spot in the creation. The beauty of its streets and mansions is only excelled by the liveliness of its inhabitants It is a complete Cythera, full of the finest women in Spain; the Cadiz belles being the Lancashire witches of their land."—*Lord B. to his Mother*, 1809.]

Tread on each other's kibes. A long adieu
He bids to sober joy that here sojourns:
Naught interrupts the riot, though in lieu
Of true devotion monkish incense burns,
And love and prayer unite, or rule the hour by turns.

LXVIII.

The Sabbath comes, a day of blessed rest:
What hallows it upon this Christian shore?
Lo! it is sacred to a solemn feast:
Hark! heard you not the forest-monarch's roar?
Crashing the lance, he snuffs the spouting gore
Of man and steed, o'erthrown beneath his horn;
The throng'd arena shakes with shouts for more;
Yells the mad crowd o'er entrails freshly torn,
Nor shrinks the female eye, nor even affects to mourn.

LXIX.

The seventh day this; the jubilee of man.
London! right well thou know'st the day of prayer.
Then thy spruce citizen, washed artisan,
And smug apprentice gulp their weekly air:
Thy coach of hackney, whiskey, one-horse chair,
And humblest gig through sundry suburbs whirl:
To Hampstead, Brentford, Harrow make repair;
Till the tired jade the wheel forgets to hurl,
Provoking envious gibe from each pedestrian churl.

LXX.

Some o'er thy Thamis row the ribbon'd fair,
Others along the safer turnpike fly;
Some Richmond-hill ascend, some scud to Ware,
And many to the steep of Highgate hie.

[1] [" —Monkish temples share
The hours misspent, and all in turns is love and prayer."—MS.

Ask ye, Bœotian shades! the reason why?[1]
'Tis to the worship of the solemn horn,
Grasp'd in the holy hand of mystery,
In whose dread name both men and maids are sworn,
And consecrate the oath[2] with draught, and dance
till morn.[3]

LXXI.

All have their fooleries—not alike are thine,
Fair Cadiz, rising o'er the dark-blue sea!
Soon as the matin bell proclaimeth nine,
Thy saint adorers count the rosary:
Much is the VIRGIN teased to shrive them free
(Well do I ween the only virgin there)
From crimes as numerous as her beadsmen be;
Then to the crowded circus forth they fare: [share
Young, old, high, low, at once the same diversion

[1] This was written at Thebes, and consequently in the best situation for asking and answering such a question; not as the birthplace of Pindar, but as the capital of Bœotia, where the first riddle was compounded and solved.

[2] [Lord Byron alludes to a ridiculous custom which formerly prevailed at the public-houses in Highgate, of administering a burlesque oath to all travellers of the middling rank who stopped there. The party was sworn on a pair of horns, fastened, "never to kiss the maid when he could kiss the mistress; never to eat brown bread when he could get white; never to drink small beer when he could get strong;" with many other injunctions of the like kind,—to all which was added the saving clause,—"unless you like it best."]

[3] [In thus mixing up the light with the solemn, it was the intention of the poet to imitate Ariosto. But it is far easier to rise, with grace, from the level of a strain generally familiar, into an occasional short burst of pathos or splendour, than to interrupt thus a prolonged tone of solemnity by any descent into the ludicrous or burlesque. In the former case, the transition may have the effect of softening or elevating; while, in the latter, it almost invariably shocks;—for the same reason, perhaps, that a trait of pathos or high feeling, in comedy, has a peculiar charm; while the intrusion of comic scenes into tragedy, however sanctioned

LXXII.

The lists are oped, the spacious area clear'd,
Thousands on thousands piled are seated round;
Long ere the first loud trumpet's note is heard,
Ne vacant space for lated wight is found:
Here dons, grandees, but chiefly dames abound,
Skill'd in the ogle of a roguish eye,
Yet ever well inclined to heal the wound;
None through their cold disdain are doom'd to die,
As moon-struck bards complain, by Love's sad archery.

LXXIII.

Hush'd is the din of tongues—on gallant steeds,
With milk-white crest, gold spur, and light-poised
lance,
Four cavaliers prepare for venturous deeds,
And lowly bending to the lists advance;
Rich are their scarfs, their chargers featly prance:
If in the dangerous game they shine to-day,
The crowd's loud shout and ladies' lovely glance,
Best prize of better acts, they bear away,
And all that kings or chiefs e'er gain their toils repay.

LXXIV.

In costly sheen and gaudy cloak array'd,
But all afoot, the light-limb'd Matadore
Stands in the centre, eager to invade
The lord of lowing herds; but not before
The ground, with cautious tread, is traversed o'er,
Lest aught unseen should lurk to thwart his speed
His arms a dart, he fights aloof, nor more
Can man achieve without his friendly steed—
Alas! too oft condemn'd for him to bear and bleed

among us by habit and authority, rarely fails to offend. The poet was himself convinced of the failure of the experiment, and in none of the succeeding cantos of Childe Harold repeated it.—MOORE.]

LXXV.

Thrice sounds the clarion; lo! the signal falls,
The den expands, and Expectation mute
Gapes round the silent circle's peopled walls.
Bounds with one lashing spring the mighty brute,
And, wildly staring, spurns, with sounding foot,
The sand, nor blindly rushes on his foe:
Here, there, he points his threatening front, to suit
His first attack, wide waving to and fro
His angry tail; red rolls his eye's dilated glow.

LXXVI.

Sudden he stops; his eye is fix'd: away,
Away, thou heedless boy! prepare the spear:
Now is thy time, to perish, or display
The skill that yet may check his mad career.
With well-timed croupe[1] the nimble coursers veer;
On foams the bull, but not unscathed he goes;
Streams from his flank the crimson torrent clear:
He flies, he wheels, distracted with his throes;
Dart follows dart; lance, lance; loud bellowings speak his woes.

LXXVII.

Again he comes; nor dart nor lance avail,
Nor the wild plunging of the tortured horse;
Though man and man's avenging arms assail,
Vain are his weapons, vainer in his force.
One gallant steed is stretch'd a mangled corse:
Another hideous sight! unseam'd appears,
His gory chest unveils life's panting source;
Though death-struck, still his feeble frame he rears;
Staggering, but stemming all, his lord unharm'd he bears.

[1] ["The croupe is a particular leap taught in the manège."—MS.]

LXXVIII.

Foil'd, bleeding, breathless, furious to the last,
Full in the centre stands the bull at bay,
Mid wounds, and clinging dart, and lances brast,
And foes disabled in the brutal fray:
And now the matadores around him play,
Shake the red cloak, and poise the ready brand:
Once more through all he bursts his thundering way—
Vain rage! the mantle quits the conynge hand,
Wraps his fierce eye—'tis past—he sinks upon the sand![1]

LXXIX.

Where his vast neck just mingles with the spine.
Sheathed in his form the deadly weapon lies.
He stops—he starts—disdaining to decline:
Slowly he falls, amidst triumphant cries,
Without a groan, without a struggle dies.
The decorated car appears—on high
The corse is piled—sweet sight for vulgar eyes—[2]
Four steeds that spurn the rein, as swift as shy,
Hurl the dark bulk along, scarce seen in dashing by.

[1] [The reader will do well to compare Lord Byron's animated picture of the popular "sport" of the Spanish nation, with the very circumstantial details contained in the charming "Letters of Don Leucadio Doblado," (*i. e.* the Rev. Blanco White,) published in 1822. So inveterate was, at one time, the rage of the people for this amusement, that even boys mimicked its features in their play. In the slaughter-house itself the professional bull-fighter gave public lessons; and such was the force of depraved custom, that ladies of the highest rank were not ashamed to appear amidst the filth and horror of the shambles. The Spaniards received this sport from the Moors, among whom it was celebrated with great pomp and splendour. See various Notes to Mr. Lockhart's Collection of Ancient Spanish Ballads, 1822.]

[2] ["The trophy corse is reared—disgusting prize—
Or, "The corse is reared—sparkling the chariot flies."—MS.]

LXXX.

Such the ungentle sport that oft invites
The Spanish maid, and cheers the Spanish swain,
Nurtured in blood betimes, his heart delights
In vengeance, gloating on another's pain.
What private feuds the troubled village stain!
Though now one phalanx'd host should meet the foe,
Enough, alas! in humbler homes remain,
To meditate 'gainst friends the secret blow,
For some slight cause of wrath, whence life's warm stream must flow.[1]

LXXXI.

But Jealousy has fled: his bars, his bolts,
His wither'd sentinel, Duenna sage!
And all whereat the generous soul revolts,
Which the stern dotard deem'd he could encage,
Have pass'd to darkness with the vanish'd age.
Who late so free as Spanish girls were seen,
(Ere War uprose in his volcanic rage,)
With braided tresses bounding o'er the green,
While on the gay dance shone Night's lover-loving queen?

LXXXII.

Oh! many a time and oft, had Harold loved,
Or dream'd he loved, since rapture is a dream;
But now his wayward bosom was unmoved,
For not yet had he drunk of Lethe's stream;

[1] ["The Spaniards are as revengeful as ever. At Santa Otella I heard a young peasant threaten to stab a woman, (an old one, to be sure, which mitigates the offence,) and was told, on expressing some small surprise, that this ethic was by no means uncommon."—MS.]

And lately had he learn'd with truth to deem
Love has no gift so grateful as his wings:
How fair, how young, how soft soe'er he seem,
Full from the fount of Joy's delicious springs[1]
Some bitter o'er the flowers its bubbling venom flings.[2]

LXXXIII.

Yet to the beauteous form he was not blind,
Though now it moved him as it moves the wise;
Not that Philosophy on such a mind
E'er deign'd to bend her chastely-awful eyes:
But Passion raves itself to rest, or flies;
And Vice, that digs her own voluptuous tomb,
Had buried long his hopes, no more to rise:
Pleasure's pall'd victim! life-abhorring gloom
Wrote on his faded brow cursed Cain's unresting doom.

LXXXIV.

Still he beheld, nor mingled with the throng;
But view'd them not with misanthropic hate:
Fain would he now have join'd the dance, the song;
But who may smile that sinks beneath his fate?
Naught that he saw his sadness could abate:
Yet once he struggled 'gainst the demon's sway,
And as in Beauty's bower he pensive sate,
Pour'd forth this unpremeditated lay,
To charms as fair as those that soothed his happier day.

1 "Medio de fonte leporum
Surgit amari aliquid quod in ipsis floribus angat."—LUC.

2 ["Full from the heart of Joy's delicious springs
Some bitter bubbles up, and e'en on roses stings."—MS.]

TO INEZ.

1.

Nay, smile not at my sullen brow ;
  Alas ! I cannot smile again :
Yet Heaven avert that ever thou
  Shouldst weep, and haply weep in vain.

2

And dost thou ask what secret woe
  I bear, corroding joy and youth ?
And wilt thou vainly seek to know
  A pang, even thou must fail to soothe ?

3.

It is not love, it is not hate,
  Nor low Ambition's honours lost,
That bids me loathe my present state,
  And fly from all I prized the most :

4.

It is that weariness which springs
  From all I meet, or hear, or see :
To me no pleasure Beauty brings ;
  Thine eyes have scarce a charm for me

5.

It is that settled, ceaseless gloom
  The fabled Hebrew wanderer bore ;
That will not look beyond the tomb,
  But cannot hope for rest before.

6.

What exile from himself can flee ? [1]
  To zones though more and more remote,

[1] ["What exile from himself can flee ?
  To other zones, howe'er remote,
Still, still pursuing clings to me
  The blight of life — the demon Thought." — MS.]

Still, still pursues, where'er I be,
The blight of life—the demon Thought.[1]

7.

Yet others rapt in pleasure seem,
And taste of all that I forsake ;
Oh ! may they still of transport dream,
And ne'er, at least like me, awake !

8.

Through many a clime 'tis mine to go,
With many a retrospection cursed;
And all my solace is to know,
Whate'er betides, I've known the worst.

9.

What is that worst? Nay, do not ask—
In pity from the search forbear:
Smile on—nor venture to unmask
Man's heart, and view the hell that's there.[2]

[1] [" Written January 25, 1810."—MS.]

[2] [In place of this song, which was written at Athens, January 25, 1810, and which contains, as Moore says, " some of the dreariest touches of sadness that ever Byron's pen let fall," we find, in the first draught of the Canto, the following:—

1.

Oh never talk again to me
Of northern climes and British ladies;
It has not been your lot to see,
Like me, the lovely girl of Cadiz.
Although her eye be not of blue,
Nor fair her locks, like English lasses,
How far its own expressive hue
The languid azure eye surpasses!

2.

Prometheus-like, from heaven she stole
The fire, that through those silken lashes
In darkest glances seems to roll,
From eyes that cannot hide their flashes:

LXXXV.

Adieu, fair Cadiz ! yea, a long adieu !
Who may forget how well thy walls have stood ?
When all were changing thou alone wert true,
First to be free and last to be subdued :
And if amidst a scene, a shock so rude,

And as along her bosom steal
In lengthen'd flow her raven tresses,
You'd swear each clustering lock could feel,
And curl'd to give her neck caresses.

3.

Our English maids are long to woo,
And frigid even in possession ;
And if their charms be fair to view,
Their lips are slow at Love's confession:
But born beneath a brighter sun,
For love ordain'd the Spanish maid is,
And who,—when fondly, fairly won,—
Enchants you like the girl of Cadiz ?

4.

The Spanish maid is no coquette,
Nor joys to see a lover tremble ;
And if she love, or if she hate,
Alike she knows not to dissemble.
Her heart can ne'er be bought or sold—
Howe'er it beats, it beats sincerely ;
And, though it will not bend to gold,
'Twill love you long and love you dearly.

5.

The Spanish girl that meets your love
Ne'er taunts you with a mock denial,
For every thought is bent to prove
Her passion in the hour of trial.
When thronging foemen menace Spain
She dares the deed and shares the danger ;
And should her lover press the plain,
She hurls the spear, her love's avenger.

Some native blood was seen thy streets to dye;
A traitor only fell beneath the feud:[1]
Here all were noble, save Nobility;
None hugg'd a conqueror's chain, save fallen Chivalry!

LXXXVI.

Such be the sons of Spain, and strange her fate!
They fight for freedom who were never free;
A kingless people for a nerveless state,
Her vassals combat when their chieftains flee,
True to the veriest slaves of treachery:
Fond of a land which gave them naught but life,
Pride points the path that leads to liberty;
Back to the struggle, baffled in the strife,
War, war is still the cry, "War even to the knife!"[2]

6.

And when, beneath the evening star,
She mingles in the gay bolero,
Or sings to her attuned guitar
Of Christian knight or Moorish hero,
Or counts her beads with fairy hand
Beneath the twinkling rays of Hesper,
Or joins devotion's choral band,
To chant the sweet and hallow'd vesper;—

7.

In each her charms the heart must move
Of all who venture to behold her;
Then let not maids less fair reprove
Because her bosom is not colder:
Through many a clime 'tis mine to roam,
Where many a soft and melting maid is,
But none abroad and few at home,
May match the dark-eyed girl of Cadiz.

[1] Alluding to the conduct and death of Solano, the governor of Cadiz, in May, 1809.

[2] "War to the knife." Palafox's answer to the French general at the siege of Saragoza. [In his proclamations, also, he stated

LXXXVII.

Ye, who would more of Spain and Spaniards know,
Go, read whate'er is writ of bloodiest strife:
Whate'er keen vengeance urged on foreign foe
Can act, is acting there against man's life:
From flashing scimitar to secret knife,
War mouldeth there each weapon to his need—
So may he guard the sister and the wife,
So may he make each cursed oppressor bleed—
So may such foes deserve the most remorseless deed![1]

that, should the French commit any robberies, devastations, and murders, no quarter should be given them. The dogs by whom he was beset, he said, scarcely left him time to clean his sword from their blood, but they still found their grave at Saragoza. All his addresses were in the same spirit. "His language," says Mr. Southey, "had the high tone, and something of the inflation of Spanish romance, suiting the character of those to whom it was directed." See *History of the Peninsular War*, vol. iii. p. 152.]

[1] The Canto, in the original MS., closes with the following stanzas:—

Ye who would more of Spain and Spaniards know,
Sights, saints, antiques, arts, anecdotes, and war,
Go! hie ye hence to Paternoster Row—
Are they not written in the Book of Carr,*
Green Erin's knight and Europe's wandering star!
Then listen, readers, to the Man of Ink,
Hear what he did, and sought, and wrote afar;
All these are coop'd within one quarto's brink,
This borrow, steal,—don't buy,—and tell us what you think.

There may you read, with spectacles on eyes,
How many Wellesleys did embark for Spain,
As if therein they meant to colonize,
How many troops y-crossed the laughing main

* Porphyry said, that the prophecies of Daniel were written after their completion, and such may be my fate here; but it requires no second sight to foretell a tome: the first glimpse of the knight was enough. [In a letter written from Gibraltar, August 6, 1809, to his friend Hodgson, Lord Byron says, "I have seen Sir John Carr at Seville and Cadiz; and, like Swift's barber, have been down on my knees to beg he would not put me into black and white."]

LXXXVIII.

Flows there a tear of pity for the dead?
Look o'er the ravage of the reeking plain;
Look on the hands with female slaughter red;
Then to the dogs resign the unburied slain,
Then to the vulture let each corse remain;
Albeit unworthy of the prey-bird's maw,
Let their bleached bones, and blood's unbleaching stain,
Long mark the battle-field with hideous awe:
Thus only may our sons conceive the scenes we saw!

That ne'er beheld the sad return again:
How many buildings are in such a place,
How many leagues from this to yonder plain,
How many relics each cathedral grace,
And where Giralda stands on her gigantic base.

There may you read (Oh, Phœbus, save Sir John!
That there my words prophetic may not err)
All that was said, or sung, or lost, or won,
By vaunting Wellesley or by blundering Frere,
He that wrote half the "Needy Knifegrinder."*
Thus poesy the way to grandeur paves—
Who would not such diplomatists prefer?
But cease, my Muse, thy speed some respite craves,
Leave legates to their house, and armies to their graves.

Yet here of —— mention may be made,
Who for the Junta modell'd sapient laws,
Taught them to govern ere they were obey'd;
Certes, fit teacher to command, because
His soul Socratic no Xantippe awes;
Bless'd with a dame in Virtue's bosom nursed,—
With her let silent admiration pause!—
True to her second husband and her first;
On such unshaken fame let Satire do its worst.

---

* [The "Needy Knifegrinder," in the Antijacobin, was a joint production of Messrs. Frere and Canning.]

LXXXIX.

Nor yet, alas! the dreadful work is done;
Fresh legions pour adown the Pyrenees:
It deepens still, the work is scarce begun,
Nor mortal eye the distant end foresees.
Fallen nations gaze on Spain; if freed, she frees
More than her fell Pizarros once enchain'd:
Strange retribution! now Columbia's ease
Repairs the wrongs that Quito's sons sustain'd,
While o'er the parent clime prowls Murder unre-
strain'd.

XC.

Not all the blood at Talavera shed,
Not all the marvels of Barossa's fight,
Not Albuera lavish of the dead,
Have won for Spain her well-asserted right.
When shall her Olive-Branch be free from blight?
When shall she breathe her from the blushing toil?
How many a doubtful day shall sink in night,
Ere the Frank robber turn him from his spoil,
And Freedom's stranger-tree grow native of the soil!

XCI.

And thou, my friend![1]—since unavailing woe
Bursts from my heart, and mingles with the strain—
Had the sword laid thee with the mighty low,
Pride might forbid e'en Friendship to complain:

[1] The Honourable John Wingfield, of the Guards, who died of a fever at Coimbra, (May 14, 1811.) I had known him ten years, the better half of his life, and the happiest part of mine. In the short space of one month, I have lost *her* who gave me being, and most of those who had made that being tolerable. To me the lines of Young are no fiction:—

"Insatiate archer! could not one suffice?
Thy shaft flew thrice, and thrice my peace was slain,
And thrice ere thrice yon moon had fill'd her horn.

But thus unlaurell'd to descend in vain,
By all forgotten, save the lonely breast,
And mix unbleeding with the boasted slain,
While Glory crowns so many a meaner crest!
What hadst thou done to sink so peacefully to rest?

I should have ventured a verse to the memory of the late Charles Skinner Matthews, Fellow of Downing College, Cambridge, were he not too much above all praise of mine. His powers of mind, shown in the attainment of greater honours, against the ablest candidates, than those of any graduate on record at Cambridge, have sufficiently established his fame on the spot where it was acquired; while his softer qualities live in the recollection of friends who loved him too well to envy his superiority.—[This and the following stanza were added in August, 1811. In one of his schoolboy poems, entitled "Childish Recollections," Lord Byron has thus drawn the portrait of young Wingfield:—

"Alonzo, best and dearest of my friends,
Thy name ennobles him who thus commends:
From this fond tribute thou canst gain no praise;
The praise is his who now that tribute pays.
Oh! in the promise of thy early youth,
If hope anticipates the words of truth,
Some loftier bard shall sing thy glorious name,
To build his own upon thy deathless fame,
Friend of my heart, and foremost of the list
Of those with whom I lived supremely blest,
Oft have we drain'd the font of ancient lore,
Though drinking deeply, thirsting still for more;
Yet when confinement's lingering hour was done,
Our sports, our studies, and our souls were one.
In every element, unchanged, the same,
All, all that brothers should be, but the name."

Matthews, the idol of Lord Byron at college, was drowned, while bathing in the Cam, on the 2d of August. The following passage of a letter from Newstead to his friend Scrope Davies, written immediately after the event, bears the impress of strong and even agonized feelings:—"My dearest Davies, some curse hangs over me and mine. My mother lies a corpse in the house; one of my best friends is drowned in a ditch; what can I say, or think, or do? I received a letter from him the day before yesterday. My dear Scrope, if you can spare a moment do come down to me—I

XCII.

Oh, known the earliest, and esteem'd the most![1]
Dear to a heart where naught was left so dear!
Though to my hopeless days forever lost,
In dreams deny me not to see thee here!
And Morn in secret shall renew the tear
Of Consciousness awaking to her woes,
And Fancy hover o'er thy bloodless bier,
Till my frail frame return to whence it rose,
And mourn'd and mourner lie united in repose

XCIII.

Here is one fytte of Harold's pilgrimage:
Ye who of him may further seek to know,
Shall find some tidings in a future page,
If he that rhymeth now may scribble moe.
Is this too much? stern critic! say not so:
Patience! and ye shall hear what he beheld
In other lands, where he was doom'd to go:
Lands that contain the monuments of Eld,
Ere Greece and Grecian arts by barbarous hands were quell'd.[2]

want a friend. Matthews's last letter was written on Friday,—on Saturday he was not. In ability, who was like Matthews? How did we all shrink before him! You do me but justice in saying I would have risked my paltry existence to have preserved his. This very evening did I mean to write, inviting him, as I invite you, my very dear friend, to visit me. What will our poor Hobhouse feel? His letters breathe but of Matthews. Come to me, Scrope, I am almost desolate—left almost alone in the world!" Matthews was the son of John Matthews, Esq., (the representative of Herefordshire, in the parliament of 1802—1806,) and brother of the author of "The Diary of an Invalid," also untimely snatched away.]

1 ["Beloved the most."—MS.]

2 ["Dec. 30th, 1809."—MS.]

CHILDE HAROLD'S PILGRIMAGE

CANTC THE SECOND.

CHILDE HAROLD'S PILGRIMAGE.

CANTO THE SECOND.

I.

Come, blue-eyed maid of heaven!—but thou, alas!
Didst never yet one mortal song inspire—
Goddess of Wisdom! here thy temple was,
And is, despite of war and wasting fire,[1]
And years that bade thy worship to expire:
But worse than steel, and flame, and ages slow,
Is the dread sceptre and dominion dire
Of men who never felt the sacred glow [bestow.
That thoughts of thee and thine on polish'd breasts

[1] Part of the Acropolis was destroyed by the explosion of a magazine during the Venetian siege.—[On the highest part of Lycabettus, as Chandler was informed by an eyewitness, the Venetians, in 1687, placed four mortars and six pieces of cannon, when they battered the Acropolis. One of the bombs was fatal to some of the sculpture on the west front of the Parthenon. "In 1667," says Mr. Hobhouse, "every antiquity of which there is now any trace in the Acropolis was in a tolerable state of pre servation. This great temple might, at that period, be called entire;—having been previously a Christian church, it was then a mosque, the most beautiful in the world. The portion yet standing cannot fail to fill the mind of the most indifferent spectator with sentiments of astonishment and awe; and the same reflections arise upon the sight even of the enormous masses of marble ruins which are spread upon the area of the temple."]

II.

Ancient of days! august Athena![1] where,
Where are thy men of might? thy grand in soul?
Gone—glimmering through the dream of things
that were:
First in the race that led to Glory's goal,
They won and pass'd away—is this the whole?
A schoolboy's tale, the wonder of an hour!
The warrior's weapon and the sophist's stole
Are sought in vain, and o'er each mouldering tower,
Dim with the mist of years, gray flits the shade of power.

[1] We can all feel, or imagine the regret with which the ruins of cities, once the capitals of empires, are beheld: the reflections suggested by such objects are too trite to require recapitulation. But never did the littleness of man and the vanity of his very best virtues, of patriotism to exalt, and of valour to defend his country, appear more conspicuous than in the record of what Athens was, and the certainty of what she now is. This theatre of contention between mighty factions, of the struggles of orators, the exaltation and deposition of tyrants, the triumph and punishment of generals, is now become a scene of petty intrigue and perpetual disturbance, between the bickering agents of certain British nobility and gentry. "The wild foxes, the owls and serpents in the ruins of Babylon," were surely less degrading than such inhabitants. The Turks have the plea of conquest for their tyranny, and the Greeks have only suffered the fortune of war, incidental to the bravest; but how are the mighty fallen, when two painters contest the privilege of plundering the Parthenon, and triumph in turn, according to the tenor of each succeeding firman! Sylla could but punish, Philip subdue, and Xerxes burn Athens; but it remained for the paltry antiquarian, and his despicable agents, to render her contemptible as himself and his pursuits. The Parthenon, before its destruction in part by fire, during the Venetian siege, had been a temple, a church, and a mosque. In each point of view it is an object of regard; it changed its worshippers; but still it was a place of worship thrice sacred to devotion: its violation is a triple sacrifice. But—

"Man, proud man,
Dress'd in a little brief authority,
Plays such fantastic tricks before high heaven
As make the angels weep."

III.

Son of the morning, rise! approach you here!
Come—but molest not yon defenceless urn·
Look on this spot—a nation's sepulchre!
Abode of gods, whose shrines no longer burn.
Even gods must yield—religions take their turn:
'Twas Jove's—'tis Mahomet's—and other creeds
Will rise with other years, till man shall learn
Vainly his incense soars, his victim bleeds; [reeds.[1]
Poor child of Doubt and Death, whose hope is built on

IV.

Bound to the earth, he lifts his eye to heaven—
Is't not enough, unhappy thing, to know
Thou art? Is this a boon so kindly given,
That being, thou wouldst be again, and go,

[1] [In the original MS. we find the following note to this and the five succeeding stanzas, which had been prepared for publication, but was afterwards withdrawn, "from a fear," says the poet, "that it might be considered rather as an attack, than a defence of religion."—"In this age of bigotry, when the puritan and priest have changed places, and the wretched Catholic is visited with the 'sins of his fathers,' even unto generations far beyond the pale of the commandment, the cast of opinion in these stanzas will, doubtless, meet with many a contemptuous anathema. But let it be remembered, that the spirit they breathe is desponding, not sneering, skepticism; that he who has seen the Greek and Moslem superstitions contending for mastery over the former shrines of Polytheism—who has left in his own 'Pharisees, thanking God that they are not like publicans and sinners,' and Spaniards in theirs, abhorring the heretics, who have holpen them in their need,—will be not a little bewildered, and begin to think, that as only one of them can be right, they may, most of them, be wrong. With regard to morals, and the effect of religion on mankind, it appears, from all historical testimony, to have had less effect in making them love their neighbours, than inducing that cordial Christian abhorrence between sectaries and schismatics. The Turks and Quakers are the most tolerant: if an Infidel pays his heratch to the former, he may pray how, when, and where he pleases; and the mild tenets and devout demeanour of the latter, make their ives the truest commentary on the Sermon on the Mount."]

Thou know'st not, reck'st not to what region, so
On earth no more, but mingled with the skies?
Still wilt thou dream[1] on future joy and woe?
Regard and weigh yon dust before it flies:
That little urn saith more than thousand homilies.

V.

Or burst the banish'd hero's lofty mound;
Far on the solitary shore he sleeps:[2]
He fell, and falling nations mourn'd around;
But now not one of saddening thousands weeps,
Nor warlike worshipper his vigil keeps
Where demi-gods appear'd, as records tell.
Remove yon skull from out the scatter'd heaps:
Is that a temple where a God may dwell?
Why, even the worm at last disdains her shatter'd cell!

VI.

Look on its broken arch, its ruin'd wall,
Its chambers desolate, and portals foul:
Yes, this was once Ambition's airy hall,
The dome of Thought, the palace of the Soul:
Behold through each lack-lustre, eyeless hole,
The gay recess of Wisdom and of Wit,
And Passion's host, that never brook'd control:
Can all saint, sage, or sophist ever writ,
People this lonely tower, this tenement refit?

[1] ["Still wilt thou harp."—MS.]

[2] It was not always the custom of the Greeks to burn their dead; the greater Ajax, in particular, was interred entire. Almost all the chiefs became gods after their decease; and he was indeed neglected, who had not annual games near his tomb, or festivals in honour of his memory by his countrymen, as Achilles, Brasidas, &c., and at last even Antinöus, whose death was as heroic as his life was infamous.

VII.

Well didst thou speak, Athena's wisest son!
"All that we know is, nothing can be known."
Why should we shrink from what we cannot shun?
Each hath his pang, but feeble sufferers groan
With brain-born dreams of evil all their own.
Pursue what Chance or Fate proclaimeth best;
Peace waits us on the shores of Acheron:
There no forced banquet claims the sated guest,
But Silence spreads the couch of every welcome rest.

VIII.

Yet if, as holiest men have deem'd, there be
A land of souls beyond that sable shore,
To shame the doctrine of the Sadducee
And sophists, madly vain of dubious lore;
How sweet it were in concert to adore
With those who made our mortal labours light!
To hear each voice we fear'd to hear no more!
Behold each mighty shade reveal'd to sight,
The Bactrian, Samian sage, and all who taught the right![1]

IX.

There, thou!—whose love and life together fled,
Have left me here to love and live in vain—
Twined with my heart, and can I deem thee dead
When busy Memory flashes on my brain?

[1] [In the original MS., for this magnificent stanza, we find what follows:—

"Frown not upon me, churlish priest! that I
Look not for life, where life may never be;
I am no sneerer at thy fantasy:
Thou pitiest me,—alas! I envy thee,
Thou bold discoverer in an unknown sea,
Of happy isles and happier tenants there;
I ask thee not to prove a Sadducee;
Still dream of Paradise, thou know'st not where,
But lovest too well to bid thine erring brother share."]

Well—I will dream that we may meet again,
And woo the vision to my vacant breast:
If aught of young Remembrance then remain,
Be as it may Futurity's behest,
For me 'twere bliss enough to know thy spirit blest![1]

X.

Here let me sit upon this massy stone,[2]
The marble column's yet unshaken base;
Here, son of Saturn! was thy favourite throne:[3]
Mightiest of many such! Hence let me trace
The latent grandeur of thy dwelling-place.
It may not be: nor even can Fancy's eye
Restore what Time hath labour'd to deface.
Yet these proud pillars claim no passing sigh;
Unmov'd the Moslem sits, the light Greek carols by.

XI.

But who, of all the plunderers of yon fane
On high, where Pallas linger'd, loath to flee

[1] [Lord Byron wrote this stanza at Newstead, in October, 1811, on hearing of the death of his Cambridge friend, young Eddlestone; "making," he says, "the sixth, within four months, of friends and relations that I have lost between May and the end of August."]

[2] ["The thought and the expression," says Professor Clarke, in a letter to the poet, "are here so truly Petrarch's, that I would ask you whether you ever read,—

Poi quando 'l vero sgombra
Quel dolce error pur li medesmo assido,
Me freddo, pietra morta in pietra viva;
In guisa d' uom chè pensi e piange e scriva.'

'Thus rendered by Wilmot,—

'But when rude truth destroys
The loved illusion of the dreamed sweets,
I sit me down on the cold rugged stone,
Less cold, less dead than I, and think and weep alone.'"]

[3] The temple of Jupiter Olympius, of which sixteen columns, entirely of marble, yet survive: originally there were one hundred and fifty. These columns, however, are by many supposed to have belonged to the Pantheon.

The latest relic of her ancient reign;
The last, the worst, dull spoiler, who was he?
Blush, Caledonia! such thy sons could be!
England! I joy no child he was of thine:
Thy free-born men should spare what once was free;
Yet they could violate each saddening shrine,
And bear these altars o'er the long-reluctant brine.[1]

XII.

But most the modern Pict's ignoble boast,
To rive what Goth and Turk, and Time hath spared;[2]
Cold as the crags upon his native coast,[3]
His mind as barren and his heart as hard,
Is he whose head conceived, whose hand prepared
Aught to displace Athena's poor remains:
Her sons too weak the sacred shrine to guard,
Yet felt some portion of their mother's pains,[4]
And never knew, till then, the weight of despot's chains.

XIII.

What! shall it e'er be said by British tongue
Albion was happy in Athena's tears?
Though in thy name the slave her bosom wrung,
Tell not the deed to blushing Europe's ears;

[1] The ship was wrecked in the Archipelago.

[2] See Appendix, Note A, for some strictures on the removal of the works of art from Athens.

[3] ["Cold and accursed as his native coast."—MS.]

[4] I cannot resist availing myself of the permission of my friend Dr. Clarke, whose name requires no comment with the public, but whose sanction will add tenfold weight to my testimony, to insert the following extract from a very obliging letter of his to me, as a note to the above lines:—"When the last of the Metopes was taken from the Parthenon, and, in moving of it, great part of the superstructure with one of the triglyphs was thrown down by the workmen whom Lord Elgin employed, the disdar, who beheld the mischief done in the building, took his pipe from his mouth. dropped a tear, and, in a supplicating tone of voice, said to Lusieri. Τέλος!—I was present." The disdar alluded to was the fathe' of the present disdar.

The ocean queen, the free Britannia, bears
The last poor plunder from a bleeding land:
Yes, she, whose generous aid her name endears,
Tore down those remnants with a harpy's hand,
Which envious Eld forbore, and tyrants left to stand.[1]

XIV.

Where was thine Ægis, Pallas! that appall'd
Stern Alaric and Havoc on their way?[2]
Where Peleus' son? whom hell in vain enthrall'd,
His shades from hades upon that dreary day
Bursting to light in terrible array!
What! could not Pluto spare the chief once more,
To scare a second robber from his prey?
Idly he wander'd on the Stygian shore,
Nor now preserved the walls he loved to shield before

[1] [After stanza xiii. the original MS. has the following:—

"Come, then, ye classic thanes of each degree,
Dark Hamilton and sullen Aberdeen,
Come pilfer all the Pilgrim loves to see,
All that yet consecrates the fading scene:
Oh! better were it ye had never been,
Nor ye, nor Elgin, nor that lesser wight,
The victim sad of vase-collecting spleen,
House-furnisher withal, one Thomas hight,
Than ye should bear one stone from wrong'd Athena's site

"Or will the gentle dilettanti crew
Now delegate the task to digging Gell,
That mighty limner of a bird's-eye view,
How like to nature let his volumes tell;
Who can with him the folio's limits swell
With all the author saw, or said he saw?
Who can topographize or delve so well?
No boaster he, nor impudent and raw,
His pencil, pen, and shade, alike without a flaw."]

[2] According to Zosimus, Minerva and Achilles frightened Alaric from the Acropolis; but others relate that the Gothic king was nearly as mischievous as the Scottish peer.—See Chandler.

XV.

Cold is the heart, fair Greece! that looks on thee,
Nor feels as lovers o'er the dust they loved;
Dull is the eye that will not weep to see
Thy walls defaced, thy mouldering shrines removed
By British hands, which it had best behooved
To guard those relics ne'er to be restored.
Cursed be the hour when from their isle they roved,
And once again thy hapless bosom gored,
And snatch'd thy shrinking gods to northern climes abhorr'd!

XVI.

But where is Harold? shall I then forget
To urge the gloomy wanderer o'er the wave?
Little reck'd he of all that men regret;
No loved-one now in feign'd lament could rave;
No friend the parting hand extended gave,
Ere the cold stranger pass'd to other climes:
Hard is his heart whom charms may not enslave;
But Harold felt not as in other times,
And left without a sigh the land of war and crimes.

XVII.

He that has sail'd upon the dark-blue sea
Has view'd at times, I ween, a full fair sight;
When the fresh breeze is fair as breeze may be,
The white sail set, the gallant frigate tight;
Masts, spires, and strand retiring to the right,
The glorious main expanding o'er the bow,
The convoy spread like wild swans in their flight,
The dullest sailer wearing bravely now,
So gayly curl the waves before each dashing prow

XVIII.

And, oh! the little warlike world within!
The well-reeved guns, the netted canopy,[1]
The hoarse command, the busy humming din,
When, at a word, the tops are mann'd on high:
Hark, to the boatswain's call, the cheering cry!
While through the seaman's hand the tackle glides,
Or schoolboy midshipman that, standing by,
Strains his shrill pipe as good or ill betides,
And well the docile crew that skilful urchin guides.

XIX.

White is the glassy deck, without a stain,
Where on the watch the staid lieutenant walks:
Look on that part which sacred doth remain
For the lone chieftain, who majestic stalks,
Silent and feared by all—not oft he talks
With aught beneath him, if he would preserve
That strict restraint, which, broken, ever balks
Conquest and Fame: but Britons rarely swerve
From law, however stern, which tends their strength to nerve.[2]

XX.

Blow! swiftly blow, thou keel-compelling gale!
Till the broad sun withdraws his lessening ray;
Then must the pennant-bearer slacken sail,
That lagging barks may make their lazy way.
Ah! grievance sore, and listless, dull delay,
To waste on sluggish hulks the sweetest breeze!
What leagues are lost, before the dawn of day,
Thus loitering pensive on the willing seas,
The flapping sail haul'd down to halt for logs like these

[1] To prevent blocks or splinters from falling on deck during action.

[2] ["From Discipline's stern law," &c.—MS.]

XXI.

The moon is up; by Heaven, a lovely eve!
Long streams of light o'er dancing waves expand,
Now lads on shore may sigh, and maids believe·
Such be our fate when we return to land!
Meantime some rude Arion's restless hand
Wakes the brisk harmony that sailors love;[1]
A circle there of merry listeners stand,
Or to some well-known measure featly move,
Thoughtless, as if on shore they still were free to rove.

XXII.

Through Calpe's straits survey the steepy shore;
Europe and Afric on each other gaze!
Lands of the dark-eyed maid and dusky Moor
Alike beheld beneath pale Hecate's blaze:
How softly on the Spanish shore she plays,
Disclosing rock and slope, and forest brown,
Distinct, though darkening with her waning phase;
But Mauritania's giant shadows frown,
From mountain-cliff to coast descending sombre down.

XXIII.

'Tis night, when Meditation bids us feel
We once have loved, though love is at an end:
The heart, lone mourner of its baffled zeal,
Though friendless now, will dream it had a friend.[2]
Who with the weight of years would wish to bend.
When Youth itself survives young Love and Joy?
Alas! when mingling souls forget to blend,
Death hath but little left him to destroy!
Ah! happy years! once more who would not be a boy?

[1] ["Plies the brisk instrument that sailors love."—MS.]
[2] ["Bleeds the lone heart, once boundless in its zeal,
And friendless now, yet dreams it had a friend."—MS.]

XXIV.

Thus bending o'er the vessel's laving side,
To gaze on Dian's wave-reflected sphere,
The soul forgets her schemes of Hope and Pride,
And flies unconscious o'er each backward year.
None are so desolate but something dear,
Dearer than self, possesses or possess'd
A thought and claims the homage of a tear;
A flashing pang! of which the weary breast
Would still, albeit in vain, the heavy heart divest.

XXV.

To sit on rocks, to muse o'er flood and fell,
To slowly trace the forest's shady scene,
Where things that own not man's dominion dwell,
And mortal foot hath ne'er or rarely been;
To climb the trackless mountain all unseen,
With the wild flock that never needs a fold;
Alone o'er steeps and foaming falls to lean;
This is not solitude; 'tis but to hold
Converse with nature's charms, and view her stores unroll'd.

XXVI.

But midst the crowd, the hum, the shock of men,
To hear, to see, to feel, and to possess,
And roam along, the world's tired denizen,
With none who bless us, none whom we can bless;
Minions of splendour shrinking from distress!
None that, with kindred consciousness endued,
If we were not, would seem to smile the less,
Of all that flatter'd, follow'd, sought, and sued;
This is to be alone; this, this is solitude!

XXVII.

More blest the life of godly eremite,
Such as on lonely Athos may be seen,[1]
Watching at eve upon the giant height,
Which look o'er waves so blue, skies so serene,
That he who there at such an hour hath been
Will wistful linger on that hallow'd spot;
Then slowly tear him from the witching scene,
Sigh forth one wish that such had been his lot,
hen turn to hate a world he had almost forgot.

XXVIII.

Pass we the long, unvarying course, the track
Oft trod, that never leaves a trace behind;
Pass we the calm, the gale, the change, the tack,
And each well known caprice of wave and wind;
Pass we the joys and sorrows sailors find,
Coop'd in their winged sea-girt citadel;
The foul, the fair, the contrary, the kind,
As breezes rise and fall and billows swell,
Till on some jocund morn—lo, land! and all is well:

XXIX.

But not in silence pass Calypso's isles,[2]
The sister tenants of the middle deep;

[1] [One of Lord Byron's chief delights was, as he himself states in one of his journals, after bathing in some retired spot, to seat himself on a high rock above the sea, and there remain for hours, gazing upon the sky and the waters. "He led the life," says Sir Egerton Brydges, "as he wrote the strains, of a true poet. He could sleep, and very frequently did sleep, wrapped up in his rough great coat, on the hard boards of a deck, while the winds and the waves were roaring round him on every side, and could subsist on a crust and a glass of water. It would be difficult to persuade me, that he who is a coxcomb in his manners, and artificial in his habits of life, could write good poetry."

[2] Goza is said to have been the island of Calypso.—["The

There for the weary still a haven smiles,
Though the fair goddess long hath ceased to weep,
And o'er her cliffs a fruitless watch to keep
For him who dared prefer a mortal bride:
Here, too, his boy essay'd the dreadful leap
Stern Mentor urged from high to yonder tide;
While thus of both bereft, the nymph-queen doubly sigh'd.

XXX.

Her reign is past, her gentle glories gone:
But trust not this: too easy youth, beware!
A mortal sovereign holds her dangerous throne,
And thou mayst find a new Calypso there.
Sweet Florence! could another ever share
This wayward, loveless heart, it would be thine:
But check'd by every tie, I may not dare
To cast a worthless offering at thy shrine,
Nor ask so dear a breast to feel one pang for mine.

XXXI.

Thus Harold deem'd, as on that lady's eye[1]
He look'd, and met its beam without a thought,
Save Admiration glancing harmless by:
Love kept aloof, albeit not far remote,
Who knew his votary often lost and caught,
But knew him as his worshipper no more,
And ne'er again the boy his bosom sought:
Since now he vainly urged him to adore,
Well deem'd the little god his ancient sway was o'er.

identity of the habitation assigned by poets to the nymph Calypso has occasioned much discussion and variety of opinion. Some place it at Malta, and some at Goza."—*Sir R. C. Hoare's Classical Tour.*]

[1] ["Thus Harold spoke," &c.—MS.]

XXXII.

Fair Florence[1] found, in sooth with some amaze,
One who, 'twas said, still sigh'd to all he saw,
Withstand, unmoved, the lustre of her gaze,
Which others hail'd with real or mimic awe,
Their hope, their doom, their punishment, their law;
All that gay Beauty from her bondsmen claims:
And much she marvell'd that a youth so raw
Nor felt, nor feign'd at least, the oft-told flames,
Which, though sometimes they frown, yet rarely anger dames.

XXXIII.

Little knew she that seeming marble heart,
Now mask'd in silence or withheld by pride,
Was not unskilful in the spoiler's art,[2]
And spread its snares licentious far and wide;[3]
Nor from the base pursuit had turn'd aside,
As long as aught was worthy to pursue:
But Harold on such arts no more relied;
And had he doted on those eyes so blue,
Yet never would he join the lover's whining crew.

[1] [For an account of this accomplished but eccentric lady, whose acquaintance the poet formed at Malta, see Miscellaneous Poems, September, 1809, "To Florence."—"In one so imaginative as Lord Byron, who, while he infused so much of his life into his poetry, mingled also not a little of poetry with his life, it is difficult," says Moore, "in unravelling the texture of his feelings, to distinguish at all times between the fanciful and the real. His description *here*, for instance, of the unmoved and 'loveless heart,' with which he contemplated even the charms of this attractive person, is wholly at variance with the statements in many of his letters; and, above all, with one of the most graceful of his lesser poems, addressed to this same lady, during a thunder-storm on his road to Zitza."]

[2] [Against this line it is sufficient to set the poet's own declaration, in 1821.—"I am not a Joseph, nor a Scipio; but I can safely affirm, that I never in my life seduced any woman."]

[3] ["We have here another instance of his propensity to self

XXXIV.

Not much he kens, I ween, of woman's breast,
Who thinks that wanton thing is won by sighs;
What careth she for hearts when once possess'd?
Do proper homage to thine idol's eyes;
But not too humbly, or she will despise
Thee and thy suit, though told in moving tropes:
Disguise even tenderness, if thou art wise;
Brisk Confidence[1] still best with woman copes:
Pique her and soothe in turn, soon Passion crowns thy hopes.

XXXV.

'Tis an old lesson; Time approves it true,
And those who know it best, deplore it most;
When all is won that all desire to woo,
The paltry prize is hardly worth the cost:
Youth wasted, minds degraded, honour lost,
These are thy fruits, successful Passion! these!
If, kindly cruel, early Hope is crost,
Still to the last it rankles, a disease,
Not to be cured when Love itself forgets to please.

XXXVI.

Away! nor let me loiter in my song,
For we have many a mountain-path to tread,
And many a varied shore to sail along,
By pensive Sadness, not by Fiction, led—
Climes, fair withal as ever mortal head
Imagined in its little schemes of thought;
Or e'er in new Utopias were ared,
To teach man what he might be, or he ought;
If that corrupted thing could ever such be taught.

misrepresentation. However great might have been the irregularities of his college life, such phrases as 'the spoiler's art,' and 'spreading snares,' were in no wise applicable to them."—MOORE.]

[1] ["Brisk Impudence," &c.—MS.]

XXXVII.

Dear Nature is the kindest mother still,
Though always changing in her aspect mild;
From her bare bosom let me take my fill,
Her never-weaned, though not her favour'd child.
Oh! she is fairest in her features wild,
Where nothing polish'd dares pollute her path:
To me by day or night she ever smiled,
Though I have mark'd her when none other hath,
And sought her more and more, and loved her best in
wrath.

XXXVIII.

Land of Albania! where Iskander rose,
Theme of the young, and beacon of the wise,
And he his namesake, whose oft-baffled foes
Shrunk from his deeds of chivalrous emprize:
Land of Albania![1] let me bend mine eyes
On thee, thou rugged nurse of savage men!
The cross descends, thy minarets arise,
And the pale crescent sparkles in the glen.
Through many a cypress grove within each city's ken

XXXIX.

Childe Harold sail'd, and pass'd the barren spot,
Where sad Penelope o'erlook'd the wave;[2]
And onward view'd the mount, nor yet forgot,
The lover's refuge, and the Lesbian's grave.

[2] See Appendix, Note [B].

[2] Ithaca.—["Sept. 24th," says Mr. Hobhouse, "we were in the channel, with Ithaca, then in the hands of the French, to the west of us. We were close to it, and saw a few shrubs on a brown heathy land, two little towns in the hills, scattered amongst trees, and a windmill or two, with a tower on the heights. That Ithaca was not very strongly garrisoned you will easily believe, when I tell, that a month afterwards, when the Ionian Islands were invested by a British squadron, it was surrendered into the hands of a sergeant and seven men." For a very curious account

Dark Sappho ! could not verse immortal save
That breast imbued with such immortal fire ?
Could she not live who life eternal gave ?
If life eternal may await the lyre, [aspire.
That only heaven to which Earth's children may

XL.

'Twas on a Grecian autumn's gentle eve
Childe Harold hail'd Leucadia's cape afar ;[1]
A spot he longed to see nor cared to leave :
Oft did he mark the scene of vanish'd war,
Actium, Lepanto, fatal Trafalgar ;[2]
Mark them unmoved, for he would not delight
(Born beneath some remote inglorious star)
In themes of bloody fray, or gallant fight, [wight.
But loath'd the bravo's trade, and laughed at martial

XLI.

But when he saw the evening star above
Leucadia's far projecting rock of woe,
And hail'd the last resort of fruitless love,
He felt, or deem'd he felt, no common glow :
And as the stately vessel glided slow
Beneath the shadow of that ancient mount,
He watched the billows' melancholy flow,

of the state of the kingdom of Ulysses in 1816, see Williams's Travels, vol. ii. p. 427.]

[1] Leucadia, now Santa Maura. From the promontory (the Lover's Leap) Sappho is said to have thrown herself.—[" Sept. 28th, we doubled the promontory of Santa Maura, and saw the precipice which the fate of Sappho, the poetry of Ovid, and the rocks so formidable to the ancient mariners, have made forever memorable."—HOBHOUSE.]

[2] Actium and Trafalgar need no further mention. The battle of Lepanto, equally bloody and considerable, but less known, was fought in the Gulf of Patras. Here the author of Don Quixote lost his left hand.

And, sunk albeit in thought as he was wont,
More placid seem'd his eye, and smooth his pallid front.[1]

XLII.

Morn dawns; and with it stern Albania's hills,
Dark Suli's rocks, and Pindus' inland peak,
Robed half in mist, bedew'd with snowy rills,
Array'd in many a dun and purple streak,
Arise; and, as the clouds along them break,
Disclose the dwelling of the mountaineer:
Here roams the wolf, the eagle whets his beak,
Birds, beasts of prey, and wilder men appear,
And gathering storms around convulse the closing year.

XLIII.

Now Harold felt himself at length alone,
And bade to Christian tongues a long adieu;
Now he adventured on a shore unknown,
Which all admire, but many dread to view:
His breast was arm'd 'gainst fate, his wants were few,
Peril he sought not, but ne'er shrank to meet:
The scene was savage, but the scene was new;
This made the ceaseless toil of travel sweet, [heat.
Beat back keen winter's blast, and welcomed summer's

XLIV.

Here the red cross, for still the cross is here,
Though sadly scoff'd at by the circumcised,
Forgets that pride to pamper'd priesthood dear;
Churchman and votary alike despised.
Foul Superstition! howsoe'er disguised.
Idol, saint, virgin, prophet crescent, cross,
For whatsoever symbol thou art prized,
Thou sacerdotal gain, but general loss!
Who from true worship's gold can separate thy dross?

1 [" And roused him more from thought than he was wont,
While Pleasure almost seemed to smooth his placid front."—MS.]

XLV.

Ambracia's gulf behold, where once was lost
A world for woman, lovely, harmless thing!
In yonder rippling bay, their naval host
Did many a Roman chief and Asian king[1]
To doubtful conflict, certain slaughter bring:
Look where the second Cæsar's trophies rose:[2]
Now, like the hands that rear'd them, withering:
Imperial anarchs, doubling human woes!
God! was thy globe ordain'd for such to win and lose?

XLVI.

From the dark barriers of that rugged clime,
Even to the centre of Illyria's vales,
Childe Harold pass'd o'er many a mount sublime,
Through lands scarce noticed in historic tales;
Yet in famed Attica such lovely dales
Are rarely seen; nor can fair Tempe boast
A charm they know not; loved Parnassus fails,
Though classic ground and consecrated most, [coast.
To match some spots that lurk within this lowering

XLVII.

He pass'd bleak Pindus, Acherusia's lake,[3]
And left the primal city of the land,

[1] It is said, that, on the day previous to the battle of Actium, Antony had thirteen kings at his levee.—["To-day" (Nov. 12,) "I saw the remains of the town of Actium, near which Antony lost the world, in a small bay, where two frigates could hardly manœuvre: a broken wall is the sole remnant. On another part of the gulf stand the ruins of Nicopolis, built by Augustus, in honour of his victory."—*Lord Byron to his Mother*, 1809.]

[2] Nicopolis, whose ruins are most extensive, is at some distance from Actium, where the wall of the Hippodrome survives in a few fragments. These ruins are large masses of brickwork, the bricks of which are joined by interstices of mortar, as large as the bricks themselves, and equally durable.

[3] According to Pouqueville, the lake of Yanina: but Pouqueville is always out.

And onwards did his further journey take
To greet Albania's chief,[1] whose dread command
Is lawless law; for with a bloody hand
He sways a nation, turbulent and bold:
Yet here and there some daring mountain-band
Disdain his power, and from their rocky hold
Hurl their defiance far, nor yield, unless to gold.[2]

XLVIII.

Monastic Zitza![3] from thy shady brow,
Thou small but favour'd spot of holy ground!
Where'er we gaze, around, above, below,
What rainbow tints, what magic charms are found!
Rock, river, forest, mountain, all abound,
And bluest skies that harmonize the whole:
Beneath, the distant torrent's rushing sound
Tells where the volumed cataract doth roll [soul.
Between those hanging rocks, that shock yet please the

[1] The celebrated Ali Pasha. Of this extraordinary man there is an incorrect account in Pouqueville's Travels.—[" I left Malta in the Spider brig-of-war, on the 21st of September, and arrived in eight days at Prevesa. I thence have traversed the interior of the province of Albania, on a visit to the pasha, as far as Tepaleen, his highness's country palace, where I stayed three days. The name of the pasha is Ali, and he is considered a man of the first abilities: he governs the whole of Albania, (the ancient Illyricum,) Epirus, and part of Macedonia."—*Lord B. to his Mother.*]

[2] Five thousand Suliotes, among the rocks and in the castle of Suli, withstood thirty thousand Albanians for eighteen years; the castle at last was taken by bribery. In this contest there were several acts performed not unworthy of the better days of Greece.

[3] The convent and village of Zitza are four hours' journey from Joannina, or Yanina, the capital of the pashalick. In the valley the river Kalamus (once the Acheron) flows, and, not far from Zitza, forms a fine cataract. The situation is perhaps the finest in Greece, though the approach to Delvinachi and parts of Acarnania and Ætolia may contest the palm. Delphi, Parnassus, and, in Attica, even Cape Colonna and Port Raphti, are very inferior; as also every scene in Ionia, or the Troad: I am almost inclined to add the approach to Constantinople; but, from the different fea

XLIX.

Amidst the grove that crowns yon tufted hill,
Which, were it not for many a mountain nigh
Rising in lofty ranks, and loftier still,
Might well itself be deem'd of dignity,
The convent's white walls glisten fair on high:
Here dwells the caloyer,[1] nor rude is he,
Nor niggard of his cheer; the passer by
Is welcome still; nor heedless will he flee
From hence, if he delight kind Nature's sheen to see.

L.

Here in the sultriest season let him rest,
Fresh is the green beneath those aged trees;
Here winds of gentlest wing will fan his breast,
From heaven itself he may inhale the breeze:
The plain is far beneath—oh! let him seize
Pure pleasure while he can: the scorching ray
Here pierceth not, impregnate with disease:
Then let his length the loitering pilgrim lay,
And gaze, untired, the morn, the noon, the eve away.

tures of the last, a comparison can hardly be made. [" Zitza," says the poet's companion, "is a village inhabited by Greek peasants. Perhaps there is not in the world a more romantic prospect than that which is viewed from the summit of the hill. The foreground is a gentle declivity, terminating on every side in an extensive landscape of green hills and dale, enriched with vineyards, and dotted with frequent flocks."]

[1] The Greek monks are so called.—[" We went into the monastery," says Mr. Hobhouse, " after some parley with one of the monks, through a small door plated with iron, on which the marks of violence were very apparent, and which, before the country had been tranquillized under the powerful government of Ali, had been battered in vain by the troops of robbers then, by turns, infesting every district. The prior, an humble, meek-mannered man, entertained us in a warm chamber with grapes, and a pleasant white wine, not trodden out, as he told us, by the feet, but pressed from the grape by the hand; and we were so

LI.

Dusky and huge, enlarging on the sight,
Nature's volcanic amphitheatre,[1]
Chimæra's alps extend from left to right:
Beneath a living valley seems to stir; [fir
Flocks play, trees wave, streams flow, the mountain-
Nodding above; behold black Acheron![2]
Once consecrated to the sepulchre.
Pluto! if this be hell I look upon, [none
Close shamed Elysium's gates, my shade shall seek for

LII.

Ne city's towers pollute the lovely view;
Unseen is Yanina, though not remote,
Veil'd by the screen of hills: here men are few,
Scanty the hamlet, rare the lonely cot:
But, peering down each precipice, the goat
Browseth; and, pensive o'er his scattered flock,
The little shepherd in his white capote[3]
Doth lean his boyish form along the rock,
Or in his cave awaits the tempest's short-lived shock.

LIII.

Oh! where, Dodona! is thine aged grove,
Prophetic fount, and oracle divine?
What valley echoed the response of Jove?
What trace remaineth of the Thunderer's shrine?
All, all forgotten—and shall man repine
That his frail bonds to fleeting life are broke?
Cease, fool! the fate of gods may well be thine:
Wouldst thou survive the marble or the oak?
When nations, tongues, and worlds must sink beneath
the stroke!

well pleased with every thing about us, that we agreed to lodge with him on our return from the vizier."]

1 The Chimariot mountains appear to have been volcanic.

2 Now called Kalamas.

3 Albanese cloak.

LIV.

Epirus' bounds recede, and mountains fail;
Tired of up-gazing still, the wearied eye
Reposes gladly on as smooth a vale
As ever Spring yclad in grassy dye:
Even on a plain no humble beauties lie,
Where some bold river breaks the long expanse,
And woods along the banks are waving high,
Whose shadows in the glassy waters dance, [trance.
Or with the moonbeam sleep in midnight's solemn

LV.

The sun had sunk behind vast Tomerit,[1]
And Laos wide and fierce came roaring by;[2]
The shades of wonted night were gathering yet,
When, down the steep banks winding warily,
Childe Harold saw, like meteors in the sky,
The glittering minarets of Tepalen,
Whose walls o'erlook the stream; and drawing nigh,
He heard the busy hum of warrior-men [glen.[3]
Swelling the breeze that sigh'd along the lengthening

[1] Anciently Mount Tomarus.

[2] The river Laos was full at the time the author passed it; and, immediately above Tepaleen, was to the eye as wide as the Thames at Westminster; at least in the opinion of the author and his fellow-traveller. In the summer it must be much narrower. It certainly is the finest river in the Levant; neither Achelous, Alpheus, Acheron, Scamander, nor Cayster, approached it in breadth or beauty.

[3] ["Ali Pasha, hearing that an Englishman of rank was in his dominions, left orders, in Yanina, with the commandant, to provide a house, and supply me with every kind of necessary *gratis*. I rode out on the vizier's horses, and saw the palaces of himself and grandsons. I shall never forget the singular scene on entering Tepaleen, at five in the afternoon, (Oct. 11,) as the sun was going down. It brought to my mind (with some change of *dress*, however) Scott's description of Branksome Castle in his Lay, and the feudal system. The Albanians in their dresses (the most

LVI.

He pass'd the sacred harem's silent tower,
And underneath the wide o'erarching gate
Survey'd the dwelling of this chief of power,
Where all around proclaim'd his high estate.
Amidst no common pomp the despot sate,
While busy preparation shook the court;
Slaves, eunuchs, soldiers, guests, and santons wait;
Within a palace, and without, a fort;
Here men of every clime appear to make resort.

LVII.

Richly caparison'd, a ready row
Of armed horse, and many a warlike store,
Circled the wide-extending court below;
Above, strange groups adorn'd the corridore;
And oft-times through the area's echoing door,
Some high-capp'd Tartar spurr'd his steed away:
The Turk, the Greek, the Albanian, and the Moor,
Here mingled in their many-hued array,
While the deep war-drum's sound announced the close of day.

magnificent in the world, consisting of a long white kilt, gold-worked cloak, crimson velvet gold-laced jacket and waistcoat, silver-mounted pistols and daggers;) the Tartars, with their high caps; the Turks in their vast pelisses and turbans; the soldiers and black slaves with the horses, the former in groups, in an immense large open gallery, in front of the palace, the latter placed in a kind of cloister below it; two hundred steeds ready caparisoned to move in a moment; couriers entering or passing out with despatches; the kettle-drums beating; boys calling the hour from the minaret of the mosque;—altogether, with the singular appearance of the building itself, formed a new and delightful spectacle to a stranger. I was conducted to a very handsome apartment, and my health inquired after by the vizier's secretary à la mode Turque."—*Byron Letters.*]

LVIII.

The wild Albanian kirtled to his knee
With shawl-girt head and ornamented gun,
The gold-embroidered garments, fair to see;
The crimson-scarfed men of Macedon;
The Delhi with his cap of terror on,
And crooked glaive; the lively, supple Greek;
And swarthy Nubia's mutilated son;
The bearded Turk, that rarely deigns to speak,
Master of all around, too potent to be meek,

LIX.

Are mix'd conspicuous: some recline in groups,
Scanning the motley scene that varies round;
There some grave Moslem to devotion stoops,
And some that smoke, and some that play, are found;
Here the Albanian proudly treads the ground;
Half whispering there the Greek is heard to prate;
Hark! from the mosque the nightly solemn sound,
The Muezzin's call doth shake the minaret,
"There is no god but God!—to prayer—lo! God is great!"[1]

LX.

Just at this season Ramazani's fast[2]
Through the long day its penance did maintain:

[1] ["On our arrival at Tepaleen, we were lodged in the palace. During the night we were disturbed by the perpetual carousal which seemed to be kept up in the gallery, and by the drum, and the voice of the 'Muezzin,' or chanter, calling the Turks to prayers from the minaret of the mosque attached to the palace. The chanter was a boy, and he sang out his hymn in a sort of loud melancholy recitative. He was a long time repeating the purport of these few words: 'God most high! I bear witness that there is no god but God, and Mahomet is his prophet: come to prayer; come to the asylum of salvation: great God! there is no God but God!"—HOBHOUSE.]

[2] ["We were a little unfortunate in the time we chose for travelling, for it was during the Ramazan, or Turkish Lent, which

But when the lingering twilight hour was past,
Revel and feast assumed the rule again:
Now all was bustle, and the menial train
Prepared and spread the plenteous board within;
The vacant gallery now seem'd made in vain,
But from the chambers came the mingling din,
As page and slave anon were passing out and in.

LXI.

Here woman's voice is never heard: apart,
And scarce permitted, guarded, veil'd, to move,
She yields to one her person and her heart,
Tamed to her cage, nor feels a wish to rove:
For, not unhappy in her master's love,
And joyful in a mother's gentlest cares,
Blest cares! all other feelings far above!
Herself more sweetly rears the babe she bears,
Who never quits the breast, no meaner passion shares

LXII.

In marble-paved pavilion, where a spring
Of living water from the centre rose,
Whose bubbling did a genial freshness fling,
And soft voluptuous couches breathed repose,
ALI reclined, a man of war and woes:[1]

fell this year in October, and was hailed at the rising of the new moon, on the evening of the 8th, by every demonstration of joy: but although, during this month, the strictest abstinence is observed in the daytime, yet with the setting of the sun the feasting commences: then is the time for paying and receiving visits, and for the amusements of Turkey, puppet-shows, jugglers, dancers, and story-tellers."—HOBHOUSE.]

[1] ["On the 12th, I was introduced to Ali Pasha. I was dressed in a full suit of staff uniform, with a very magnificent sabre, &c The vizier received me in a large room paved with marble; a fountain was playing in the centre; the apartment was surrounded by scarlet ottomans. He received me standing, a wonderful compliment from a Mussulman, and made me sit down on his right hand. His first question was, why, at so early an age, I left my country? He then said, the English minister, Captain Leake, had

Yet in his lineaments ye cannot trace,
While Gentleness her milder radiance throws
Along that aged venerable face, [grace.
The deeds that lurk beneath, and stain him with dis-

LXIII.

It is not that yon hoary lengthened beard
Ill suits the passions which belong to youth;
Love conquers age—so Hafiz hath averr'd,
So sings the Teian, and he sings in sooth—
But crimes that scorn the tender voice of ruth,
Beseeming all men ill, but most the man
In years, have mark'd him with a tiger's tooth;[1]
Blood follows blood, and through their mortal span,
In bloodier acts conclude those who with blood began.[2]

told him I was of a great family, and desired his respects to my mother; which I now, in the name of Ali Pasha, present to you. He said he was certain I was a man of birth, because I had small ears, curling hair, and little white hands. He told me to consider him as a father whilst I was in Turkey, and said he looked on me as his own son. Indeed, he treated me like a child, sending me almonds and sugared sherbet, fruit, and sweetmeats, twenty times a day. I then, after coffee and pipes, retired."—*B. to his Mother.*]

[1] [Mr. Hobhouse describes the vizier as "a short man, about five feet five inches in height, and very fat; possessing a very pleasing face, fair and round, with blue quick eyes, not at all settled into a Turkish gravity." Dr. Holland happily compares the spirit which lurked under Ali's usual exterior, as "the fire of a stove, burning fiercely under a smooth and polished surface." When the doctor returned from Albania, in 1813, he brought a letter from the pasha to Lord Byron. "It is," says the poet, "in Latin, and begins 'Excellentissime, *necnon* Carissime,' and ends about a gun he wants made for him. He tells me that, last spring, he took a town, a hostile town, where, forty-two years ago, his mother and sisters were treated as Miss Cunegunde was by the Bulgarian cavalry. He takes the town, selects all the survivors of the exploit—children, grandchildren, &c., to the tune of six hundred, and has them shot before his face. So much for 'dearest friend.'"]

[2] [The fate of Ali was precisely such as the poet anticipated.

LXIV.

Mid many things most new to ear and eye
The pilgrim rested here his weary feet,
And gazed around on Moslem luxury,[1]
Till quickly wearied with that spacious seat
Of Wealth and Wantonness, the choice retreat
Of sated Grandeur from the city's noise:
And were it humbler it in sooth were sweet;
But Peace abhorreth artificial joys, [destroys.
And Pleasure, leagued with Pomp, the zest of both

LXV.

Fierce are Albania's children, yet they lack
Not virtues, were those virtues more mature.
Where is the foe that ever saw their back?
Who can so well the toil of war endure?
Their native fastnesses not more secure
Than they in doubtful time of troublous need·
Their wrath how deadly! but their friendship sure,
When Gratitude or Valour bids them bleed,
Unshaken rushing on where'er their chief may lead.

For a circumstantial account of his assassination, in February, 1822, see Walsh's "Journey from Constantinople to England," p. 60. His head was sent to Constantinople, and exhibited at the gates of the seraglio. As the name of Ali had made a considerable noise in England, in consequence of his negotiations with Sir Thomas Maitland, and still more, perhaps, these stanzas of Lord Byron, a merchant of Constantinople thought it would be no bad speculation to purchase the head and consign it to a London showman; but this scheme was defeated by the piety of an old servant of the pasha, who bribed the executioner with a higher price, and bestowed decent sepulture on the relic.]

1 ["Childe Harold with the chief held colloquy,
Yet what they spake it boots not to repeat,
Converse may little charm strange ear or eye;
Albeit he rested in that spacious seat
Of Moslem luxury," &c.—MS.]

LXVI.

Childe Harold saw them in their chieftain's tower
Thronging to war in splendour and success;
And after viewed them, when, within their power,
Himself a while the victim of distress;
That saddening hour when bad men hotlier press:
But these did shelter him beneath their roof,
When less barbarians would have cheer'd him less,
And fellow-countrymen have stood aloof[1]—
In aught that tries the heart how few withstand the
proof!

LXVII.

It chanced that adverse winds once drove his bark
Full on the coast of Suli's shaggy shore,
When all around was desolate and dark;
To land was perilous, to sojourn more;
Yet for a while the mariners forbore,
Dubious to trust where treachery might lurk:
At length they ventured forth, though doubting sore
That those who loathe alike the Frank and Turk
Might once again renew their ancient butcher-work.

LXVIII.

Vain fear! the Suliotes stretch'd the welcome hand,
Led them o'er rocks and past the dangerous swamp,
Kinder than polish'd slaves, though not so bland,
And piled the hearth, and wrung their garments
damp,
And fill'd the bowl, and trimm'd the cheerful lamp,
And spread their fare; though homely, all they had
Such conduct bears Philanthropy's rare stamp—
To rest the weary and to soothe the sad,
Doth lesson happier men, and shames at least the bad.

[1] Alluding to the wreckers of Cornwall.

LXIX.

It came to pass, that when he did address
Himself to quit at length this mountain-land,
Combined marauders halfway barr'd egress,
And wasted far and near with glaive and brand;
And therefore did he take a trusty band
To traverse Acarnania's forest wide,
In war well season'd, and with labours tann'd,
Till he did greet white Achelous' tide,
And from his further bank Ætolia's wolds espied.

LXX.

Where lone Utraikey forms its circling cove,
And weary waves retire to gleam at rest,
How brown the foliage of the green hill's grove,
Nodding at midnight o'er the calm bay's breast,
As winds come lightly whispering from the west,
Kissing, not ruffling, the blue deep's serene :—
Here Harold was received a welcome guest;
Nor did he pass unmoved the gentle scene, [glean
For many a joy could he from Night's soft presence

LXXI.

On the smooth shore the night-fires brightly blazed,
The feast was done, the red wine circling fast,[1]
And he that unawares had there ygazed,
With gaping wonderment had stared aghast;
For ere night's midmost, stillest hour was past,
The native revels of the troop began;
Each Palikar[2] his sabre from him cast,
And bounding hand in hand, man link'd to man,
Yelling their uncouth dirge, long daunced the kirtled clan.[3]

[1] The Albanian Mussulmans do not abstain from wine, and indeed, very few of the others.

[2] Palikar, shortened when addressed to a single person, from Παλικαρι, a general name for a soldier amongst the Greeks and Albanese who speak Romaic: it means, properly, "a lad."

[3] [The following is Mr. Hobhouse's animated description of

LXXII.

Childe Harold at a little distance stood,
And view'd, but not displeased, the revelrie,
Nor hated harmless mirth, however rude:
In sooth it was no vulgar sight to see
Their barbarous, yet their not indecent, glee;
And, as the flames along their faces gleam'd,
Their gestures nimble, dark eyes flashing free,
The long wild locks that to their girdles stream'd,
While thus in concert they this lay half sang, half screamed:—[1]

this scene:—"In the evening the gates were secured, and preparations were made for feeding our Albanians. A goat was killed and roasted whole, and four fires were kindled in the yard, round which the soldiers seated themselves in parties. After eating and drinking, the greatest part of them assembled round the largest of the fires, and whilst ourselves and the elders of the party were seated on the ground, danced round the blaze, to their own songs, with astonishing energy. All their songs were relations of some robbing exploits. One of them, which detained them more than an hour, began thus—'When we set out from Parga, there were sixty of us:' then came the burden of the verse,—

'Robbers all at Parga!—Robbers all at Parga!'
'Κλεφτεις ποτε Παργα!—Κλεφτεις ποτε Παργα!'

and, as they roared out this stave, they whirled round the fire, dropped, and rebounded from their knees, and again whirled round, as the chorus was again repeated. The rippling of the waves upon the pebbly margin where we were seated, filled up the pauses of the song with a milder, and not more monotonous music. The night was very dark; but, by the flashes of the fires, we caught a glimpse of the woods, the rocks, and the lake, which, together with the wild appearance of the dancers, presented us with a scene that would have made a fine picture in the hands of such an artist as the author of the Mysteries of Udolpho. As we were acquainted with the character of the Albanians, it did not at all diminish our pleasure to know, that every one of our guard had been robbers, and some of them a very short time before. It was eleven o'clock before we had retired to our room, at which time the Albanians, wrapping themselves up in their capotes, went to sleep round the fires."]

[1] [For a specimen of the Albanian or Arnaout dialect of the Illyric see Appendix, Note [C].]

1.

TAMBOURGI! Tambourgi![1] thy 'larum afar
Gives hope to the valiant, and promise of war;
All the sons of the mountains arise at the note,
Chimariot, Illyrian, and dark Suliote![2]

2.

Oh! who is more brave than a dark Suliote,
In his snowy camese and his shaggy capote?
To the wolf and the vulture he leaves his wild flock,
And descends to the plain like the stream from the rock.

3.

Shall the sons of Chimari, who never forgive
The fault of a friend, bid an enemy live?
Let those guns so unerring such vengeance forego?
What mark is so fair as the breast of a foe?

4.

Macedonia sends forth her invincible race;
For a time they abandon the cave and the chase:
But those scarfs of blood-red shall be redder, before
The sabre is sheathed and the battle is o'er.

5.

Then the pirates of Parga that dwell by the waves,
And teach the pale Franks what it is to be slaves,
Shall leave on the beach the long galley and oar,
And track to his covert the captive on shore.

6.

I ask not the pleasures that riches supply,
My sabre shall win what the feeble must buy;
Shall win the young bride with her long flowing hair,
And many a maid from her mother shall tear.

[1] Drummer.

[2] These stanzas are partly taken from different Albanese songs, as far as I was able to make them out by the expositior of the Albanese in Romaic and Italian.

7.

I love the fair face of the maid in her youth,
Her caresses shall lull me, her music shall soothe;
Let her bring from the chamber her many-toned lyre
And sing us a song on the fall of her sire.

8.

Remember the moment when Previsa fell,[1]
The shrieks of the conquer'd, the conquerors' yell;
The roofs that we fired, and the plunder we shared,
The wealthy we slaughter'd, the lovely we spared.

9.

I talk not of mercy, I talk not of fear;
He neither must know who would serve the vizier:
Since the days of our prophet the Crescent ne'er saw
A chief ever glorious like Ali Pashaw.

10.

Dark Muchtar his son to the Danube is sped,
Let the yellow-hair'd[2] Giaours[3] view his horsetail[4]
with dread.
When his Delhis[5] come dashing in blood o'er the banks,
How few shall escape from the Muscovite ranks!

11.

Selictar![6] unsheathe then our chief's scimitār:
Tambourgi! thy 'larum gives promise of war.
Ye mountains, that see us descend to the shore,
Shall view us as victors, or view us no more!

[1] It was taken by storm from the French.
[2] Yellow is the epithet given to the Russians.
[3] Infidel.
[4] The insignia of a pasha.
[5] Horsemen, answering to our forlorn hope.
[6] Sword-bearer.

LXXIII.

Fair Greece! sad relic of departed worth!
Immortal, though no more; though fallen great!
Who now shall lead thy scattered children forth,
And long accustom'd bondage uncreate?
Not such thy sons who whilome did await,
The hopeless warriors of a willing doom,
In bleak Thermopylæ's sepulchral strait—
Oh! who that gallant spirit shall resume,
Leap from Eurotas' banks, and call thee from the tomb?

LXXIV.

Spirit of freedom! when on Phyle's brow[2]
Thou sat'st with Thrasybulus and his train,
Couldst thou forbode the dismal hour which now
Dims the green beauties of thine Attic plain?
Not thirty tyrants now enforce the chain,
But every carle can lord it o'er thy land;
Nor rise thy sons, but idly rail in vain,
Trembling beneath the scourge of Turkish hand;
From birth till death enslaved; in word, in deed, unmann'd.

LXXV.

In all save form alone, how changed! and who
That marks the fire still sparkling in each eye,
Who but would deem their bosoms burn'd anew
With thy unquenched beam, lost Liberty!
And many dream withal the hour is nigh
That gives them back their fathers' heritage:
For foreign arms and aid they fondly sigh,
Nor solely dare encounter hostile rage,
Or tear their name defiled from Slavery's mournful page.

[1] Some Thoughts on the present state of Greece and Turkey will be found in the Appendix, Notes [D] and [E].

[2] Phyle, which commands a beautiful view of Athens, has still considerable remains: it was seized by Thrasybulus, previous to the expulsion of the Thirty.

LXXVI.

Hereditary bondsmen! know ye not
Who would be free themselves must strike the blow?
By their right arms the conquest must be wrought?
Will Gaul or Muscovite redress ye? no!
True, they may lay your proud despoilers low,
But not for you will Freedom's altars flame.
Shades of the Helots! triumph o'er your foe!
Greece! change thy lords, thy state is still the same,
Thy glorious day is o'er, but not thine years of shame.

LXXVII.

The city won for Allah from the Giaour,
The Giaour from Othman's race again may wrest;
And the serai's impenetrable tower
Receive the fiery Frank, her former guest;[1]
Or Wahab's revel brood who dared divest
The prophet's[2] tomb of all its pious spoil,
May wind their path of blood along the West;
But ne'er will freedom seek this fated soil,
But slave succeed to slave through years of endless toil.

LXXVIII.

Yet mark their mirth—ere lenten days begin
That penance which their holy rites prepare
To shrive from man his weight of mortal sin,
By daily abstinence and nightly prayer;
But ere his sackcloth garb Repentance wear,
Some days of joyaunce are decreed to all,
To take of pleasaunce each his secret share,
In motley robe to dance at masking ball,
And join the mimic train of merry Carnival.

[1] When taken by the Latins, and retained for several years.

[2] Mecca and Medina were taken some time ago by the Wahabees, a sect yearly increasing.

LXXIX.

And whose more rife with merriment than thine,
Oh Stamboul![1] once the empress of their reign?
Though turbans now pollute Sophia's shrine,
And Greece her very altars eyes in vain:
(Alas! her woes will still pervade my strain!)
Gay were her minstrels once, for free her throng,
All felt the common joy they now must feign,
Nor oft I've seen such sights, nor heard such song,
As woo'd the eye, and thrill'd the Bosphorus along.[2]

[1] [Of Constantinople Lord Byron says,—"I have seen the ruins of Athens, of Ephesus, and Delhi; I have traversed great part of Turkey and many other parts of Europe, and some of Asia; but I never beheld a work of nature or art which yielded an impression like the prospect on each side, from the Seven Towers to the end of the Golden Horn."]

[2] ["The view of Constantinople," says Mr. Rose, "which appeared intersected by groves of cypress, (for such is the effect of its great burial-grounds planted with these trees,) its gilded domes and minarets reflecting the first rays of the sun; the deep blue sea 'in which it glassed itself,' and *that* sea covered with beautiful boats and barges darting in every direction in perfect silence, amid sea-fowl, who sat at rest upon the waters, altogether conveyed such an impression as I had never received, and probably never shall again receive, from the view of any other place." The following sonnet, by the same author, has been so often quoted, that, but for its exquisite beauty, we should not have ventured to reprint it here:—

"A glorious form thy shining city wore,
Mid cypress thickets of perennial green,
With minaret and golden dome between,
While thy sea softly kiss'd its grassy shore:
Darting across whose blue expanse was seen
Of sculptured barks and galleys many a score;
Whence noise was none save that of plashing oar;
Nor word was spoke, to break the calm serene.
Unheard is whisker'd boatman's hail or joke;
Who, mute as Sinbad's man of copper, rows,
And only intermits the sturdy stroke,
When fearless gull too nigh his pinnace goes.
I, hardly conscious if I dream'd or woke,
Mark'd that strange piece of action and repose."]

LXXX.

Loud was the lightsome tumult on the shore,
Oft Music changed, but never ceased her tone,
And timely echo'd back the measured oar,
And rippling waters made a pleasant moan:
The queen of tides on high consenting shone,
And when a transient breeze swept o'er the wave,
'Twas, as if darting from her heavenly throne,
A brighter glance her form reflected gave,
Till sparkling billows seem'd to light the banks they lave.

LXXXI.

Glanced many a light caique along the foam,
Danced on the shore the daughters of the land,
Ne thought had man or maid of rest or home,
While many a languid eye and thrilling hand
Exchanged the look few bosoms may withstand,
Or gently press'd, return'd the pressure still:
Oh Love! young Love! bound in thy rosy band,
Let sage or cynic prattle as he will,
These hours, and only these, redeem Life's years of ill!

LXXXII.

But, midst the throng in merry masquerade,
Lurk there no hearts that throb with secret pain,
Even through the closest searment half betray'd?
To such the gentle murmurs of the main
Seem to re-echo all they mourn in vain;
To such the gladness of the gamesome crowd
Is source of wayward thought and stern disdain:
How do they loathe the laughter idly loud,
And long to change the robe of revel for the shroud!

LXXXIII.

This must he feel, the true-born son of Greece,
If Greece one true-born patriot still can boast:
Not such as prate of war, but skulk in peace,
The bondsman's peace, who sighs for all he lost,
Yet with smooth smile his tyrant can accost,
And wield the slavish sickle, not the sword:
Ah! Greece! they love thee least who owe thee most;
Their birth, their blood, and that sublime record
Of hero sires, who shame thy now degenerate horde!

LXXXIV.

When riseth Lacedemon's hardihood,
When Thebes Epaminondas rears again,
When Athens' children are with hearts endued,
When Grecian mothers shall give birth to men,
Then mayst thou be restored; but not till then.
A thousand years scarce serve to form a state;
An hour may lay it in the dust: and when
Can man its shatter'd splendour renovate,
Recall its virtues back, and vanquish Time and Fate?

LXXXV.

And yet how lovely in thine age of woe,
Land of lost gods and godlike men, art thou!
Thy vales of evergreen, thy hills of snow,[1]
Proclaim thee Nature's varied favourite now:
Thy fanes, thy temples to thy surface bow,
Commingling slowly with heroic earth,
Broke by the share of every rustic plough:
So perish monuments of mortal birth,
So perish all in turn, save well-recorded Worth;

[1] On many of the mountains, particularly Liakura, the snow never is entirely melted, notwithstanding the intense heat of the summer; but I never saw it lie on the plains, even in the winter

LXXXVI.

Save where some solitary column mourns
Above its prostrate brethren of the cave;[1]
Save where Tritonia's airy shrine adorns
Colonna's cliff,[2] and gleams along the wave;
Save o'er some warrior's half-forgotten grave,
Where the gray stones and unmolested grass
Ages, but not oblivion, feebly brave,
While strangers only not regardless pass,
Lingering like me, perchance, to gaze, and sigh
"Alas!"

[1] Of Mount Pentelicus, from whence the marble was dug that constructed the public edifices of Athens. The modern name is Mount Mendeli. An immense cave, formed by the quarries, still remains, and will till the end of time.

[2] In all Attica, if we except Athens itself and Marathon, there is no scene more interesting than Cape Colonna. To the antiquary and artist, sixteen columns are an inexhaustible source of observation and design; to the philosopher, the supposed scene of some of Plato's conversations will not be unwelcome; and the traveller will be struck with the beauty of the prospect over "Isles that crown the Ægean deep:" but, for an Englishman, Colonna has yet an additional interest, as the actual spot of Falconer's Shipwreck. Pallas and Plato are forgotten, in the recollection of Falconer and Campbell:—

"Here in the dead of night by Lonna's steep,
The seaman's cry was heard along the deep."

This temple of Minerva may be seen at sea from a great distance. In two journeys which I made, and one voyage to Cape Colonna, the view from either side, by land, was less striking than the approach from the isles. In our second land excursion, we had a narrow escape from a party of Mainotes, concealed in the caverns beneath. We were told afterwards, by one of their prisoners, subsequently ransomed, that they were deterred from attacking us by the appearance of my two Albanians: conjecturing very sagaciously, but falsely, that we had a complete guard of these Arnaouts at hand, they remained stationary, and thus saved our party, which was too small to have opposed any effectual resistance Colonna is no less a resort of painters than of pirates; there

LXXXVII.

Yet are thy skies as blue, thy crags as wild;
Sweet are thy groves, and verdant are thy fields,
Thine olive ripe as when Minerva smiled,
And still his honied wealth Hymettus yields;
There the blithe bee his fragrant fortress builds,
The freeborn wanderer of thy mountain-air;
Apollo still thy long, long summer gilds,
Still in his beam Mendeli's marbles glare;
Art, Glory, Freedom fail, but Nature still is fair.[1]

LXXXVIII.

Where'er we tread 'tis haunted, holy ground;
No earth of thine is lost in vulgar mould,
But one vast realm of wonder spreads around,
And all the Muse's tales seem truly told,
Till the sense aches with gazing to behold
The scenes our earliest dreams have dwelt upon:
Each hill and dale, each deepening glen and wold
Defies the power which crush'd thy temples gone:
Age shakes Athena's tower, but spares gray Marathon.

"The hireling artist plants his paltry desk,
And makes degraded nature picturesque."
(See Hodgson's Lady Jane Grey, &c.)

But there Nature, with the aid of Art, has done that for herself. I was fortunate enough to engage a very superior German artist; and hope to renew my acquaintance with this and many other Levantine scenes, by the arrival of his performances.

[1] [The following passage, in Harris's Philosophical Inquiries, contains the pith of this stanza:—"Notwithstanding the various fortunes of Athens, as a city, Attica is still famous for olives, and Mount Hymettus for honey. Human institutions perish, but Nature is permanent." I recollect having once pointed out this coincidence to Lord Byron, but he assured me that he had never seen this work of Harris.—MOORE.]

LXXXIX.

The sun, the soil, but not the slave, the same;
Unchanged in all except its foreign lord—
Preserves alike its bounds and boundless fame
The battle-field, where Persia's victim horde
First bow'd beneath the brunt of Hellas' sword,
As on the morn to distant Glory dear,
When Marathon became a magic word;[1]
Which uttered, to the hearer's eye appear
The camp, the host, the fight, the conqueror's career.

XC.

The flying Mede, his shaftless broken bow;
The fiery Greek, his red pursuing spear;
Mountains above, Earth's, Ocean's plain below;
Death in the front, Destruction in the rear!
Such was the scene—what now remaineth here?
What sacred trophy marks the hallow'd ground,
Recording Freedom's smile and Asia's tear?
The rifled urn, the violated mound,
The dust thy courser's hoof, rude stranger! spurns around.

XCI.

Yet to the remnants of thy splendour past
Shall pilgrims, pensive, but unwearied, throng;

[1] "Siste Viator—heroa calcas!" was the epitaph on the famous Count Merci;—what then must be our feelings when standing on the tumulus of the two hundred (Greeks) who fell on Marathon? The principal barrow has recently been opened by Fauvel: few or no relics, as vases, &c. were found by the excavator. The plain of Marathon was offered to me for sale at the sum of sixteen thousand piastres, about nine hundred pounds! Alas!—"Expende—quot *libras* in duce summo—invenies!"—was the dust of Miltiades worth no more? It could scarcely have fetched less if sold by *weight*.

Long shall the voyager, with th' Ionian blast,
Hail the bright clime of battle and of song;
Long shall thine annals and immortal tongue
Fill with thy fame the youth of many a shore;
Boast of the aged! lesson of the young!
Which sages venerate and bards adore,
As Pallas and the Muse unveil their awful lore.

XCII.

The parted bosom clings to wonted home,
If aught that's kindred cheer the welcome hearth.
He that is lonely, hither let him roam,
And gaze complacent on congenial earth.
Greece is no lightsome land of social mirth:
But he whom Sadness sootheth may abide,
And scarce regret the region of his birth,
When wandering slow by Delphi's sacred side,
Or gazing o'er the plains where Greek and Persian died.[1]

XCIII.

Let such approach this consecrated land,
And pass in peace along the magic waste;
But spare its relics—let no busy hand
Deface the scenes, already how defaced!
Not for such purpose were these altars placed:
Revere the remnants nations once revered:
So may our country's name be undisgraced,
So mayst thou prosper where thy youth was rear'd,
By every honest joy of love and life endear'd!

XCIV.

For thee, who thus in too protracted song
Hast soothed thine idlesse with inglorious lays,

[1] [The original MS. closes with this stanza. The rest was added while the canto was passing through the press.]

Soon shall thy voice be lost amid the throng
Of louder minstrels in these later days:
To such resign the strife for fading bays—
Ill may such contest now the spirit move
Which heeds nor keen reproach nor partial praise,
Since cold each kinder heart that might approve,
And none are left to please where none are left to love.

XCV.

Thou too art gone, thou loved and lovely one!
Whom youth and youth's affections bound to me;
Who did for me what none beside have done,
Nor shrank from one albeit unworthy thee.
What is my being? thou hast ceased to be!
Nor stay'd to welcome here thy wanderer home,
Who mourns o'er hours which we no more shall see—
Would they had never been, or were to come!
Would he had ne'er return'd to find fresh cause to roam!

XCVI.

Oh! ever loving, lovely, and beloved!
How selfish Sorrow ponders on the past,
And clings to thoughts now better far removed!
But Time shall tear thy shadow from me last.
All thou couldst have of mine, stern Death! thou hast;
The parent, friend, and now the more than friend:
Ne'er yet for one thine arrows flew so fast,
And grief with grief continuing still to blend,
Hath snatch'd the little joy that life had yet to lend

XCVII.

Then must I plunge again into the crowd,
And follow all that Peace disdains to seek?
Where Revel calls, and Laughter, vainly loud,
False to the heart, distorts the hollow cheek,

To leave the flagging spirit doubly weak;
Still o'er the features, which perforce they cheer,
To feign the pleasure or conceal the pique;
Smiles form the channel of a future tear,
Or raise the writhing lip with ill-dissembled sneer.

XCVIII.

What is the worst of woes that wait on age?
What stamps the wrinkle deeper on the brow?
To view each loved one blotted from life's page,
And be alone on earth, as I am now.[1]
Before the Chastener humbly let me bow,
O'er hearts divided and o'er hopes destroy'd:
Roll on, vain days! full reckless may ye flow,
Since Time hath reft whate'er my soul enjoy'd,
And with the ills of Eld mine earlier years alloy'd.

[1] [This stanza was written October 11, 1811; upon which day the poet, in a letter to a friend, says,—"I have been again shocked with a death, and have lost one very dear to me in happier times; but 'I have almost forgot the taste of grief,' and 'supped full of horrors' till I have become callous, nor have I a tear left for an event which, five years ago, would have bowed down my head to the earth. It seems as though I were to experience in my youth the greatest misery of age. My friends fall around me, and I shall be left a lonely tree before I am withered. Other men can always take refuge in their families: I have no resource but my own reflections, and they present no prospect here or hereafter, except the selfish satisfaction of surviving my friends. I am indeed very wretched, and you will excuse my saying so, as you know I am not apt to cant of sensibility." In reference to this stanza, "Surely," said Professor Clarke to the author of the "Pursuits of Literature," "Lord Byron cannot have experienced such keen anguish as these exquisite allusions to what older men may have felt seem to denote."—"I fear he has," answered Matthias; "he could not otherwise have written such a poem."]

CHILDE HAROLD'S PILGRIMAGE.

CANTO THE THIRD.

"Afin que cette application vous forçât de penser à autre chose; il n'y a en vérité de remède que celui-là et le temps."—*Lettre du Roi de Prusse à D'Alembert, Sept.* 7, 1776.

CHILDE HAROLD'S PILGRIMAGE.

CANTO THE THIRD.[1]

I.

Is thy face like thy mother's, my fair child!
ADA! sole daughter of my house and heart?[2]
When last I saw thy young blue eyes they smiled
And when we parted,—not as now we part,
But with a hope.—
Awaking with a start,
The waters heave around me; and on high
The winds lift up their voices: I depart,
Whither I know not;[3] but the hour's gone by,
When Albion's lessening shores could grieve or glad
mine eye.

[1] ["Begun July 10th, 1816. Diodati, near Lake of Geneva."—MS.]

[2] [In a hitherto unpublished letter, dated Verona, November 6, 1816, Lord Byron says—"By the way, *Ada's* name (which I found in our pedigree, under King John's reign) is the same with that of the sister of Charlemagne, as I redde, the other day, in a book treating on the Rhine."]

[3] [Lord Byron quitted England, for the second and last time, on the 25th of April, 1816, attended by William Fletcher and Robert Rushton, the "yeoman" and "page" of Canto I.; his physician, Dr. Polidori; and a Swiss valet.]

II.

Once more upon the waters! yet once more!
And the waves bound beneath me as a steed
That knows his rider.[1] Welcome to the roar!
Swift be their guidance, wheresoe'er it lead!
Though the strain'd mast should quiver as a reed,
And the rent canvass fluttering strew the gale,[2]
Still must I on; for I am as a weed,
Flung from the rock, on Ocean's foam to sail
Where'er the surge may sweep, the tempest's breath
prevail.

III.

In my youth's summer I did sing of one,
The wandering outlaw of his own dark mind;
Again I seize the theme, then but begun,
And bear it with me, as the rushing wind
Bears the cloud onwards: in that tale I find
The furrows of long thought, and dried-up tears,
Which, ebbing, leave a sterile track behind,
O'er which all heavily the journeying years
Plod the last sands of life,—where not a flower ap-
pears.

[1] [In the "Two Noble Kinsmen" of Beaumont and Fletcher, (a play to which the picture of passionate friendship delineated in the characters of Palamon and Arcite would be sure to draw the attention of Byron in his boyhood,) we find the following passage:—

"Oh, never
Shall we two exercise, like twins of Honour,
Our arms again, and *feel our fiery horses*
Like proud seas under us."

Out of this somewhat forced simile, by a judicious transposition of the comparison, and by the substitution of the more definite word "waves" for "seas," Lord Byron's clear and noble thought has been produced.—MOORE.]

[2] ["And the rent canvass tattering."—MS.]

IV.

Since my young days of passion—joy, or pain,
Perchance my heart and harp have lost a string,
And both may jar: it may be, that in vain
I would essay as I have sung to sing.
Yet, though a dreary strain, to this I cling,
So that it wean me from the weary dream
Of selfish grief or gladness—so it fling
Forgetfulness around me—it shall seem
To me, though to none else, a not ungrateful theme.

V.

He who, grown aged in this world of woe,
In deeds, not years, piercing the depths of life,
So that no wonder waits him; nor below
Can love or sorrow, fame, ambition, strife,
Cut to his heart again with the keen knife
Of silent, sharp endurance: he can tell
Why thought seeks refuge in lone caves, yet rife
With airy images, and shapes which dwell
Still unimpair'd, though old, in the soul's haunted cell.

VI.

'Tis to create, and in creating live
A being more intense, that we endow
With form our fancy, gaining as we give
The life we image, even as I do now.
What am I? Nothing: but not so art thou,
Soul of my thought! with whom I traverse earth,
Invisible but gazing, as I glow
Mix'd with thy spirit, blended with thy birth,
And feeling still with thee in my crush'd feelings' dearth.

VII.

Yet must I think less wildly:—I *have* thought
Too long and darkly, till my brain became,
In its own eddy, boiling and o'erwrought,
A whirling gulf of phantasy and flame:
And thus, untaught in youth my heart to tame,
My springs of life were poison'd. 'Tis too late!
Yet am I changed; though still enough the same
In strength to bear what time can not abate,
And feed on bitter fruits without accusing Fate.

VIII.

Something too much of this:—but now 'tis past,
And the spell closes with its silent seal.
Long absent HAROLD reappears at last;
He of the breast which fain no more would feel,
Wrung with the wounds which kill not, but ne'er heal;
Yet Time, who changes all, had alter'd him
In soul and aspect as in age:[1] years steal
Fire from the mind as vigour from the limb;
And life's enchanted cup but sparkles near the brim.

[1] ["The first and second cantos of Childe Harold's Pilgrimage produced, on their appearance in 1812, an effect upon the public, at least equal to any work which has appeared within this or the last century, and placed at once upon Lord Byron's head the garland for which other men of genius have toiled long, and which they have gained late. He was placed pre-eminent among the literary men of his country by general acclamation. It was amidst such feelings of admiration that he entered the public stage. Every thing in his manner, person, and conversation, tended to maintain the charm which his genius had flung around him; and those admitted to his conversation, far from finding that the inspired poet sunk into ordinary mortality, felt themselves attached to him, not only by many noble qualities, but by the interest of a mysterious, undefined, and almost painful curiosity. A countenance exquisitely modelled to the expression of feeling and passion, and exhibiting the remarkable contrast of very dark hair and eyebrows, with a light and expressive eye, presented to the physiog-

IX.

His had been quaff'd too quickly, and he found
The dregs were wormwood ; but he fill'd again,
And from a purer fount, on holier ground,
And deem'd its spring perpetual ; but in vain !
Still round him clung invisibly a chain
Which gall'd forever, fettering though unseen,
And heavy though it clank'd not; worn with pain,
Which pined although it spoke not, and grew keen,
Entering with every step he took through many a scene.

X.

Secure in guarded coldness, he had mix'd
Again in fancied safety with his kind,
And deem'd his spirit now so firmly fix'd
And sheath'd with an invulnerable mind,
That, if no joy, no sorrow lurk'd behind ;
And he, as one, might midst the many stand
Unheeded, searching through the crowd to find
Fit speculation ; such as in strange land
He found in wonder-works of God and Nature's hand,

nomist the most interesting subject for the exercise of his art. The predominating expression was that of deep and habitual thought, which gave way to the most rapid play of features when he engaged in interesting discussion ; so that a brother poet compared them to the sculpture of a beautiful alabaster vase, only seen to perfection when lighted up from within. The flashes of mirth, gayety, indignation, or satirical dislike, which frequently animated Lord Byron's countenance, might, during an evening's conversation, be mistaken, by a stranger, for the habitual expression, so easily and so happily was it formed for them all ; but those who had an opportunity of studying his features for a length of time, and upon various occasions, both of rest and emotion, will agree that their proper language was that of melancholy. Sometimes shades of this gloom interrupted even his gayest and most happy moments."—SIR WALTER SCOTT.]

XI.

But who can view the ripened rose, nor seek
To wear it? who can curiously behold
The smoothness and the sheen of beauty's cheek,
Nor feel the heart can never all grow old?
Who can contemplate Fame through clouds unfold
The star which rises o'er her steep, nor climb?
Harold once more within the vortex, roll'd
On with the giddy circle, chasing Time,
Yet with a nobler aim than in his youth's fond prime.

XII.

But soon he knew himself the most unfit
Of men to herd with man; with whom he held
Little in common; untaught to submit
His thoughts to others, though his soul was quell'd
In youth by his own thoughts; still uncompell'd,
He would not yield dominion of his mind
To spirits against whom his own rebell'd;
Proud though in desolation; which could find
A life within itself, to breathe without mankind.

XIII.

Where rose the mountains, there to him were friends;
Where roll'd the ocean, thereon was his home;
Where a blue sky, and glowing clime, extends,
He had the passion and the power to roam;
The desert, forest, cavern, breaker's foam,
Were unto him companionship; they spake
A mutual language, clearer than the tome
Of his land's tongue, which he would oft forsake
For Nature's pages glass'd by sunbeams on the lake.

XIV.

Like the Chaldean, he could watch the stars,
Till he had peopled them with beings bright
As their own beams; and earth, and earth-born jars,
And human frailties, were forgotten quite:
Could he have kept his spirit to that flight
He had been happy; but this clay will sink
Its spark immortal, envying it the light
To which it mounts, as if to break the link [brink.
That keeps us from yon heaven which woos us to its

XV.

But in man's dwellings he became a thing
Restless and worn, and stern and wearisome,
Droop'd as a wild born falcon with clipp'd wing,
To whom the boundless air alone were home:
Then came his fit again, which to o'ercome,
As eagerly the barr'd-up bird will beat
His breast and beak against his wiry dome
Till the blood tinge his plumage, so the heat
Of his impeded soul would through his bosom eat.

XVI.

Self-exiled Harold[1] wanders forth again,
With naught of hope left, but with less of gloom;
The very knowledge that he lived in vain,
That all was over on this side the tomb,

[1] ["In the third canto of Childe Harold there is much inequality. The thoughts and images are sometimes laboured; but still they are a very great improvement upon the first two cantos. Lord Byron here speaks in his own language and character, not in the tone of others;—he is describing, not inventing; therefore he has not, and cannot have, the freedom with which fiction is composed. Sometimes he has a conciseness which is very powerful, but almost abrupt. From trusting himself alone, and working out his own deep-buried thoughts, he now, perhaps, fell into a habit of labouring, even where there was no occasion to labour. In the first sixteen stanzas there is yet a mighty but groaning

Had made Despair a smilingness assume [wreck,
Which, though 'twere wild,—as on the plunder'd
When mariners would madly meet their doom
With draughts intemperate on the sinking deck,—
Did yet inspire a cheer, which he forbore to check.[1]

XVII.

Stop!—for thy tread is on an empire's dust!
An earthquake's spoil is sepulchred below!
Is the spot mark'd with no colossal bust?
Nor column trophied for triumphal show?
None; but the moral's truth tells simpler so,
As the ground was before, thus let it be;—
How that red rain hath made the harvest grow!
And is this all the world has gain'd by thee,
Thou first and last of fields! king-making Victory?

burst of dark and appalling strength. It was unquestionably the unexaggerated picture of a most tempestuous and sombre, but magnificent soul."—BRYDGES.]

[1] [These stanzas—in which the author, adopting more distinctly the character of Childe Harold than in the original poem, assigns the cause why he has resumed his pilgrim's staff, when it was hoped he had sat down for life a denizen of his native country, —abound with much moral interest and poetical beauty. The commentary through which the meaning of this melancholy tale is rendered obvious, is still in vivid remembrance; for the errors of those who excel their fellows in gifts and accomplishments are not soon forgotten. Those scenes, ever most painful to the bosom, were rendered yet more so by public discussion; and it is at least possible that amongst those who exclaimed most loudly on this unhappy occasion, were some in whose eyes literary superiority exaggerated Lord Byron's offence. The scene may be described in a few words:—the wise condemned—the good regretted—the multitude, idly or maliciously inquisitive, rushed from place to place, gathering gossip, which they mangled and exaggerated while they repeated it; and impudence, ever ready to hitch itself into notoriety, *hooked on*, as Falstaff enjoins Bardolph, blustered, bullied, and talked of "pleading a cause," and "taking a side."—SIR WALTER SCOTT.]

XVIII.

And Harold stands upon this place of skulls,
The grave of France, the deadly Waterloo!
How in an hour the power which gave annuls
Its gifts, transferring fame as fleeting too!
In "pride of place"[1] here last the eagle flew,
Then tore with bloody talon the rent plain,[2]
Pierced by the shaft of banded nations through;
Ambition's life and labours all were vain; [chain.
He wears the shatter'd links of the world's broken

XIX.

Fit retribution! Gaul may champ the bit
And foam in fetters;—but is earth more free?
Did nations combat to make *one* submit;
Or league to teach all kings true sovereignty?
What! shall reviving Thraldom again be
The patch'd-up idol of enlighten'd days!
Shall we, who struck the lion down, shall we
Pay the wolf homage? proffering lowly gaze
And servile knees to thrones? No; *prove* before ye
praise!

[1] "Pride of place" is a term of falconry, and means the highest pitch of flight. See Macbeth, &c.

"An eagle towering in his pride of place," &c.

[2] [In the original draught of this stanza, (which, as well as the preceding one, was written after a visit to the field of Waterloo,) the lines stood—

"Here his last flight the haughty eagle flew,
Then tore with bloody beak the fatal plain."—

On seeing these lines, Mr. Reinagle sketched a spirited chained eagle, grasping the earth with his *talons*. The circumstance being mentioned to Lord Byron, he wrote thus to a friend at Brussels —"Reinagle is a better poet and a better ornithologist than I am eagles, and all birds of prey, attack with their talons, and not with their beaks: and I have altered the line thus:—

'Then tore with bloody talon the rent plain.'

This is, I think, a better line, besides its poetical justice."]

XX.

If not, o'er one fallen despot boast no more!
In vain fair cheeks were furrow'd with hot tears
For Europe's flowers, long rooted up before
The trampler of her vineyards; in vain years
Of death, depopulation, bondage, fears,
Have all been borne, and broken by the accord
Of roused-up millions: all that most endears
Glory, is when the myrtle wreathes a sword
Such as Harmodius[1] drew on Athens' tyrant lord.

XXI.

There was a sound of revelry by night,
And Belgium's capital had gather'd then
Her beauty and her chivalry, and bright
The lamps shone o'er fair women and brave men;
A thousand hearts beat happily; and when
Music arose with its voluptuous swell,
Soft eyes look'd love to eyes which spake again,
And all went merry as a marriage-bell;[3]
But hush! hark! a deep sound strikes like a rising knell!

[1] See the famous song on Harmodius and Aristogiton. The best English translation is in Bland's Anthology, by Mr. (now Lord Chief Justice) Denman,—

"With myrtle my sword will I wreathe," &c.

[2] [There can be no more remarkable proof of the greatness of Lord Byron's genius, than the spirit and interest he has contrived to communicate to his picture of the often-drawn and difficult scene of the breaking up from Brussels before the great battle. It is a trite remark, that poets generally fail in the representation of great events, where the interest is recent, and the particulars are consequently clearly and commonly known. It required some courage to venture on a theme beset with so many dangers, and deformed with the wrecks of so many former adventurers. See, however, with what easy strength he enters upon it, and with how much grace he gradually finds his way back to his own peculiar vein of sentiment and diction!—JEFFREY.]

[3] On the night previous to the action, it is said that a ball was given at Brussels.—[The popular error of the Duke of Wellington

XXII.

Did ye not hear it?—No; 'twas but the wind
Or the car rattling o'er the stony street;
On with the dance! let joy be unconfined;
No sleep till morn, when Youth and Pleasure meet
To chase the glowing hours with flying feet—
But hark!—that heavy sound breaks in once more,
As if the clouds its echo would repeat;
And nearer, clearer, deadlier than before!
Arm! arm! it is—it is the cannon's opening roar!

XXIII.

Within a window'd niche of that high hall
Sate Brunswick's fated chieftain; he did hear
That sound the first amidst the festival,
And caught its tone with Death's prophetic ear;
And when they smiled because he deem'd it near,
His heart more truly knew that peal too well
Which stretched his father on a bloody bier,[1]
And roused the vengeance blood alone could quell:
He rush'd into the field, and, foremost fighting, fell.[2]

having been *surprised*, on the eve of the battle of Waterloo, at a ball given by the Dutchess of Richmond, at Brussels, was first corrected on authority, in the History of Napoleon Bonaparte, which forms a portion of the "Family Library." The duke had received intelligence of Napoleon's decisive operations, and it was intended to put off the ball; but, on reflection, it seemed highly important that the people of Brussels should be kept in ignorance as to the course of events, and the duke not only desired that the ball should proceed, but the general officers received his commands to appear at it—each taking care to quit the apartment as quietly as possible at ten o'clock, and proceed to join his respective division *en route*.]

1 [The father of the Duke of Brunswick, who fell at Quatre-bras, received his death-wound at Jena.]

2 [This stanza is very grand, even from its total unadornment. It is only a versification of the common narrative: but here may well be applied a position of Johnson, that "where truth is sufficient to fill the mind, fiction is worse than useless."—Brydges.]

XXIV.

Ah! then and there was hurrying to and fro,
And gathering tears and tremblings of distress,
And cheeks all pale, which but an hour ago
Blush'd at the praise of their own loveliness
And there were sudden partings, such as press
The life from out young hearts, and choking sighs
Which ne'er might be repeated; who could guess
If ever more should meet those mutual eyes,
Since upon night so sweet such awful morn could rise!

XXV.

And there was mounting in hot haste: the steed,
The mustering squadron, and the clattering car,
Went pouring forward with impetuous speed,
And swiftly forming in the ranks of war;
And the deep thunder peal on peal afar;
And near, the beat of the alarming drum
Roused up the soldier ere the morning star;
While throng'd the citizens with terror dumb,
Or whispering, with white lips—"The foe! They come! they come!"

XXVI.

And wild and high the "Cameron's gathering" rose!
The war-note of Lochiel, which Albyn's hills
Have heard, and heard, too, have her Saxon foes:—
How in the noon of night that pibroch thrills,
Savage and shrill! But with the breath which fills
Their mountain-pipe, so fill the mountaineers
With the fierce native daring which instils
The stirring memory of a thousand years,
And Evan's, Donald's[1] fame rings in each clansman's ears!

[1] Sir Evan Cameron, and his descendant Donald, the "gentle Lochiel" of the "forty-five."

XXVII.

And Ardennes[1] waves above them her green leaves,
Dewy with nature's tear-drops, as they pass,
Grieving, if aught inanimate e'er grieve,
Over the unreturning brave,—alas!
Ere evening to be trodden like the grass
Which now beneath them, but above shall grow
In its next verdure, when this fiery mass
Of living valour, rolling on the foe
And burning with high hope, shall moulder cold and low.

XXVIII.

Last noon beheld them full of lusty life,
Last eve in Beauty's circle proudly gay,
The midnight brought the signal sound of strife,
The morn the marshalling in arms,—the day
Battle's magnificently-stern array!
The thunder-clouds close o'er it, which when rent,
The earth is cover'd thick with other clay,
Which her own clay shall cover, heap'd and pent
Rider and horse,—friend, foe,—in one red burial blent![2]

[1] The wood of Soignies is supposed to be a remnant of the forest of Ardennes, famous in Boiardo's Orlando, and immortal in Shakspeare's "As you like it." It is also celebrated in Tacitus, as being the spot of successful defence by the Germans against the Roman encroachments. I have ventured to adopt the name connected with nobler associations than those of mere slaughter.

[2] [Childe Harold, though he shuns to celebrate the victory of Waterloo, gives us here a most beautiful description of the evening which preceded the battle of Quatre Bras, the alarm which called out the troops, and the hurry and confusion which preceded their march. I am not sure that any verses in our language surpass, in vigour and in feeling, this most beautiful description.—SIR WALTER SCOTT.]

XXIX.

Their praise is hymn'd by loftier harps than mine;
Yet one I would select from that proud throng,
Partly because they blend me with his line,
And partly that I did his sire some wrong,[1]
And partly that bright names will hallow song;
And his was of the bravest, and when shower'd
The death-bolts deadliest the thinn'd files along,
Even where the thickest of war's tempest lower'd,
They reach'd no nobler breast than thine, young, gallant Howard![2]

XXX.

There have been tears and breaking hearts for thee,
And mine were nothing, had I such to give;
But when I stood beneath the fresh green tree,
Which living waves where thou didst cease to live,
And saw around me the wide field revive
With fruits and fertile promise, and the spring
Come forth her work of gladness to contrive,
With all her reckless birds upon the wing,
I turn'd from all she brought to those she could not bring.[3]

[1] [See English Bards and Scotch Reviewers.]

[2] ["In the late battles, like all the world, I have lost a connection—poor Frederick Howard, the best of his race. I had little intercourse of late years with his family; but I never saw or heard but good of him."—*Lord B. to Mr. Moore.*]

[3] My guide from Mont St. Jean over the field seemed intelligent and accurate. The place where Major Howard fell was not far from two tall and solitary trees, (there was a third cut down, or shivered in the battle,) which stand a few yards from each other at a pathway's side. Beneath these he died and was buried. The body has since been removed to England. A small hollow for the present marks where it lay, but will probably soon be effaced; the plough has been upon it, and the grain is. After pointing out the different spots where Picton and other gallant men had perished; the guide said, "Here Major Howard lay; I was near him when

XXXI.

I turn'd to thee, to thousands, of whom each
And one as all a ghastly gap did make
In his own kind and kindred, whom to teach
Forgetfulness were mercy for their sake;
The Archangel's trump, not Glory's, must awake
Those whom they thirst for; though the sound of Fame
May for a moment soothe, it cannot slake
The fever of vain longing, and the name
So honour'd but assumes a stronger, bitterer claim.

XXXII.

They mourn, but smile at length; and, smiling, mourn:
The tree will wither long before it fall;
The hull drives on, though mast and sail be torn;
The roof-tree sinks, but moulders on the hall
In massy hoariness; the ruin'd wall
Stands when its wind-worn battlements are gone;
The bars survive the captive they enthral;
The day drags through though storms keep out the sun;
And thus the heart will break, yet brokenly live on:

wounded." I told him my relationship, and he seemed then still more anxious to point out the particular spot and circumstances. The place is one of the most marked in the field, from the peculiarity of the two trees above mentioned. I went on horseback twice over the field, comparing it with my recollection of similar scenes. As a plain, Waterloo seems marked out for the scene of some great action, though this may be mere imagination: I have viewed with attention those of Platea, Troy, Mantinea. Leuctra, Chæronea, and Marathon; and the field around Mont St. Jean and Hougoumont appears to want little but a better cause, and that undefinable but impressive halo which the lapse of ages throws around a celebrated spot, to vie in interest with any or all of these, except, perhaps, the last mentioned.

XXXIII.

Even as a broken mirror, which the glass
In every fragment multiplies; and makes
A thousand images of one that was
The same, and still the more, the more it breaks;
And thus the heart will do which not forsakes,
Living in shatter'd guise, and still, and cold,
And bloodless, with its sleepless sorrow aches,
Yet withers on till all without is old,
Showing no visible sign, for such things are untold.[1]

XXXIV.

There is a very life in our despair,
Vitality of poison,—a quick root
Which feeds these deadly branches; for it were
As nothing did we die; but life will suit
Itself to Sorrow's most detested fruit,
Like to the apples[2] on the Dead Sea's shore,
All ashes to the taste: did man compute
Existence by enjoyment, and count o'er
Such hours 'gainst years of life,—say, would he name
threescore?

XXXV.

The psalmist number'd out the years of man:
They are enough; and if thy tale be *true*,
Thou, who didst grudge him even that fleeting span,
More than enough, thou fatal Waterloo!

[1] [There is a richness and energy in this passage, which is peculiar to Lord Byron, among all modern poets; a throng of glowing images, poured forth at once, with a facility and profusion, which must appear mere wastefulness to more economical writers, and a certain negligence and harshness of diction, which can belong only to an author who is oppressed with the exuberance and rapidity of his conceptions.—JEFFREY.]

[2] The (fabled) apples on the brink of the lake Asphaltes were said to be fair without, and, within, ashes. Vide Tacitus, Histor. lib. v. 7.

Millions of tongues record thee, and anew
Their children's lips shall echo them, and say—
"Here, where the sword united nations drew,
Our countrymen were warring on that day!"
And this is much, and all which will not pass away.

XXXVI.

There sunk the greatest, nor the worst of men,
Whose spirit antithetically mix'd
One moment of the mightiest, and again
On little objects with like firmness fix'd,
Extreme in all things! hadst thou been betwixt,
Thy throne had still been thine, or never been;
For daring made thy rise as fall: thou seek'st
Even now to reassume the imperial mien,
And shake again the world, the Thunderer of the
scene!

XXXVII.

Conqueror and captive of the earth art thou!
She trembles at thee still, and thy wild name
Was ne'er more bruited in men's minds than now
That thou art nothing, save the jest of Fame,
Who woo'd thee once, thy vassal, and became
The flatterer of thy fierceness, till thou wert
A god unto thyself; nor less the same
To the astounded kingdoms all inert,
Who deem'd thee for a time whate'er thou didst
assert.

XXXVIII.

Oh, more or less than man—in high or low,
Battling with nations, flying from the field;
Now making monarchs' necks thy footstool, now
More than thy meanest soldier taught to yield.

An empire thou couldst crush, command, rebuild,
But govern not thy pettiest passion, nor,
However deeply in men's spirits skill'd,
Look through thine own, nor curb the lust of war,
Nor learn that tempted Fate will leave the loftiest
star.

XXXIX.

Yet well thy soul hath brook'd the turning tide
With that untaught innate philosophy,
Which, be it wisdom, coldness, or deep pride,
Is gall and wormwood to an enemy.
When the whole host of hatred stood hard by,
To watch and mock thee shrinking, thou hast smiled
With a sedate and all-enduring eye;—
When Fortune fled her spoil'd and favourite child,
He stood unbow'd beneath the ills upon him piled.

XL.

Sager than in thy fortunes; for in them
Ambition steel'd thee on too far to show
That just habitual scorn, which could contemn
Men and their thoughts; 'twas wise to feel, not so
To wear it ever on thy lip and brow,
And spurn the instruments thou wert to use
Till they were turn'd unto thine overthrow;
'Tis but a worthless world to win or lose;
So hath it proved to thee, and all such lot who choose.

XLI.

If, like a tower upon a headlong rock,
Thou hadst been made to stand or fall alone,
Such scorn of man had help'd to brave the shock;
But men's thoughts were the steps which paved
thy throne,

Their admiration thy best weapon shone;
The part of Philip's son was thine, not then
(Unless aside thy purple had been thrown)
Like stern Diogenes to mock at men;
For sceptred cynics earth were far too wide a den.[1]

XLII.

But quiet to quick bosoms is a hell,
And *there* hath been thy bane; there is a fire
And motion of the soul which will not dwell
In its own narrow being, but aspire
Beyond the fitting medium of desire;
And, but once kindled, quenchless evermore,
Preys upon high adventure, nor can tire
Of aught but rest; a fever at the core,
Fatal to him who bears, to all who ever bore.

XLIII.

This makes the madmen who have made men mad
By their contagion; conquerors and kings,
Founders of sects and systems, to whom add
Sophists, bards, statesmen, all unquiet things
Which stir too strongly the soul's secret springs,
And are themselves the fools to those they fool;
Envied, yet how unenviable! what stings
Are theirs! One breast laid open were a school
Which would unteach mankind the lust to shine or rule:

[1] The great error of Napoleon, "if we have writ our annals true," was a continued obtrusion on mankind of his want of all community of feeling for or with them; perhaps more offensive to human vanity than the active cruelty of more trembling an suspicious tyranny. Such were his speeches to public assemblies as well as individuals; and the single expression which he is said to have used on returning to Paris after the Russian winter had destroyed his army, rubbing his hands over a fire, "This is pleasanter than Moscow," would probably alienate more favour from his cause than the destruction and reverses which led to the remark.

XLIV.

Their breath is agitation, and their life
A storm whereon they ride, to sink at last,
And yet so nursed and bigoted to strife,
That should their days, surviving perils past.
Melt to calm twilight, they feel overcast
With sorrow and supineness, and so die;
Even as a flame unfed, which runs to waste
With its own flickering, or a sword laid by,
Which eats into itself, and rusts ingloriously.

XLV.

He who ascends to mountain-tops, shall find
The loftiest peaks most wrapt in clouds and snow;
He who surpasses or subdues mankind,
Must look down on the hate of those below.
Though high *above* the sun of glory glow,
And far *beneath* the earth and ocean spread,
Round him are icy rocks, and loudly blow
Contending tempests on his naked head,
And thus reward the toils which to those summits led.[1]

[1] [This is certainly splendidly written, but we trust it is not true. From Macedonia's madman to the Swede—from Nimrod to Bonaparte,—the hunters of men have pursued their sport with as much gayety, and as little remorse, as the hunters of other animals; and have lived as cheerily in their days of action, and as comfortable in their repose, as the followers of better pursuits. It would be strange, therefore, if the other active, but more innocent spirits, whom Lord Byron has here placed in the same predicament, and who share all their sources of enjoyment, without the guilt and the hardness which they cannot fail of contracting, should be more miserable or more unfriended than those splendid curses of their kind; and it would be passing strange, and pitiful, if the most precious gifts of Providence should produce only unhappiness, and mankind regard with hostility their greatest benefactors.—JEFFREY.]

XLVI.

Away with these! true Wisdom's world will be
Within its own creation, or in thine,
Maternal Nature! for who teems like thee,
Thus on the banks of thy majestic Rhine?
There Harold gazes on a work divine,
A blending of all beauties; streams and dells,
Fruit, foliage, crag, wood, cornfield, mountain, vine,
And chiefless castles breathing stern farewells
From gay but leafy walls, where Ruin greenly dwells.

XLVII.

And there they stand, as stands a lofty mind,
Worn, but unstooping to the baser crowd,
All tenantless, save to the crannying wind,
Or holding dark communion with the cloud.
There was a day when they were young and proud,
Banners on high, and battles pass'd below;
But they who fought are in a bloody shroud,
And those which waved are shredless dust ere now,
And the bleak battlements shall bear no future blow.

XLVIII.

Beneath these battlements, within those walls
Power dwelt amidst her passions; in proud state
Each robber chief upheld his armed halls,
Doing his evil will, nor less elate
Than mightier heroes of a longer date.
What want these outlaws[1] conquerors should have?
But History's purchased page to call them great?
A wider space, an ornamented grave?
Their hopes were not less warm, their souls were full
as brave.

[1] "What wants that knave that a king should have?" was King James's question on meeting Johnny Armstrong and his followers in full accoutrements.—See the Ballad.

XLIX.

In their baronial feuds and single fields,
What deeds of prowess unrecorded died!
And Love, which lent a blazon to their shields,
With emblems well devised by amorous pride,
Through all the mail of iron hearts would glide;
But still their flame was fierceness, and drew on
Keen contest and destruction near allied,
And many a tower, for some fair mischief won,
Saw the discolour'd Rhine beneath its ruin run.

L.

But thou, exulting and abounding river!
Making thy waves a blessing as they flow
Through banks whose beauty would endure forever
Could man but leave thy bright creation so,
Nor its fair promise from the surface mow
With the sharp scythe of conflict,—then to see
Thy valley of sweet waters, were to know
Earth paved like heaven; and to seem such to me,
Even now what wants thy stream?—that it should Lethe be.

LI.

A thousand battles have assail'd thy banks,
But these and half their fame have pass'd away,
And Slaughter heap'd on high his weltering ranks;
Their very graves are gone, and what are they?
Thy tide wash'd down the blood of yesterday,
And all was stainless, and on thy clear stream
Glass'd with its dancing light the sunny ray;
But o'er the blacken'd memory's blighting dream
Thy waves would vainly roll, all sweeping as they seem.

LII.

Thus Harold inly said, and passed along,
Yet not insensibly to all which here
Awoke the jocund birds to early song
In glens which might have made even exile dear:
Though on his brow were graven lines austere,
And tranquil sternness which had ta'en the place
Of feelings fierier far but less severe,
Joy was not always absent from his face,
But o'er it in such scenes would steal with transient trace.

LIII.

Nor was all love shut from him, though his days
Of passion had consumed themselves to dust.
It is in vain that we would coldly gaze
On such as smile upon us; the heart must
Leap kindly back to kindness, though disgust
Hath wean'd it from all worldlings: thus he felt,
For there was soft remembrance, and sweet trust
In one fond breast, to which his own would melt,
And in its tenderer hour on that his bosom dwelt.

LIV.

And he had learn'd to love,—I know not why,
For this in such as him seems strange of mood,—
The helpless looks of blooming infancy,
Even in its earliest nurture; what subdued,
To change like this, a mind so far imbued
With scorn of man, it little boots to know;
But thus it was; and though in solitude
Small power the nipp'd affections have to grow.
In him this glow'd when all beside had ceased to glow.

LV.

And there was one soft breast, as hath been said,
Which unto his was bound by stronger ties
Than the church links withal; and, though unwed,
That love was pure, and far above disguise,
Had stood the test of mortal enmities
Still undivided, and cemented more
By peril, dreaded most in female eyes;
But this was firm, and from a foreign shore [pour!
Well to that heart might his these absent greetings

1.

The castled crag of Drachenfels[1]
Frowns o'er the wide and winding Rhine,
Whose breast of waters broadly swells
Between the banks which bear the vine,
And hills all rich with blossom'd trees,
And fields which promise corn and wine,
And scatter'd cities crowning these,
Whose far white walls along them shine,
Have strew'd a scene, which I should see
With double joy wert *thou* with me.[2]

2.

And peasant girls, with deep-blue eyes,
And hands which offer early flowers,
Walk smiling o'er this paradise;
Above, the frequent feudal towers

[1] The castle of Drachenfels stands on the highest summit of "the Seven Mountains," over the Rhine banks: it is in ruins, and connected with some singular traditions. It is the first in view on the road from Bonn, but on the opposite side of the river; on this bank, nearly facing it, are the remains of another, called the Jew's Castle, and a large cross, commemorative of the murder of a chief by his brother. The number of castles and cities along the course of the Rhine on both sides is very great, and their situations remarkably beautiful.

[2] [These verses were written on the banks of the Rhine, in

Through green leaves lift their walls of gray,
And many a rock which steeply lowers,
And noble arch in proud decay,
Look o'er this vale of vintage-bowers;
But one thing want these banks of Rhine,—
Thy gentle hand to clasp in mine!

3.

I send the lilies given to me;
Though long before thy hand they touch,
I know that they must wither'd be,
But yet reject them not as such;
For I have cherish'd them as dear,
Because they yet may meet thine eye,
And guide thy soul to mine even here,
When thou behold'st them drooping nigh,
And know'st them gathered by the Rhine,
And offer'd from my heart to thine!

4.

The river nobly foams and flows,
The charm of this enchanted ground,
And all its thousand turns disclose
Some fresher beauty varying round:
The haughtiest breast its wish might bound
Through life to dwell delighted here;
Nor could on earth a spot be found
To nature and to me so dear,
Could thy dear eyes in following mine
Still sweeten more these banks of Rhine!

LVI.

By Coblentz, on a rise of gentle ground,
There is a small and simple pyramid,
Crowning the summit of the verdant mound;
Beneath its base are heroes' ashes hid,

May. The original pencilling is before us. It is needless to observe, that they were addressed by the poet to his sister]

Our enemy's—but let not that forbid
Honour to Marceau! o'er whose early tomb
Tears, big tears gush'd from the rough soldier's lid,
Lamenting and yet envying such a doom,
Falling for France, whose rights he battled to resume.

LVII.

Brief, brave, and glorious was his young career,—
His mourners were two hosts, his friends and foes;
And fitly may the stranger lingering here
Pray for his gallant spirit's bright repose;
For he was Freedom's champion, one of those,
The few in number, who had not o'erstept
The charter to chastise which she bestows
On such as wield her weapons; he had kept
The whiteness of his soul, and thus men o'er him wept.[1]

[1] The monument of the young and lamented General Marceau (killed by a rifle-ball at Alterkirchen, on the last day of the fourth year of the French republic) still remains as described. The inscriptions on his monument are rather too long, and not required: his name was enough; France adored, and her enemies admired; both wept over him. His funeral was attended by the generals and detachments from both armies. In the same grave General Hoche is interred, a gallant man also in every sense of the word; but though he distinguished himself greatly in battle, *he* had not the good fortune to die there: his death was attended by suspicions of poison. A separate monument (not over his body, which is buried by Marceau's) is raised for him near Andernach, opposite to which one of his most memorable exploits was performed, in throwing a bridge to an island on the Rhine. The shape and style are different from that of Marceau's, and the inscription more simple and pleasing:—"The Army of the Sambre and Meuse to its Commander-in-chief, Hoche." This is all, and as it should be Hoche was esteemed among the first of France's earlier generals, before Bonaparte monopolized her triumphs. He was the destined commander of the invading army of Ireland.

LVIII.

Here Ehrenbreitstein,[1] with her shatter'd wall
Black with the miner's blast, upon her height
Yet shows of what she was, when shell and ball
Rebounding idly on her strength did light:
A tower of victory! from whence the flight
Of baffled foes was watch'd along the plain:
But Peace destroy'd what War could never blight,
And laid those proud roofs bare to Summer's rain—
On which the iron shower for years had pour'd in vain.

LIX.

Adieu to thee, fair Rhine! How long delighted
The stranger fain would linger on his way!
Thine is a scene alike where souls united
Or lonely Contemplation thus might stray;
And could the ceaseless vultures cease to prey
On self-condemning bosoms, it were here,
Where Nature, nor too sombre nor too gay,
Wild but not rude, awful yet not austere,
Is to the mellow Earth as Autumn to the year.

LX.

Adieu to thee again! a vain adieu!
There can be no farewell to scene like thine,
The mind is colour'd by thy every hue;
And if reluctantly the eyes resign

[1] Ehrenbreitstein, *i. e.* "the broad stone of honour," one of the strongest fortresses in Europe, was dismantled and blown up by the French at the truce of Leoben. It had been, and could only be, reduced by famine or treachery. It yielded to the former aided by surprise. After having seen the fortifications of Gibraltar and Malta, it did not much strike by comparison; but the situation is commanding. General Marceau besieged it in vain for some time, and I slept in a room where I was shown a window at which he is said to have been standing observing the progress of the siege by moonlight, when a ball struck immediately below it.

Their cherish'd gaze upon thee, lovely Rhine![1]
'Tis with the thankful glance of parting praise;
More mighty spots may rise—more glaring shine,
But none unite in one attaching maze
The brilliant, fair, and soft,—the glories of old days,

LXI.

The negligently grand, the fruitful bloom
Of coming ripeness, the white city's sheen,
The rolling stream, the precipice's gloom,
The forest's growth, and Gothic walls between,
The wild rocks shaped as they had turrets been,
In mockery of man's art; and these withal
A race of faces happy as the scene,
Whose fertile bounties here extend to all,
Still springing o'er thy banks, though empires near
them fall.

LXII.

But these recede. Above me are the Alps,
The palaces of Nature, whose vast walls
Have pinnacled in clouds their snowy scalps,
And throned Eternity in icy halls
Of cold sublimity, where forms and falls
The avalanche—the thunderbolt of snow!
All that expands the spirit, yet appals,
Gather around these summits, as to show
How Earth may pierce to Heaven, yet leave vain
man below.

[1] [On taking Hockheim, the Austrians, in one part of the engagement, got to the brow of the hill, whence they had their first view of the Rhine. They instantly halted—not a gun was fired—not a voice heard: but they stood gazing on the river with those feelings which the events of the last fifteen years at once called up. Prince Schwartzenberg rode up to know the cause of this sudden stop; then they gave three cheers, rushed after the enemy, and drove them into the water.]

LXIII.

But ere these matchless heights I dare to scan,
There is a spot should not be pass'd in vain,—
Morat! the proud, the patriot field! where man
May gaze on ghastly trophies of the slain,
Nor blush for those who conquer'd on that plain;
Here Burgundy bequeath'd his tombless host,
A bony heap, through ages to remain,
Themselves their monument;—the Stygian coast
Unsepulchred they roam'd, and shriek'd each wandering ghost.[1]

LXIV.

While Waterloo with Cannæ's carnage vies,
Morat and Marathon twin names shall stand;
They were true Glory's stainless victories,
Won by the unambitious heart and hand
Of a proud, brotherly, and civic band,
All unbought champions in no princely cause
Of vice-entail'd Corruption; they no land
Doom'd to bewail the blasphemy of laws
Making kings' rights divine, by some Draconic clause.

[1] The chapel is destroyed, and the pyramid of bones diminished to a small number by the Burgundian legion in the service of France; who anxiously effaced this record of their ancestors' less successful invasions. A few still remain, notwithstanding the pains taken by the Burgundians for ages, (all who passed that way removing a bone to their own country,) and the less justifiable larcenies of the Swiss postilions, who carried them off to sell for knife-handles; a purpose for which the whiteness imbibed by the bleaching of years had rendered them in great request. Of these relics I ventured to bring away as much as may have made a quarter of a hero, for which the sole excuse is, that if I had not, the next passer-by might have perverted them to worse uses than the careful preservation which I intend for them.

LXV.

By a lone wall a lonelier column rears
A gray and grief-worn aspect of old days;
'Tis the last remnant of the wreck of years,
And looks as with the wild, bewilder'd gaze
Of one to stone converted by amaze,
Yet still with consciousness; and there it stands
Making a marvel that it not decays,
When the coeval pride of human hands,
Levell'd Aventicum,[1] hath strew'd her subject lands.

LXVI.

And there—oh! sweet and sacred be the name!—
Julia—the daughter, the devoted—gave
Her youth to Heaven; her heart, beneath a claim
Nearest to Heaven's, broke o'er a father's grave.
Justice is sworn 'gainst tears, and hers would crave
The life she lived in; but the judge was just,
And then she died on him she could not save.
Their tomb was simple and without a bust,
And held within their urn one mind, one heart, one dust.[2]

[1] Aventicum, near Morat, was the Roman capital of Helvetia, where Avenches now stands.

[2] Julia Alpinula, a young Aventian priestess, died soon after a vain endeavour to save her father, condemned to death as a traitor by Aulus Cæcina. Her epitaph was discovered many years ago;—it is thus:—"Julia Alpinula: Hic jaceo. Infelicis patris infelix proles. Deæ Aventiæ Sacerdos. Exorare patris necem non potui: Male mori in fatis ille erat. Vixi annos XXIII."—I know of no human composition so affecting as this, nor a history of deeper interest. These are the names and actions which ought not to perish, and to which we turn with a true and healthy tenderness, from the wretched and glittering detail of a confused mass of conquests and battles, with which the mind is roused for a time to a false and feverish sympathy, from whence it recurs at length with all the nausea consequent on such intoxication.

LXVII.

But these are deeds which should not pass away,
And names that must not wither, though the earth
Forgets her empires with a just decay, [birth;
The enslavers and the enslaved, their death and
The high, the mountain-majesty of worth
Should be, and shall, survivor of its woe,
And from its immortality look forth
In the sun's face, like yonder Alpine snow,[1]
Imperishably pure beyond all things below.

LXVIII.

Lake Leman woos me with its crystal face,[2]
The mirror where the stars and mountains view
The stillness of their aspect in each trace
Its clear depth yields of their far height and hue:
There is too much of man here, to look through
With a fit mind the might which I behold;
But soon in me shall Loneliness renew
Thoughts hid, but not less cherish'd than of old,
Ere mingling with the herd had penn'd me in their fold.

[1] This is written in the eye of Mont Blanc, (June 3d, 1816,) which even at this distance dazzles mine.—(July 20th.) I this day observed for some time the distinct reflection of Mont Blanc and Mont Argentière in the calm of the lake, which I was crossing in my boat; the distance of these mountains from their mirror is sixty miles.

[2] In the exquisite lines which the poet, at this time, addressed to his sister, there is the following touching stanza:—

"I did remind thee of our own dear lake,
By the old hall which may be mine no more.
Leman's is fair; but think not I forsake
The sweet remembrance of a dearer shore:
Sad havoc Time must with my memory make
Ere *that* or *thou* can fade these eyes before;
Though, like all things which I have loved, they are
Resign'd forever, or divided far."

LXIX.

To fly from, need not be to hate, mankind:
All are not fit with them to stir and toil,
Nor is it discontent to keep the mind
Deep in its fountain, lest it overboil
In the hot throng, where we become the spoil
Of our infection, till too late and long
We may deplore and struggle with the coil,
In wretched interchange of wrong for wrong
Midst a contentious world, striving where none are strong.

LXX.

There, in a moment, we may plunge our years
In fatal penitence, and in the blight
Of our own soul turn all our blood to tears,
And colour things to come with hues of Night;
The race of life becomes a hopeless flight
To those that walk in darkness: on the sea,
The boldest steer but where their ports invite,
But there are wanderers o'er Eternity
Whose bark drives on and on, and anchor'd ne'er shall be.

LXXI.

Is it not better, then, to be alone,
And love earth only for its earthly sake?
By the blue rushing of the arrowy Rhone,[1]
Or the pure bosom of its nursing lake,

[1] The colour of the Rhone at Geneva is blue, to a depth of tint which I have never seen equalled in water, salt or fresh, except in the Mediterranean and Archipelago.—[See Don Juan, c. xiv. st 87, for a beautiful comparison:—

"There was no great disparity of years,
Though much in temper; but they never clash'd:
They moved like stars united in their spheres,
Or like the Rhone by Leman's waters wash'd,

Which feeds it as a mother who doth make
A fair but froward infant her own care,
Kissing its cries away as these awake;—
Is it not better thus our lives to wear,
Than join the crushing crowd, doom'd to inflict or
bear?

LXXII.

I live not in myself, but I become
Portion of that around me; and to me
High mountains are a feeling,[1] but the hum
Of human cities torture: I can see
Nothing to loathe in nature, save to be
A link reluctant in a fleshly chain,
Class'd among creatures, when the soul can flee,
And with the sky, the peak, the heaving plain
Of ocean, or the stars, mingle, and not in vain.

LXXIII.

And thus I am absorb'd, and this is life;
I look upon the peopled desert past,
As on a place of agony and strife,
Where, for some sin, to sorrow I was cast,

Where mingled and yet separate appears
The river from the lake, all bluely dash'd
Through the serene and placid glassy deep,
Which fain would lull its river child to sleep."—]

[1] ["Mr. Hobhouse and myself are just returned from a journey of lakes and mountains. We have been to the Grindelwald, and the Jungfrau, and stood on the summit of the Wengen Alp; and seen torrents of 900 feet in fall, and glaciers of all dimensions; we have heard shepherds' pipes, and avalanches, and looked on the clouds foaming up from the valleys below us like the spray of the ocean of hell. Chamouni, and that which it inherits, we saw a month ago; but, though Mont Blanc is higher, it is not equal in wildness to the Jungfrau, the Eighers, the Shreckhorn, and the Rose Glaciers."—*B. Letters*, Sept. 1816.]

To act and suffer, but remount at last
With a fresh pinion; which I feel to spring,
Though young, yet waxing vigorous, as the blast
Which it would cope with, on delighted wing,
Spurning the clay-cold bonds which round our being
cling.

LXXIV.

And when, at length, the mind shall be all free
From what it hates in this degraded form,
Reft of its carnal life, save what shall be
Existent happier in the fly and worm,—
When elements to elements conform,
And dust is as it should be, shall I not
Feel all I see, less dazzling, but more warm?
The bodiless thought? the Spirit of each spot?
Of which, even now, I share at times the immortal lot?

LXXV.

Are not the mountains, waves, and skies, a part
Of me and of my soul, as I of them?
Is not the love of these deep in my heart
With a pure passion? should I not contemn
All objects, if compared with thee? and stem
A tide of suffering, rather than forego
Such feelings for the hard and worldly phlegm
Of those whose eyes are only turn'd below,
Gazing upon the ground, with thoughts which dare
not glow?

LXXVI.

But this is not my theme; and I return
To that which is immediate, and require
Those who find contemplation in the urn,
To look on One, whose dust was once all fire,
A native of the land where I respire

The clear air for a while—a passing guest,
Where he became a being,—whose desire
Was to be glorious; 'twas a foolish quest,
The which to gain and keep he sacrificed all rest.

LXXVII.

Here the self-torturing sophist, wild Rousseau,[1]
The apostle of affliction, he who threw
Enchantment over passion, and from woe
Wrung overwhelming eloquence, first drew
The breath which made him wretched; yet he knew
How to make madness beautiful, and cast
O'er erring deeds and thoughts a heavenly hue[2]
Of words, like sunbeams, dazzling as they past
The eyes, which o'er them shed tears feelingly and fast.

[1] ["I have traversed all Rousseau's ground with the 'Héloïse' before me, and am struck to a degree that I cannot express with the force and accuracy of his descriptions, and the beauty of their reality. Meillerie, Clarens, and Vevay, and the Château de Chillon, are places of which I shall say little; because all I could say must fall short of the impressions they stamp."—*B. Letters.*]

[2] ["It is evident that the impassioned parts of Rousseau's romance had made a deep impression upon the feelings of the noble poet. The enthusiasm expressed by Lord Byron is no small tribute to the power possessed by Jean Jacques over the passions: and, to say truth, we needed some such evidence; for, though almost ashamed to avow the truth,—still, like the barber of Midas, we must speak or die,—we have never been able to feel the interest or discover the merit of this far-famed performance. That there is much eloquence in the letters we readily admit: there lay Rousseau's strength. But his lovers, the celebrated St. Preux and Julie, have, from the earliest moment we have heard the tale (which we well remember) down to the present hour, totally failed to interest us. There might be some constitutional hardness of heart: but like Lance's pebble-hearted cur, Crab, we remained dry-eyed while all wept around us. And still, on resuming the volume, even now, we can see little in the loves of these two tiresome pedants to interest our feelings for either of them. To state our opinion in language (see Burke's Reflections) much better than our own, we are unfortunate enough to regard this far-famed history of philosophical gallantry as an 'unfash-

LXXVIII

His love was passion's essence—as a tree
On fire by lightning; with ethereal flame
Kindled he was, and blasted; for to be
Thus, and enamour'd, were in him the same.
But his was not the love of living dame,
Nor of the dead who rise upon our dreams,
But of ideal beauty, which became
In him existence, and o'erflowing teems
Along his burning page, distemper'd though it seems

LXXIX.

This breathed itself to life in Julie, *this*
Invested her with all that's wild and sweet;
This hallow'd, too, the memorable kiss[1]
Which every morn his fever'd lip would greet,
From hers, who but with friendship his would meet;
But to that gentle touch, through brain and breast
Flash'd the thrill'd spirit's love-devouring heat;
In that absorbing sigh perchance more blest
Than vulgar minds may be with all they seek possest.[2]

ioned, indelicate, sour, gloomy, ferocious medley of pedantry and lewdness; of metaphysical speculations, blended with the coarsest sensuality.' "—SIR WALTER SCOTT.]

[1] This refers to the account in his "Confessions" of his passion for the Comtesse d'Houdetot, (the mistress of St. Lambert,) and his long walk every morning, for the sake of the single kiss which was the common salutation of French acquaintance. Rousseau's description of his feelings on this occasion may be considered as the most passionate, yet not impure, description and expression of love that ever kindled into words; which, after all, must be felt, from their very force, to be inadequate to the delineation: a painting can give no sufficient idea of the ocean.

[2] [" Lord Byron's character of Rousseau is drawn with great force, great power of discrimination, and great eloquence. I know not that he says any thing which has not been said before:—but what he says issues, apparently, from the recesses of his own mind. It is a little laboured, which, possibly, may be caused by the form of the stanza into which it was necessary to throw it; but it

LXXX.

His life was one long war with self-sought foes,
Or friends by him self-banish'd; for his mind
Had grown Suspicion's sanctuary, and chose,
For its own cruel sacrifice, the kind
'Gainst whom he raged with fury strange and blind.
But he was frenzied,—wherefore, who may know?
Since cause might be which skill could never find;
But he was frenzied by disease or woe, [show.
To that worst pitch of all, which wears a reasoning

LXXXI.

For then he was inspired, and from him came,
As from the Pythian's mystic cave of yore,
Those oracles which set the world in flame,
Nor ceased to burn till kingdoms were no more:
Did he not this for France? which lay before
Bow'd to the inborn tyranny of years?
Broken and trembling to the yoke she bore,
Till by the voice of him and his compeers, [fears?
Roused up to too much wrath, which follows o'ergrown

LXXXII.

They made themselves a fearful monument!
The wreck of old opinions—things which grew,
Breathed from the birth of time: the veil they rent,
And what behind it lay, all earth shall view.
But good with ill they also overthrew,
Leaving but ruins, wherewith to rebuild
Upon the same foundation, and renew
Dungeons and thrones, which the same hour refill'd,
As heretofore, because ambition was self-will'd.

cannot be doubted that the poet felt a sympathy for the enthusiastic tenderness of Rousseau's genius, which he could not have recognised with such extreme fervour, except from a consciousness of having at least occasionally experienced similar emotions.'—Sir E. Brydges.]

LXXXIII.

But this will not endure, nor be endured!
Mankind have felt their strength, and made it felt.
They might have used it better, but, allured
By their new vigour, sternly have they dealt
On one another; pity ceased to melt
With her once natural charities. But they,
Who in oppression's darkness caved had dwelt,
They were not eagles, nourish'd with the day;
What marvel then, at times, if they mistook their prey?

LXXXIV.

What deep wounds ever closed without a scar?
The heart's bleed longest, and but heal to wear
That which disfigures it; and they who war
With their own hopes, and have been vanquish'd, bear
Silence, but not submission: in his lair
Fix'd Passion holds his breath, until the hour
Which shall atone for years; none need despair:
It came, it cometh, and will come,—the power
To punish or forgive—in *one* we shall be slower.

LXXXV.

Clear, placid Leman! thy contrasted lake,
With the wild world I dwelt in, is a thing
Which warns me, with its stillness, to forsake
Earth's troubled waters for a purer spring.
This quiet sail is as a noiseless wing
To waft me from distraction; once I loved
Torn ocean's roar, but thy soft murmuring
Sounds sweet as if a sister's voice reproved,
That I with stern delights should e'er have been so moved.

LXXXVI.

It is the hush of night, and all between
Thy margin and the mountains, dusk, yet clear,
Mellow'd and mingling, yet distinctly seen,
Save darken'd Jura, whose capt heights appear
Precipitously steep; and, drawing near,
There breathes a living fragrance from the shore,
Of flowers yet fresh with childhood; on the ear
Drops the light drip of the suspended oar,
Or chirps the grasshopper one good-night carol more:

LXXXVII.

He is an evening reveller, who makes
His life an infancy, and sings his fill;
At intervals, some bird from out the brakes
Starts into voice a moment, then is still.
There seems a floating whisper on the hill,
But that is fancy, for the starlight dews
All silently their tears of love instil,
Weeping themselves away, till they infuse
Deep into Nature's breast the spirit of her hues.[1]

[1] [During Lord Byron's stay in Switzerland, he took up his residence at the Campagne-Diodati, in the village of Coligny. It stands at the top of a rapidly descending vineyard; the windows commanding, one way, a noble view of the lake and of Geneva; the other, up the lake. Every evening, the poet embarked on the lake; and to the feelings created by these excursions we owe these delightful stanzas. Of his mode of passing a day, the following, from his Journal, is a pleasant specimen:—

"September 18. Called. Got up at five. Stopped at Vevay two hours. View from the churchyard superb; within it Ludlow (the regicide's) monument—black marble—long inscription; Latin, but simple. Near him Broughton (who read King Charles's sentence to Charles Stuart) is buried, with a queer and rather canting inscription. Ludlow's house shown. Walked down to the lake side; servants, carriages, saddle-horses,—all set off, and left us *plantés là*, by some mistake. Hobhouse ran on before, and overtook them. Arrived at Clarens. Went to Chillon through scenery worthy of I know not whom

LXXXVIII.

Ye stars which are the poetry of heaven!
If in your bright leaves we would read the fate
Of men and empires,—'tis to be forgiven,
That in our aspirations to be great,
Our destinies o'erleap their mortal state,
And claim a kindred with you; for ye are
A beauty and a mystery, and create
In us such love and reverence from afar,
That fortune, fame, power, life, have named themselves a star.

LXXXIX.

All heaven and earth are still—though not in sleep,
But breathless, as we grow when feeling most;
And silent, as we stand in thoughts too deep:—
All heaven and earth are still: From the high host
Of stars, to the lull'd lake and mountain-coast,
All is concenter'd in a life intense,
Where not a beam, nor air, nor leaf is lost,
But hath a part of being, and a sense
Of that which is of all Creator and defence.

went over the castle again. Met an English party in a carriage, a lady in it fast asleep—fast asleep in the most anti-narcotic spot in the world,—excellent! after a slight and short dinner, visited the Château de Clarens. Saw all worth seeing, and then descended to the 'Bosquet de Julie,' &c. &c.: our guide full of Rousseau, whom he is eternally confounding with St. Preux, and mixing the man and the book. Went again as far as Chillon, to revisit the little torrent from the hill behind it. The corporal who showed the wonders of Chillon was as drunk as Blucher, and (to my mind) as great a man: he was deaf also; and, thinking every one else so, roared out the legends of the castle so fearfully, that Hobhouse got out of humour. However, we saw things from the gallows to the dungeons. Sunset reflected in the lake. Nine o'clock—going to bed. Have to get up at five to-morrow."]—

XC.

Then stirs the feeling infinite, so felt
In solitude, where we are *least* alone;
A truth which through our being then doth melt,
And purifies from self: it is a tone,
The soul and source of music, which makes known
Eternal harmony, and sheds a charm
Like to the fabled Cytherea's zone,
Binding all things with beauty;—'twould disarm
The spectre Death, had he substantial power to harm.

XCI.

Not vainly did the early Persian make
His altar the high places and the peak
Of earth-o'ergazing mountains,[1] and thus take
A fit and unwall'd temple, there to seek
The Spirit in whose honour shrines are weak,
Uprear'd of human hands. Come, and compare
Columns and idol-dwellings, Goth or Greek,
With Nature's realms of worship, earth and air,
Nor fix on fond abodes to circumscribe thy prayer!

XCII.

The sky is changed—and such a change! Oh night,
And storm, and darkness, ye are wondrous strong,
Yet lovely in your strength, as is the light
Of a dark eye in woman! Far along,
From peak to peak, the rattling crags among
Leaps the live thunder! Not from one lone cloud,
But every mountain now hath found a tongue,
And Jura answers, through her misty shroud,
Back to the joyous Alps, who call to her aloud!

[1] See Appendix, Note [F].

XCIII.

And this is in the night:—Most glorious night!
Thou wert not sent for slumber! let me be
A sharer in thy fierce and far delight,—
A portion of the tempest and of thee![1]
How the lit lake shines, a phosphoric sea,
And the big rain comes dancing to the earth!
And now again 'tis black,—and now, the glee
Of the loud hills shakes with its mountain-mirth,
As if they did rejoice o'er a young earthquake's birth.[2]

XCIV.

Now, where the swift Rhone cleaves his way be tween
Heights which appear as lovers who have parted
In hate, whose mining depths so intervene,
That they can meet no more; though broken-hearted;
Though in their souls, which thus each other [thwarted,
Love was the very root of the fond rage
Which blighted their life's bloom, and then de-parted:—
Itself expired, but leaving them an age
Of years all winters,—war within themselves to wage.

[1] The thunder-storm to which these lines refer occurred on the 13th of June, 1816, at midnight. I have seen among the Acroceraunian mountains of Chimari, several more terrible, but none more beautiful.

[2] [This is one of the most beautiful passages of the poem. The "fierce and far delight" of a thunder-storm is here described in verse almost as vivid as its lightnings. The live thunder "leaping among the rattling crags"—the voice of mountains, as if shouting to each other—the plashing of the big rain—the gleaming of the wide lake, lighted like a phosphoric sea—present a picture of sublime terror, yet of enjoyment, often attempted, but never so well, certainly never better, brought out in poetry.—SIR WALTER SCOTT.]

XCV.

Now, where the quick Rhone thus hath cleft his way,
The mightiest of the storms hath ta'en his stand:
For here, not one, but many, make their play,
And fling their thunderbolts from hand to hand,
Flashing and cast around: of all the band,
The brightest through these parted hills hath fork'd
His lightnings,—as if he did understand,
That in such gaps as desolation work'd,
There the hot shaft should blast whatever therein lurk'd.

XCVI.

Sky, mountains, river, winds, lake, lightnings! ye!
With night, and clouds, and thunder, and a soul,
To make these felt and feeling, well may be
Things that have made me watchful; the far roll
Of your departed voices, is the knoll
Of what in me is sleepless,—if I rest.[1]
But where of ye, oh tempests! is the goal?
Are ye like those within the human breast?
Or do ye find at length, like eagles, some high nest?

[1] [The Journal of his Swiss tour, which Lord Byron kept for his sister, closes with the following mournful passage:—"In the weather, for this tour, of thirteen days, I have been very fortunate—fortunate in a companion" (Mr. Hobhouse)—"fortunate in our prospects, and exempt from even the little petty accidents and delays which often render journeys in a less wild country disappointing. I was disposed to be pleased. I am a lover of nature, and an admirer of beauty. I can bear fatigue, and welcome privation, and have seen some of the noblest views in the world. But in all this,—the recollection of bitterness, and more especially of recent and more home desolation, which must accompany me through life, has preyed upon me here; and neither the music of the shepherd, the crashing of the avalanche, nor the torrent, the mountain, the glacier, the forest, nor the cloud, have for one moment lightened the weight upon my heart, nor enabled me to lose my own wretched identity, in the majesty, and the power, and the glory, around, above, and beneath me."]

XCVII.

Could I imbody and unbosom now
That which is most within me,—could I wreak
My thoughts upon expression, and thus throw
Soul, heart, mind, passions, feelings, strong or weak,
All that I would have sought, and all I seek,
Bear, know, feel, and yet breathe—into *one* word,
And that one word were Lightning, I would speak;
But as it is, I live and die unheard,
With a most voiceless thought, sheathing it as a sword.

XCVIII.

The morn is up again, the dewy morn,
With breath all incense, and with cheek all bloom,
Laughing the clouds away with playful scorn,
And living as if earth contain'd no tomb,—
And glowing into day: we may resume
The march of our existence: and thus I,
Still on thy shores, fair Leman! may find room
And food for meditation, nor pass by
Much, that may give us pause, if ponder'd fittingly.

XCIX.

Clarens! sweet Clarens,[1] birthplace of deep Love!
Thine air is the young breath of passionate thought;
Thy trees take root in Love; the snows above
The very glaciers have his colours caught,
And sunset into rose-hues sees them wrought

[1] [Stanzas XCIX. to CXV. are exquisite. They have every thing which makes a poetical picture of local and particular scenery perfect. They exhibit a miraculous brilliancy and force of fancy; but the very fidelity causes a little constraint and labour of language. The poet seems to have been so engrossed by the attention to give vigour and fire to the imagery, that he both neglected and disdained to render himself more harmonious by diffuser words, which, while they might have improved the effect upon the ear, might have weakened the impression upon the mind. This

By rays which sleep there lovingly: the rocks,
The permanent crags, tell here of Love, who sought
In them a refuge from the worldly shocks,
Which stir and sting the soul with hope that woos, then mocks.

C.

Clarens! by heavenly feet thy paths are trod,—
Undying Love's, who here ascends a throne
To which the steps are mountains; where the god
Is a pervading life and light,—so shown
Not on those summits solely, nor alone
In the still cave and forest; o'er the flower
His eye is sparkling, and his breath hath blown,
His soft and summer breath, whose tender power
Passes the strength of storms in their most desolate hour.[1]

CI.

All things are here of *him;* from the black pines,
Which are his shade on high, and the loud roar
Of torrents, where he listeneth, to the vines
Which slope his green path downward to the shore
Where the bow'd waters meet him, and adore,
Kissing his feet with murmurs; and the wood,
The covert of old trees with trunks all hoar,
But light leaves, young as joy, stands where it stood,
Offering to him, and his, a populous solitude

mastery over new matter—this supply of powers equal not only to an untouched subject, but that subject one of peculiar and unequalled grandeur and beauty—was sufficient to occupy the strongest poetical faculties, young as the author was, without adding to it all the practical skill of the artist. The stanzas, too on Voltaire and Gibbon are discriminative, sagacious, and just. They are among the proofs of that very great variety of talen which this Canto of Lord Byron exhibits.—SIR E. BRYDGES.]

[1] See Appendix, note [G].

CII.

A populous solitude of bees and birds,
And fairy-form'd and many-colour'd things,
Who worship him with notes more sweet than
words,
And innocently open their glad wings,
Fearless and full of life: the gush of springs,
And fall of lofty fountains, and the bend
Of stirring branches, and the bud which brings
The swiftest thought of beauty, here extend,
Mingling and made by Love, unto one mighty end

CIII.

He who hath loved not, here would learn that
lore,
And make his heart a spirit; he who knows
That tender mystery, will love the more,
For this is Love's recess, where vain men's woes,
And the world's waste, have driven him far from
those,
For 'tis his nature to advance or die;
He stands not still, but or decays, or grows
Into a boundless blessing, which may vie
With the immortal lights, in its eternity!

CIV.

'Twas not for fiction chose Rousseau this spot,
Peopling it with affections; but he found
It was the scene which passion must allot
To the mind's purified beings; 'twas the ground
Where early Love his Psyche's zone unbound,
And hallow'd it with loveliness: 'tis lone,
And wonderful, and deep, and hath a sound,
And sense, and sight of sweetness; here the Rhone
Hath spread himself a couch, the Alps have rear'd a
throne

CV.

Lausanne! and Ferney! ye have been the abodes
Of names which unto you bequeath'd a name;[1]
Mortals, who sought and found, by dangerous roads,
A path to perpetuity of fame:
They were gigantic minds, and their steep aim
Was, Titan-like, on daring doubts to pile
Thoughts which should call down thunder, and the flame
Of Heaven, again assail'd if Heaven the while
On man and man's research could deign do more than smile.

CVI.

The one was fire and fickleness, a child,
Most mutable in wishes, but in mind,
A wit as various,—gay, grave, sage, or wild,—
Historian, bard, philosopher, combined;
He multiplied himself among mankind,
The Proteus of their talents: But his own
Breathed most in ridicule,—which, as the wind,
Blew where it listed, laying all things prone,—
Now to o'erthrow a fool, and now to shake a throne.

CVII.

The other, deep and slow, exhausting thought,
And hiving wisdom with each studious year,
In meditation dwelt, with learning wrought,
And shaped his weapon with an edge severe,
Sapping a solemn creed with solemn sneer;
The lord of irony,—that master-spell,
Which stung his foes to wrath, which grew from fear,
And doom'd him to the zealot's ready hell,
Which answers to all doubts so eloquently well.

[1] Voltaire and Gibbon.

CVIII.

Yet peace be with their ashes,—for by them,
If merited, the penalty is paid;
It is not ours to judge,—far less condemn:
The hour must come when such things shall be
made
Known unto all,—or hope and dread allay'd
By slumber, on one pillow,—in the dust,
Which, thus much we are sure, must lie decay'd;
And when it shall revive, as is our trust,
'Twill be to be forgiven, or suffer what is just.

CIX.

But let me quit man's works, again to read
His Maker's, spread around me, and suspend
This page, which from my reveries I feed,
Until it seems prolonging without end.
The clouds above me to the white Alps tend,
And I must pierce them, and survey whate'er
May be permitted as my steps I bend
To their most great and growing region, where
The earth to her embrace compels the powers of
air.

CX.

Italia! too, Italia! looking on thee,
Full flashes on the soul the light of ages,
Since the fierce Carthaginian almost won thee,
To the last halo of the chiefs and sages
Who glorify thy consecrated pages;
Thou wert the throne and grave of empires; still,
The fount at which the panting mind assuages
Her thirst of knowledge, quaffing there her fill,
Flows from the eternal source of Rome's imperial
hill.

CXI.

Thus far have I proceeded in a theme
Renew'd with no kind auspices :—to feel
We are not what we have been, and to deem
We are not what we should be,—and to steel
The heart against itself; and to conceal,
With a proud caution, love, or hate, or aught,—
Passion or feeling, purpose, grief, or zeal,—
Which is the tyrant spirit of our thought,
Is a stern task of soul :—No matter,—it is taught.

CXII.

And for these words, thus woven into song,
It may be that they are a harmless wile,—
The colouring of the scenes which fleet along,
Which I would seize, in passing, to beguile
My breast, or that of others, for a while.
Fame is the thirst of youth,—but I am not
So young as to regard men's frown or smile,
As loss or guerdon of a glorious lot;
I stood and stand alone,—remember'd or forgot.

CXIII.

I have not loved the world, nor the world me;
I have not flatter'd its rank breath, nor bow'd
To its idolatries a patient knee,—
Nor coin'd my cheek to smiles,—nor cried aloud
In worship of an echo; in the crowd
They could not deem me one of such; I stood
Among them, but not of them; in a shroud
Of thoughts which were not their thoughts, and still could,
Had I not filed[1] my mind, which thus itself subdued.

[1] ——— "If it be thus,
For Banquo's issue have I *filed* my mind."—MACBETH.

CXIV.

I have not loved the world, nor the world me,—
But let us part fair foes; I do believe,
Though I have found them not, that there may be
Words which are things,—hopes which will not de-
And virtues which are merciful, nor weave [ceive,
Snares for the failing: I would also deem
O'er others' griefs that some sincerely grieve;[1]
That two, or one, are almost what they seem,—
That goodness is no name, and happiness no dream.[2]

[1] It is said by Rochefoucault, that "there is always something in the misfortunes of men's best friends not displeasing to them."

[2] ["It is not the temper and talents of the poet, but the use to which he puts them, on which his happiness or misery is grounded. A powerful and unbridled imagination is the author and architect of its own disappointments. Its fascinations, its exaggerated pictures of good and evil, and the mental distress to which they give rise, are the natural and necessary evils attending on that quick susceptibility of feeling and fancy incident to the poetical temperament. But the Giver of all talents, while he has qualified them each with its separate and peculiar alloy, has endowed the owner with the power of purifying and refining them. But, as if to moderate the arrogance of genius, it is justly and wisely made requisite, that he must regulate and tame the fire of his fancy, and descend from the heights to which she exalts him, in order to obtain ease of mind and tranquillity. The materials of happiness, that is, of such degree of happiness as is consistent with our present state, lie around us in profusion. But the man of talents must stoop to gather them, otherwise they would be beyond the reach of the mass of society, for whose benefit, as well as for his, Providence has created them. There is no royal and no poetical path to contentment and heart's ease: that by which they are attained is open to all classes of mankind, and lies within the most limited range of intellect. To narrow our wishes and desires within the scope of our powers of attainment; to consider our misfortunes, however peculiar in their character, as our inevitable share in the patrimony of Adam; to bridle those irritable feelings, which ungoverned are sure to become governors; to shun that intensity of galling and self-wounding reflection which our poet has so forcibly described in its own burning language:—

CXV.

My daughter! with thy name this song begun—
My daughter! with thy name thus much shall
end—
I see thee not—I hear thee not,—but none
Can be so wrapt in thee; thou art the friend
To whom the shadows of far years extend:
Albeit my brow thou never shouldst behold,
My voice shall with thy future visions blend,
And reach into thy heart,—when mind is cold—
A token and a tone, even from thy father's mould.

CXVI.

To aid thy mind's development,—to watch
Thy dawn of little joys,—to sit and see
Almost thy very growth,—to view thee catch
Knowledge of objects,—wonders yet to thee!
To hold thee lightly on a gentle knee,
And print on thy soft cheek a parent's kiss,—
This, it should seem, was not reserved for me;
Yet this was in my nature:—as it is,
I know not what is there, yet something like to this.

'I have thought
Too long and darkly, till my brain became,
In its own eddy, boiling and o'erwrought,
A whirling gulf of fantasy and flame'——

—to stoop, in short, to the realities of life; repent if we have offended, and pardon if we have been trespassed against; to look on the world less as our foe than as a doubtful and capricious friend, whose applause we ought as far as possible to deserve, but neither to court nor contemn—such seem the most obvious and certain means of keeping or regaining mental tranquillity.

'Semita certe
Tranquillæ per virtutem patet ːnica vitæ."—SIR W. SCOTT.]

CXVII.

Yet, though dull Hate as duty should be taught,
I know that thou wilt love me: though my name
Should be shut from thee, as a spell still fraught
With desolation,—and a broken claim:
Though the grave closed between us,—'twere th
same,
I know that thou wilt love me; though to drain
My blood from out thy being were an aim,
And an attainment,—all would be in vain,—
Still thou wouldst love me, still that more than life
retain.

CXVIII.

The child of love,—though born in bitterness,
And nurtured in convulsion. Of thy sire
These were the elements,—and thine no less.
As yet such are around thee,—but thy fire
Shall be more temper'd, and thy hope far higher.
Sweet be thy cradled slumbers! O'er the sea,
And from the mountains where I now respire,
Fain would I waft such blessing upon thee,
As, with a sigh, I deem thou might'st have been to
me![1]

[1] ["Byron, July 4th. 1816. Diodati."—MS.]

CHILDE HAROLD'S PILGRIMAGE

CANTO THE FOURTH.

Visto ho Toscana, Lombardia, Romagna,
Quel Monte che divide, e quel che serra
Italia, e un mare e l' altro, che la bagna.
Ariosto, Satira iii

TO

JOHN HOBHOUSE, ESQ. A.M. F.R.S

&c. &c. &c.

Venice, January 2, 1818.

My dear Hobhouse,

After an interval of eignt years between the composition of the first and last cantos of Childe Harold, the conclusion of the poem is about to be submitted to the public. In parting with so old a friend, it is not extraordinary that I should recur to one still older and better,—to one who has beheld the birth and death of the other, and to whom I am far more indebted for the social advantages of an enlightened friendship, than—though not ungrateful—I can, or could be, to Childe Harold, for any public favour reflected through the poem on the poet,—to one, whom I have known long, and accompanied far, whom I have found wakeful over my sickness, and kind in my sorrow, glad in my prosperity, and firm in my adversity, true in counsel and trusty in peril,—to a friend often tried and never found wanting;—to yourself.

In so doing, I recur from fiction to truth; and in dedicating to you in its complete, or at least concluded state, a poetical work which is the longest, the most thoughtful and comprehensive of my compositions, I wish to do honour to myself by the record of many years' intimacy with a man of learning, of talent, of steadiness, and of honour. It is not for minds like ours to give or to receive flattery; yet the praises of sincerity have ever been permitted to the voice of friendship; and it is not for you, nor even for others, but to relieve a heart which has not elsewhere, or lately, been so much accustomed to the encounter of goodwill as to withstand the shock firmly, that I thus attempt to commemorate your good qualities, or rather the advantages which I have derived from their exertion. Even the recurrence of the date of this letter, the anniversary of the most unfortunate day of my past existence, but which cannot poison my future while I retain the resource of your friendship, and of my own faculties, will henceforth have a more agreeable recollection for both, inasmuch as it will remind us of this my attempt to thank you for an indefatigable regard, such as few men have experienced, and no one could experience without thinking better of his species and of himself.

It has been our fortune to traverse together, at various periods, the countries of chivalry, history, and fable—Spain, Greece, Asia Minor, and Italy; and what Athens and Constantinople were to us a few years ago, Venice and Rome have been more recently. The poem also, or the pilgrim, or both, have accompanied me from first to last; and perhaps it may be a pardonable vanity which induces me to reflect with complacency on a composition which in some degree connects me with the spot where it was produced, and the objects it would fain describe; and however unworthy it may be deemed of those magical and memorable abodes, however short it may fall of our distant conceptions and immediate impressions, yet as a mark of respect for what is venerable, and of feeling for what is glorious, it has been to me a source of pleasure in the production, and I part with it with a kind of regret, which I hardly suspected that events could have left me for imaginary objects.

With regard to the conduct of the last canto, there will be found less of the pilgrim than in any of the preceding, and that little slightly, if at all, separated from the author speaking in his own person. The fact is, that I had become weary of drawing a line which every one seemed determined not to perceive: like the Chinese in Goldsmith's "Citizen of the World," whom nobody would believe to be a Chinese, it was in vain that I asserted, and imagined that I had drawn, a distinction between the author and the pilgrim: and the very anxiety to preserve this difference, and disappointment at finding it unavailing, so far crushed my efforts in the composition, that I determined to abandon it altogether—and have done so. The opinions which have been, or may be, formed on that subject, are *now* a matter of indifference: the work is to depend on itself, and not on the writer; and the author, who has no resources in his own mind beyond the reputation, transient or permanent, which is to arise from his literary efforts, deserves the fate of authors.

In the course of the following canto it was my intention, either in the text or in the notes, to have touched upon the present state of Italian literature, and perhaps of manners. But the text, within the limits I proposed, I soon found hardly sufficient for the labyrinth of external objects, and the consequent reflections; and for the whole of the notes, excepting a few of the shortest, I am indebted to yourself, and these were necessarily limited to the elucidation of the text.

It is also a delicate, and no very grateful task, to dissert upon the literature and manners of a nation so dissimilar: and requires an attention and impartiality which would induce us—though perhaps no inattentive observers, nor ignorant of the language or customs of the people amongst whom we have recently abode —to distrust, or at least defer our judgment, and more narrowly examine our information. The state of literary, as well as political party, appears to run, or to *have* run so high, that for a stranger to steer impartially between them is next to impossible. It may be enough, then, at least for my purpose, to quote from their own beautiful language—"Mi pare che in un paese tutto poetico, che vanta la lingua la più nobile ed insieme la più dolce, tutte tutte le vie diverse si possono tentare, e che sinche la patria di Alfieri e di Monti non ha perduto l' antico valore, in tutte essa dovrebbe essere la prima." Italy has great names still—Canova, Monti, Ugo Foscolo, Pindemonte, Visconti, Morelli, Cicognara, Albrizzi, Mezzophanti, Mai, Mustoxidi, Aglietti, and Vacca, will secure to the present generation an honourable place in most of the departments of Art, Science, and Belles Lettres; and in some the very highest—Europe—the world has but one Canova.

It has been somewhere said by Alfieri, that "La pianta uomo nasce più robusta in Italia che in qualunque altra terra—e che gli stessi atroci delitti che vi si commettono ne sono una prova." Without subscribing to the latter part of his proposition, a dangerous doctrine, the truth of which may be disputed on better grounds, namely, that the Italians are in no respect more ferocious than their neighbours, that man must be wilfully blind, or ignorantly heedless, who is not struck with the extraordinary capacity of this people, or, if such a word be admissible, their *capabilities*, the facility of their acquisitions, the rapidity of their conceptions, the fire of their genius, their sense of beauty, and, amidst all the disadvantages of repeated revolutions, the desolation of battles, and the despair of ages, their still unquenched "longing after immortality," —the immortality of independence And when we ourselves, in riding round the walls of Rome, heard the simple lament of the labourers' chorus, "Roma! Roma! Roma! Roma non è più come era prima," it was difficult not to contrast this melancholy dirge with the bacchanal roar of the songs of exultation still yelled from the London taverns, over the carnage of Mont St. Jean, and the betrayal of Genoa, of Italy, of France, and of the world, by men whose conduct you yourself have exposed in a work worthy of the better days of our history. For me,—

> "Non movero mai corda
> Ove la turba di sue ciance assorda."

What Italy has gained by the late transfer of nations, it were useless for Englishmen to inquire, till it becomes ascertained that England has acquired something more than a permanent army and a suspended Habeas Corpus; it is enough for them to look at home. For what they have done abroad, and especially in the South, "Verily they *will have* their reward," and at no very distant period.

Wishing you, my dear Hobhouse, a safe and agreeable return to that country whose real welfare can be dearer to none than to yourself, I dedicate to you this poem in its completed state; and repeat once more how truly I am ever,

Your obliged

And affectionate friend,

BYRON.

CHILDE HAROLD'S PILGRIMAGE.

CANTO THE FOURTH.

I.

I STOOD in Venice, on the Bridge of Sighs;[1]
A palace and a prison on each hand:
I saw from out the wave her structures rise
As from the stroke of the enchanter's wand:
A thousand years their cloudy wings expand
Around me, and a dying glory smiles
O'er the far times, when many a subject land
Look'd to the winged lion's marble piles,
Where Venice sate in state, throned on her hundred
isles!

II.

She looks a sea Cybele, fresh from ocean,[2]
Rising with her tiara of proud towers
At airy distance, with majestic motion,
A ruler of the waters and their powers:
And such she was;—her daughters had their dowers
From spoils of nations, and the exhaustless East
Pour'd in her lap all gems in sparkling showers.
In purple was she robed, and of her feast
Monarchs partook, and deem'd their dignity increased.

1 See Appendix, "Historical Notes," No. I.

2 Sabellicus, describing the appearance of Venice, has made use of the above image, which would not be poetical were it not true. —"Quo fit ut qui superne urbem contempletur, turritam telluris imaginem medio Oceano figuratam se putet inspicere."

III.

In Venice Tasso's echoes are no more,[1]
And silent rows the songless gondolier;
Her palaces are crumbling to the shore,
And music meets not always now the ear:
Those days are gone—but beauty still is here.
States fall, arts fade—but Nature doth not die,
Nor yet forget how Venice once was dear,
The pleasant place of all festivity,
The revel of the earth, the masque of Italy!

IV.

But unto us she hath a spell beyond
Her name in story, and her long array
Of mighty shadows, whose dim forms despond
Above the dogeless city's vanish'd sway;
Ours is a trophy which will not decay
With the Rialto; Shylock and the Moor,
And Pierre, cannot be swept or worn away—
The keystones of the arch! though all were o'er,
For us repeopled were the solitary shore.

V.

The beings of the mind are not of clay;
Essentially immortal, they create
And multiply in us a brighter ray
And more beloved existence: that which Fate
Prohibits to dull life, in this our state
Of mortal bondage, by these spirits supplied,
First exiles, then replaces what we hate;
Watering the heart whose early flowers have died,
And with a fresher growth replenishing the void

[1] See Appendix, "Historical Notes," No. II.

VI.

Such is the refuge of our youth and age,
The first from Hope, the last from Vacancy;
And this worn feeling peoples many a page,
And, may be, that which grows beneath mine eye.
Yet there are things whose strong reality
Outshines our fairy-land; in shape and hues
More beautiful than our fantastic sky,
And the strange constellations which the Muse
O'er her wild universe is skilful to diffuse:

VII.

I saw or dream'd of such,—but let them go,—
They came like truth, and disappear'd like dreams;
And whatsoe'er they were—are now but so:
I could replace them if I would; still teems
My mind with many a form which aptly seems
Such as I sought for, and at moments found;
Let these too go—for waking Reason deems
Such overweening phantasies unsound,
And other voices speak, and other sights surround.

VIII.

I've taught me other tongues—and in strange eyes
Have made me not a stranger; to the mind
Which is itself, no changes bring surprise;
Nor is it harsh to make, nor hard to find
A country with—ay, or without mankind;
Yet was I born where men are proud to be,
Not without cause; and should I leave behind
The inviolate island of the sage and free,
And seek me out a home by a remoter sea,

IX.

Perhaps I loved it well; and should I lay
My ashes in a soil which is not mine,
My spirit shall resume it—if we may
Unbodied choose a sanctuary. I twine
My hopes of being remember'd in my line
With my land's language: if too fond and far
These aspirations in their scope incline,—
If my fame should be, as my fortunes are,
Of hasty growth and blight, and dull Oblivion bar

X.

My name from out the temple where the dead
Are honour'd by the nations—let it be—
And light the laurels on a loftier head!
And be the Spartan's epitaph on me—
"Sparta hath many a worthier son than he."[1]
Meantime I seek no sympathies, nor need;
The thorns which I have reap'd are of the tree
I planted,—they have torn me,—and I bleed:
I should have known what fruit would spring from such a seed.

XI.

The spouseless Adriatic mourns her lord;
And, annual marriage now no more renew'd,
The Bucentaur lies rotting unrestored,
Neglected garment of her widowhood!
St. Mark yet sees his lion where he stood[2]
Stand, but in mockery of his wither'd power,
Over the proud Place where an emperor sued,
And monarchs gazed and envied in the hour
When Venice was a queen with an unequall'd dower.

[1] The answer of the mother of Brasidas, the Lacedæmonian general, to the strangers who praised the memory of her son.
[2] See Appendix, "Historical Notes," No. III.

XII.

The Suabian sued, and now the Austrian reigns—[1]
An emperor tramples where an emperor knelt;
Kingdoms are shrunk to provinces, and chains
Clank over sceptred cities; nations melt
From power's high pinnacle, when they have felt
The sunshine for a while, and downward go
Like lauwine loosen'd from the mountain's belt;
Oh for one hour of blind old Dandolo![2]
Th' octogenarian chief, Byzantium's conquering foe.

XIII.

Before St. Mark still glow his steeds of brass,
Their gilded collars glittering in the sun;
But is not Doria's menace come to pass?[3]
Are they not *bridled?*—Venice, lost and won,
Her thirteen hundred years of freedom done,
Sinks, like a sea-weed, into whence she rose!
Better be whelm'd beneath the waves, and shun,
Even in destruction's depth, her foreign foes,
From whom submission wrings an infamous repose.

XIV.

In youth she was all glory,—a new Tyre,—
Her very by-word sprung from victory,
The "Planter of the Lion,"[4] which through fire
And blood she bore o'er subject earth and sea;
Though making many slaves, herself still free,
And Europe's bulwark 'gainst the Ottomite;
Witness Troy's rival, Candia! Vouch it, ye
Immortal waves that saw Lepanto's fight!
For ye are names no time nor tyranny can blight.

[1], [2], [3] See Appendix, "Historical Notes," Nos. IV. V. VI.

[4] That is, the Lion of St. Mark, the standard of the republic which is the origin of the word Pantaloon—Piantaleone, Pan taleon, Pantaloon.

XV.

Statues of glass—all shiver'd—the long file
Of her dead Doges are declined to dust;
But where they dwelt, the vast and sumptuous pile
Bespeaks the pageant of their splendid trust;
Their sceptre broken, and their sword in rust,
Have yielded to the stranger: empty halls,
Thin streets, and foreign aspects, such as must
Too oft remind her who and what enthrals,[1]
Have flung a desolate cloud o'er Venice' lovely walls.

XVI.

When Athens' armies fell at Syracuse,
And fetter'd thousands bore the yoke of war,
Redemption rose up in the Attic Muse,[2]
Her voice their only ransom from afar:
See! as they chant the tragic hymn, the car
Of the o'ermaster'd victor stops, the reins
Fall from his hands—his idle scimitar
Starts from its belt—he rends his captive's chains,
And bids him thank the bard for freedom and his strains.

XVII.

Thus, Venice, if no stronger claim were thine,
Were all thy proud historic deeds forgot,
Thy choral memory of the bard divine,
Thy love of Tasso, should have cut the knot
Which ties thee to thy tyrants; and thy lot
Is shameful to the nations,—most of all,
Albion! to thee: the ocean queen should not
Abandon ocean's children; in the fall
Of Venice think of thine, despite thy watery wall

[1] See Appendix, "Historical Notes," No. VII.
[2] The story is told in Plutarch's Life of Nicias.

XVIII.

I loved her from my boyhood—she to me
Was as a fairy city of the heart,
Rising like water-columns from the sea,
Of joy the sojourn, and of wealth the mart;
And Otway, Radcliffe, Schiller, Shakspeare's art,[1]
Had stamp'd her image in me, and even so,
Although I found her thus, we did not part,
Perchance even dearer in her day of woe
Than when she was a boast, a marvel, and a show.

XIX.

I can repeople with the past—and of
The present there is still for eye and thought,
And meditation chasten'd down enough;
And more, it may be, than I hoped or sought;
And of the happiest moments which were wrought
Within the web of my existence, some
From thee, fair Venice! have their colours caught:
There are some feelings Time can not benumb,
Nor torture shake, or mine would now be cold and dumb.

XX.

But from their nature will the tannen grow[2]
Loftiest on loftiest and least shelter'd rocks,
Rooted in barrenness, where naught below
Of soil supports them 'gainst the Alpine shocks
Of eddying storms; yet springs the trunk, and mocks
The howling tempest, till its height and frame
Are worthy of the mountains from whose blocks
Of bleak, gray granite into life it came,
And grew a giant tree;—the mind may grow the same.

1 Venice Preserved; Mysteries of Udolpho; the Ghost-Seer, or Armenian; the Merchant of Venice; Othello.

2 *Tannen* is the plural of *tanne*, a species of fir peculiar to the

XXI.

Existence may be borne, and the deep root
Of life and sufferance make its firm abode
In bare and desolated bosoms: mute
The camel labours with the heaviest load,
And the wolf dies in silence,—not bestow'd
In vain should such example be; if they,
Things of ignoble or of savage mood,
Endure and shrink not, we of nobler clay
May temper it to bear,—it is but for a day.

XXII.

All suffering doth destroy, or is destroy'd,
Even by the sufferer; and, in each event,
Ends:—Some, with hope replenish'd and rebuoy'd,
Return to whence they came—with like intent,
And weave their web again; some, bow'd and bent,
Wax gray and ghastly, withering ere their time,
And perish with the reed on which they leant;
Some seek devotion, toil, war, good or crime,
According as their souls were form'd to sink or climb.

XXIII.

But ever and anon of griefs subdued
There comes a token like a scorpion's sting,
Scarce seen but with fresh bitterness imbued;
And slight withal may be the things which bring
Back on the heart the weight which it would fling
Aside forever: it may be a sound—
A tone of music—summer's eve—or spring—
A flower—the wind—the ocean—which shall wound,
Striking the electric chain wherewith we are darkly bound;

Alps, which only thrives in very rocky parts, where scarcely soil sufficient for its nourishment can be found. On these spots it grows to a greater height than any other mountain tree.

XXIV.

And how and why we know not, nor can trace
Home to its cloud this lightning of the mind,
But feel the shock renew'd, nor can efface
The blight and blackening which it leaves behind,
Which out of things familiar, undesign'd,
When least we deem of such, calls up to view
The spectres whom no exorcism can bind,
The cold—the changed—perchance the dead—anew,
The mourn'd, the loved, the lost—too many!—yet how few!

XXV.

But my soul wanders; I demand it back
To meditate amongst decay, and stand
A ruin amidst ruins; there to track
Fallen states and buried greatness, o'er a land
Which *was* the mightiest in its old command,
And *is* the loveliest, and must ever be
The master-mould of Nature's heavenly hand,
Wherein were cast the heroic and the free,
The beautiful, the brave—the lords of earth and sea.

XXVI.

The commonwealth of kings, the men of Rome!
And even since, and now, fair Italy!
Thou art the garden of the world, the home
Of all Art yields, and Nature[1] can decree,
Even in thy desert, what is like to thee?
Thy very weeds are beautiful, thy waste
More rich than other climes' fertility;
Thy wreck a glory, and thy ruin graced
With an immaculate charm which cannot be defaced.

[1] [The whole of this canto is rich in description of nature. The love of nature now appears as a distinct passion in Lord

XXVII.

The moon is up, and yet it is not night—
Sunset divides the sky with her—a sea
Of glory streams along the Alpine height
Of blue Friuli's mountains; heaven is free
From clouds, but of all colours seems to be
Melted to one vast iris of the west,
Where the day joins the past eternity;
While, on the other hand, meek Dian's crest
Floats through the azure air—an island of the blest![1]

XXVIII.

A single star is at her side, and reigns
With her o'er half the lovely heaven; but still
Yon sunny sea heaves brightly, and remains
Roll'd o'er the peak of the far Rhætian hill,
As day and night contending were, until
Nature reclaim'd her order:—gently flows
The deep-dyed Brenta, where their hues instil
The odorous purple of a new-born rose,
Which streams upon her stream, and glass'd within
it glows.

Byron's mind. It is a love that does not rest in beholding, nor is satisfied with describing, what is before him. It has a power and being, blending itself with the poet's very life. Though Lord Byron had, with his real eyes, perhaps seen more of nature than ever was before permitted to any great poet, yet he never before seemed to open his whole heart to her genial impulses. But in this he is changed; and in this Canto of Childe Harold, he will stand a comparison with the best descriptive poets, in this age of descriptive poetry.—WILSON.]

[1] The above description may seem fantastical or exaggerated to those who have never seen an oriental or an Italian sky, yet it is but a literal and hardly sufficient delineation of an August evening, (the eighteenth,) as contemplated in one of many rides along the banks of the Brenta, near La Mira.

XXIX.

Fill'd with the face of heaven, which, from afar,
Comes down upon the waters; all its hues,
From the rich sunset to the rising star,
Their magical variety diffuse:
And now they change; a paler shadow strews
Its mantle o'er the mountains; parting day
Dies like the dolphin, whom each pang imbues
With a new colour as it gasps away,
The last still loveliest, till—'tis gone—and all is
gray.

XXX.

There is a tomb in Arqua;—rear'd in air,
Pillar'd in their sarcophagus, repose
The bones of Laura's lover: here repair
Many familiar with his well-sung woes,
The pilgrims of his genius. He arose
To raise a language, and his land reclaim
From the dull yoke of her barbaric foes:
Watering the tree which bears his lady's name[1]
With his melodious tears, he gave himself to fame.

XXXI.

They keep his dust in Arqua, where he died;[2]
The mountain-village where his latter days
Went down the vale of years; and 'tis their
pride—
An honest pride—and let it be their praise,
To offer to the passing stranger's gaze
His mansion and his sepulchre; both plain
And venerably simple, such as raise
A feeling more accordant with his strain
Than if a pyramid form'd his monumental fane.

[1], [2] See Appendix, "Historical Notes," Nos. VIII. and IX.

XXXII.

And the soft quiet hamlet where he dwelt[1]
Is one of that complexion which seems made
For those who their mortality have felt,
And sought a refuge from their hopes decay'd
In the deep umbrage of a green hill's shade,
Which shows a distant prospect far away
Of busy cities, now in vain display'd,
For they can lure no further ; and the ray
Of a bright sun can make sufficient holiday,

XXXIII.

Developing the mountains, leaves, and flowers,
And shining in the brawling brook, where-by,
Clear as its current, glide the sauntering hours
With a calm languor, which, though to the eye
Idlesse it seem, hath its morality.
If from society we learn to live,
'Tis solitude should teach us how to die:
It hath no flatterers; vanity can give
No hollow aid; alone—man with his God must strive:

XXXIV.

Or, it may be, with demons, who impair[2]
The strength of better thoughts, and seek their prey
In melancholy bosoms, such as were
Of moody texture from their earliest day,
And loved to dwell in darkness and dismay,

[1] ["Halfway up
He built his house, whence as by stealth he caught
Among the hills a glimpse of busy life
That soothed, not stirr'd."—ROGERS.]

[2] The struggle is to the full as likely to be with demons as with our better thoughts. Satan chose the wilderness for the temptation of our Saviour. And our unsullied John Locke preferred the presence of a child to complete solitude.

Deeming themselves predestined to a doom
Which is not of the pangs that pass away;
Making the sun like blood, the earth a tomb,
The tomb a hell, and hell itself a murkier gloom.

XXXV.

Ferrara![1] in thy wide and grass-grown streets,
Whose symmetry was not for solitude,
There seems as 'twere a curse upon the seats
Of former sovereigns, and the antique brood
Of Este, which for many an age made good
Its strength within thy walls, and was of yore
Patron or tyrant, as the changing mood
Of petty power impell'd, of those who wore
The wreath which Dante's brow alone had worn before.

XXXVI.

And Tasso is their glory and their shame.
Hark to the strain! and then survey his cell!
And see how dearly earn'd Torquato's fame,
And where Alfonso bade his poet dwell:
The miserable despot could not quell

[1] [In April, 1817, Lord Byron visited Ferrara, went over the castle, cell, &c., and wrote, a few days after, the Lament of Tasso.—"One of the Ferrarese asked me," he says, in a letter to a friend, "if I knew 'Lord Byron,' an acquaintance of his, *now* at Naples. I told him 'No!' which was true both ways, for I knew not the impostor: and, in the other, no one knows himself. He stared when told that I was the real Simon Pure. Another asked me, if I had not translated Tasso. You see what Fame is; how accurate! how boundless! I don't know how others feel, but I am always the lighter and the better looked on when I have got rid of mine. It sits on me like armour on the Lord Mayor's champion and I got rid of all the husk of literature, and the attendant babble, by answering that I had not translated Tasso, but a namesake had; and, by the blessing of Heaven, I looked so little like a poet, that everybody believed me."]

The insulted mind he sought to quench, and blend
With the surrounding maniacs, in the hell
Where he had plunged it. Glory without end
Scatter'd the clouds away—and on that name attend

XXXVII.

The tears and praises of all time; while thine
Would rot in its oblivion—in the sink
Of worthless dust, which from thy boasted line
Is shaken into nothing; but the link
Thou formest in his fortunes bids us think
Of thy poor malice, naming thee with scorn—
Alfonso! how thy ducal pageants shrink
From thee! if in another station born,
Scarce fit to be the slave of him thou madest tc
mourn:

XXXVIII.

Thou! form'd to eat, and be despised, and die,
Even as the beasts that perish, save that thou
Hadst a more splendid trough and wider sty:
He! with a glory round his furrow'd brow,
Which emanated then, and dazzles now,
In face of all his foes, the Cruscan quire,
And Boileau, whose rash envy could allow[1]
Nc strain which shamed his country's creaking
lyre,
That whetstone of the teeth—monotony in wire!

XXXIX.

Peace to Torquato's injured shade! 'twas his
In life and death to be the mark where Wrong
Aim'd with her poison'd arrows; but to miss.
Oh, victor unsurpass'd in modern song!
Each year brings forth its millions; but how long

[1] See Appendix, "Historical Notes," No. X.

The tide of generations shall roll on,
And not the whole combined and countless throng
Compose a mind like thine? though all in one
Condensed their scatter'd rays, they would not form
a sun.

XL.

Great as thou art, yet parallel'd by those,
Thy countrymen, before thee born to shine,
The Bards of Hell and Chivalry: first rose
The Tuscan father's comedy divine;
Then, not unequal to the Florentine,
The southern Scott,[1] the minstrel who call'd forth
A new creation with his magic line,
And, like the Ariosto of the North,[2]
Sang ladye-love and war, romance and knightly worth.

[1] ["Scott," says Lord Byron, in his MS. Diary, for 1821, "is certainly the most wonderful writer of the day. His novels are a new literature in themselves, and his poetry as good as any—if not better (only on an erroneous system,)—and only ceased to be so popular, because the vulgar were tired of hearing 'Aristides called the Just,' and Scott the Best, and ostracised him. I know no reading to which I fall with such alacrity as a work of his. I love him, too, for his manliness of character, for the extreme pleasantness of his conversation, and his good-nature towards my self personally. May he prosper! for he deserves it. In a letter, written to Sir Walter, from Pisa, in 1822, he says—"I owe to you far more than the usual obligation for the courtesies of literature and common friendship; for you went out of your way, in 1817, to do me a service, when it required not merely kindness, but courage, to do so; to have been recorded by you in such a manner, would have been a proud memorial at any time; but at such a time, when 'All the world and his wife,' as the proverb goes, were trying to trample upon me, was something still higher to my self-esteem. Had it been a common criticism, however eloquent or panegyrical, I should have felt pleased and grateful, but not to the extent which the extraordinary good-heartedness of the whole proceeding must induce in any mind capable of such sensations."]

[2] ["I do not know whether Scott will like it, but I have called him the 'Ariosto of the North,' in my text. If he should not, say so in time"—*Lord B. to Mr. Murray*. August, 1817.]

XLI.

The lightning rent from Ariosto's bust[1]
The iron crown of laurel's mimick'd leaves;
Nor was the ominous element unjust,
For the true laurel-wreath which Glory weaves
Is of the tree no bolt of thunder cleaves,[2]
And the false semblance but disgraced his brow;
Yet still, if fondly Superstition grieves,
Know, that the lightning sanctifies below[3]
Whate'er it strikes;—yon head is doubly sacred now

XLII.

Italia! oh Italia! thou who hast
The fatal gift of beauty, which became
A funeral dower of present woes and past,
On thy sweet brow is sorrow plough'd by shame,
And annals graved in characters of flame,
Oh, God! that thou wert in thy nakedness
Less lovely or more powerful, and couldst claim
Thy right, and awe the robbers back, who press
To shed thy blood, and drink the tears of thy distress;

XLIII.

Then mightst thou more appal; or, less desired,
Be homely and be peaceful, undeplored
For thy destructive charms; then, still untired,
Would not be seen the armed torrents pour'd
Down the deep Alps; nor would the hostile horde
Of many-nation'd spoilers from the Po
Quaff blood and water; nor the stranger's sword
Be thy sad weapon of defence, and so,
Victor or vanquish'd, thou the slave of friend or foe.[4]

[1], [2], [3] See Appendix, "Historical Notes," Nos. XI. XII. XIII

[4] The two stanzas xlii. and xliii. are, with the exception of a line or two, a translation of the famous sonnet of Filicaja:—"Italia, Italia, O tu cui feo la sorte!"

XLIV.

Wandering in youth, I traced the path of him,[1]
The Roman friend of Rome's least-mortal mind,
The friend of Tully: as my bark did skim
The bright blue waters with a fanning wind,
Came Megara before me, and behind
Ægina lay, Piræus on the right,
And Corinth on the left: I lay reclined
Along the prow, and saw all these unite
In ruin, even as he had seen the desolate sight;

XLV.

For Time hath not rebuilt them, but uprear'd
Barbaric dwellings on their shatter'd site,
Which only make more mourn'd and more endear'd
The few last rays of their far-scatter'd light,
And the crush'd relics of their vanish'd might.
The Roman saw these tombs in his own age,
These sepulchres of cities, which excite
Sad wonder, and his yet surviving page
The moral lesson bears, drawn from such pilgrimage.

[1] The celebrated letter of Servius Sulpicius to Cicero, on the death of his daughter, describes as it then was, and now is, a path which I often traced in Greece, both by sea and land, in different journeys and voyages. "On my return from Asia, as I was sailing from Ægina towards Megara, I began to contemplate the prospect of the countries around me: Ægina was behind, Megara before me; Piræus on the right. Corinth on the left: all which towns, once famous and flourishing, now lie overturned and buried in their ruins. Upon this sight, I could not but think presently within myself, Alas! how we poor mortals fret and vex ourselves if any of our friends happen to die or be killed, whose life is yet so short, when the carcasses of so many noble cities lie here exposed before me in one view."—See MIDDLETON'S *Cicero*, vol. ii. p. 371.

XLVI.

That page is now before me, and on mine
His country's ruin added to the mass
Of perish'd states he mourn'd in their decline,
And I in desolation: all that *was*
Of then destruction *is*; and now, alas!
Rome—Rome imperial, bows her to the storm,
In the same dust and blackness, and we pass
The skeleton of her Titanic form,[1]
Wrecks of another world, whose ashes still are warm.

XLVII.

Yet, Italy! through every other land
Thy wrongs should ring, and shall, from side to side;
Mother of Arts! as once of arms; thy hand
Was then our guardian, and is still our guide;
Parent of our Religion! whom the wide
Nations have knelt to for the keys of heaven!
Europe, repentant of her parricide,
Shall yet redeem thee, and, all backward driven,
Roll the barbarian tide, and sue to be forgiven.

XLVIII.

But Arno wins us to the fair white walls,
Where the Etrurian Athens claims and keeps
A softer feeling for her fairy halls.
Girt by her theatre of hills, she reaps
Her corn, and wine, and oil, and Plenty leaps
To laughing life, with her redundant horn.
Along the banks where smiling Arno sweeps
Was modern Luxury of Commerce born,
And buried Learning rose, redeem'd to a new morn

[1] It is Poggio, who, looking from the Capitoline hill upon ruined Rome, breaks forth into the exclamation, "Ut nunc omni decore nudata, prostrata jacet, instar gigantei cadaveris corrupti atque undique exesi."

XLIX.

There, too, the goddess loves in stone, and fills[1]
The air around with beauty; we inhale
The ambrosial aspect, which, beheld, instils
Part of its immortality; the veil
Of heaven is half undrawn; within the pale
We stand, and in that form and face behold
What Mind can make, when Nature's self would fail;
And to the fond idolaters of old
Envy the innate flash which such a soul could mould:

L.

We gaze and turn away, and know not where,
Dazzled and drunk with beauty, till the heart[2]
Reels with its fulness; there—forever there—
Chain'd to the chariot of triumphal Art,
We stand as captives, and would not depart.
Away!—there need no words, nor terms precise,
The paltry jargon of the marble mart,
Where Pedantry gulls Folly—we have eyes
Blood—pulse—and breast, confirm the Dardan shepherd's prize.

[1] See Appendix, "Historical Notes," No. XIV.

[2] [In 1817, Lord Byron visited Florence, on his way to Rome. "I remained," he says, "*but a day*: however, I went to the two galleries, from which one returns *drunk with beauty*. The Venus is more for admiration than love; but there are sculpture and painting, which, for the first time, at all gave me an idea of what people mean by their cant about those two most artificial of the arts. What struck me most were, the mistress of Raphael, a portrait; the mistress of Titian, a portrait; a Venus of Titian in the Medici Gallery; *the* Venus; Canova's Venus, also, in the other gallery: Titian's mistress is also in the other gallery, (that is, in the Pitti Palace gallery;) the Parcæ of Michael Angelo, a picture and the Antinous, the Alexander, and one or two not very decen groups in marble; the Genius of Death, a sleeping figure, &c. &c. I also went to the Medici chapel. Fine frippery in great slabs of various expensive stones, to commemorate fifty rotten and forgotten carcasses. It is unfinished, and will remain so." We find

LI.

Appear'dst thou not to Paris in this guise?
Or to more deeply blest Anchises? or,
In all thy perfect goddess-ship, when lies
Before thee thy own vanquish'd Lord of War?
And gazing in thy face as toward a star,
Laid on thy lap, his eyes to thee upturn,
Feeding on thy sweet cheek![1] while thy lips are
With lava kisses melting while they burn, [urn![2]
Shower'd on his eyelids, brow, and mouth, as from an

the following note of a second visit to the galleries in 1821, accompanied by the author of "The Pleasures of Memory:"- -"My former impressions were confirmed; but there were too many visiters to allow me to *feel* any thing properly. When we were (about thirty or forty) all stuffed into the cabinet of gems and knick-knackeries, in a corner of one of the galleries, I told Rogers that 'it felt like being in the watch-house.' I heard one bold Briton declare to the woman on his arm, looking at the Venus of Titian, 'Well, now, that is really very fine indeed!'—an observation which, like that of the landlord in Joseph Andrews, on 'the certainty of death,' was (as the landlord's wife observed) 'extremely true.' In the Pitti Palace, I did not omit Goldsmith's prescription for a connoisseur, viz. 'that the pictures would have been better if the painter had taken more pains, and to praise the works of Peter Perugino.'"]

[1] Ὀφθαλμοὺς ἑστιᾶν.
"Atque oculos pascat uterque suos."—OVID. *Amor*. lib. ii.

[2] [The delight with which the pilgrim contemplates the ancient Greek statues at Florence, and afterwards at Rome, is such as might have been expected from any great poet, whose youthful mind had, like his, been imbued with those classical ideas and associations which afford so many sources of pleasure, through every period of life. He has gazed upon these masterpieces of art with a more susceptible, and, in spite of his disavowal, with a more learned eye, than can be traced in the effusions of any poet who had previously expressed, in any formal manner, his admiration of their beauty. It may appear fanciful to say so;—but we think the genius of Byron is, more than that of any other modern poet, akin to that peculiar genius which seems to have been diffused among all the poets and artists of ancient Greece; and in

LII.

Glowing, and circumfused in speechless love,
Their full divinity inadequate
That feeling to express, or to improve,
The gods became as mortals, and man's fate
Has moments like their brightest; but the weight
Of earth recoils upon us;—let it go!
We can recall such visions, and create,
From what has been, or might be, things which grow
Into thy statue's form, and look like gods below.

LIII.

I leave to learned fingers, and wise hands,
The artist and his ape,[1] to teach and tell
How well his connoisseurship understands
The graceful bend, and the voluptuous swell:
Let these describe the undescribable:
I would not their vile breath should crisp the stream
Wherein that image shall forever dwell;
The unruffled mirror of the loveliest dream
That ever left the sky on the deep soul to beam.

whose spirit, above all its other wonders, the great specimens of sculpture seem to have been conceived and executed. His creations, whether of beauty or of strength, are all single creations. He requires no grouping to give effect to his favourites, or to tell his story. His heroines are solitary symbols of loveliness, which require no foil; his heroes stand alone as upon marble pedestals, displaying the naked power of passion, or the wrapped up and reposing energy of grief. The artist who would illustrate, as it is called, the works of any of our other poets, must borrow the mimic splendours of the pencil. He who would transfer into another vehicle the spirit of Byron, must pour the liquid metal, or hew the stubborn rock. What he loses in ease, he will gain in power. He might draw from Medora, Gulnare, Lara, or Manfred, subjects for relievos, worthy of enthusiasm almost as great as Harold has himself displayed on the contemplation of the loveliest and the sternest relics of the inimitable genius of the Greeks.—Wilson.]

[1] [Only a week before the poet visited the Florence gallery, he

LIV.

In Santa Croce's holy precincts lie[1]
Ashes which make it holier, dust which is
Even in itself an immortality,
Though there were nothing save the past, and this,
The particle of those sublimities
Which have relapsed to chaos:—here repose
Angelo's, Alfieri's bones, and his,[2]
The starry Galileo, with his woes;
Here Machiavelli's earth return'd to whence it rose.[3]

LV.

These are four minds, which, like the elements,
Might furnish forth creation:—Italy! [rents
Time, which hath wrong'd thee with ten thousand
Of thine imperial garment, shall deny,
And hath denied, to every other sky,
Spirits which soar from ruin:—thy decay
Is still impregnate with divinity,
Which gilds it with revivifying ray;
Such as the great of yore, Canova is to-day.

wrote thus to a friend:—"I know nothing of painting. Depend upon it, of all the arts, it is the most artificial and unnatural, and that by which the nonsense of mankind is most imposed upon. I never yet saw the picture or the statue which came a league within my conception or expectation; but I have seen many mountains, and seas, and rivers, and views, and two or three women, who went as far beyond it."—*Byron Letters.*]

[1], [2], [3] See Appendix, "Historical Notes," Nos. XV. XVI. XVII.—["The church of Santa Croce contains much illustrious nothing. The tombs of Machiavelli, Michael Angelo, Galileo, and Alfieri, make it the Westminster Abbey of Italy. I did not admire any of these tombs—beyond their contents. That of Alfieri is heavy; and all of them seem to me overloaded. What is necessary but a bust and name? and perhaps a date? the last for the unchronological, of whom I am one. But all your allegory and eulogy is infernal, and worse than the long wigs of English numskulls upon Roman bodies, in the statuary of the reigns of Charles the Second, William, and Anne."—*Byron Letters*, 1817.]

LVI.

But where repose the all Etruscan three—
Dante, and Petrarch, and scarce less than they,
The Bard of Prose, creative spirit! he
Of the Hundred Tales of love—where did they lay
Their bones, distinguish'd from our common clay
In death as life? Are they resolved to dust,
And have their country's marbles naught to say.
Could not her quarries furnish forth one bust?
Did they not to her breast their filial earth intrust?

LVII.

Ungrateful Florence! Dante sleeps afar,
Like Scipio, buried by the upbraiding shore:[2]
Thy factions, in their worse than civil war,
Proscribed the bard whose name for evermore
Their children's children would in vain adore
With the remorse of ages; and the crown[3]
Which Petrarch's laureate brow supremely wore,
Upon a far and foreign soil had grown,
His life, his fame, his grave, though rifled—not thine own.

LVIII.

Boccaccio to his parent earth bequeath'd[4]
His dust,—and lies it not her great among,
With many a sweet and solemn requiem breathed
O'er him who form'd the Tuscan's siren tongue?
That music in itself, whose sounds are song,
The poetry of speech? No;—even his tomb
Uptorn, must bear the hyæna bigot's wrong,
No more amidst the meaner dead find room,
Nor claim a passing sigh, because it told for *whom!*

[1], [2], [3] [4] See Appendix, "Historical Notes," Nos. XVIII. XIX. XX. and XXI.

LIX.

And Santa Croce wants their mighty dust;
Yet for this want more noted, as of yore
The Cæsar's pageant, shorn of Brutus' bust,
Did but of Rome's best son remind her more:
Happier Ravenna! on thy hoary shore,
Fortress of falling empire! honour'd sleeps
The immortal exile;—Arqua, too, her store
Of tuneful relics proudly claims and keeps,
While Florence vainly begs her banish'd dead, and
weeps.

LX.

What is her pyramid of precious stones?[1]
Of porphyry, jasper, agate, and all hues
Of gem and marble, to encrust the bones
Of merchant-dukes? the momentary dews
Which, sparkling to the twilight stars, infuse
Freshness in the green turf that wraps the dead,
Whose names are mausoleums of the Muse,
Are gently prest with far more reverent tread
Than ever paced the slab which paves the princely
head.

LXI.

There be more things to greet the heart and eyes
In Arno's dome of Art's most princely shrine,
Where Sculpture with her rainbow sister vies;
There be more marvels yet—but not for mine;
For I have been accustom'd to entwine
My thoughts with Nature rather in the fields,
Than Art in galleries: though a work divine
Calls for my spirit's homage, yet it yields
Less than it feels, because the weapon which it wields

[1] See Appendix, "Historical Notes," No. XXII

LXII.

Is of another temper, and I roam
By Thrasimene's lake, in the defiles
Fatal to Roman rashness, more at home;
For there the Carthaginian's warlike wiles
Come back before me, as his skill beguiles
The host between the mountains and the shore,
Where Courage falls in her despairing files,
And torrents swoln to rivers with their gore,
Reek through the sultry plain, with legions scatter'd o'er.

LXIII.

Like to a forest fell'd by mountain winds;
And such the storm of battle on this day,
And such the frenzy, whose convulsion blinds
To all save carnage, that, beneath the fray,
An earthquake reel'd unheededly away![1]
None felt stern Nature rocking at his feet,
And yawning forth a grave for those who lay
Upon their bucklers for a winding sheet;
Such is the absorbing hate when warring nations meet!

LXIV.

The earth to them was as a rolling bark
Which bore them to eternity; they saw
The ocean round, but had no time to mark
The motions of their vessel; Nature's law,
In them suspended, reck'd not of the awe
Which reigns when mountains tremble, and the birds
Plunge in the clouds for refuge, and withdraw
From their down-toppling nests; and bellowing herds
Stumble o'er heaving plains, and man's dread hath no words.

[1] See Appendix, "Historical Notes," No. XXIII.—[An earth

LXV.

Far other scene is Thrasimene now;
Her lake a sheet of silver, and her plain
Rent by no ravage save the gentle plough;
Her aged trees rise thick as once the slain
Lay where their roots are; but a brook hath ta'en—
A little rill of scanty stream and bed—
A name of blood from that day's sanguine rain;
And Sanguinetto tells ye where the dead
Made the earth wet, and turn'd the unwilling waters red.[1]

LXVI.

But thou, Clitumnus! in thy sweetest wave[2]
Of the most living crystal that was e'er
The haunt of river nymph, to gaze and lave
Her limbs where nothing hid them, thou dost rear
Thy grassy banks whereon the milk-white steer
Grazes; the purest god of gentle waters!
And most serene of aspect, and most clear;
Surely that stream was unprofaned by slaughters—
A mirror and a bath for Beauty's youngest daughters!

quake which shook all Italy occurred during the battle, and was unfelt by any of the combatants.]

[1] ["The lovely peaceful mirror reflected the mountains of Monte Pulciana, and the wild fowl skimming its ample surface, touched the waters with their rapid wings, leaving circles and trains of light to glitter in gray repose. As we moved along, one set of interesting features yielded to another, and every change excited new delight. Yet, was it not among these tranquil scenes that Hannibal and Flaminius met? Was not the blush of blood upon the silver lake of Thrasimene?"—H. W. WILLIAMS.]

[2] No book of travels has omitted to expatiate on the temple of the Clitumnus, between Foligno and Spoleto; and no site, or scenery, even in Italy is more worthy a description. For an account of the dilapidation of this temple, the reader is referred to "Historical Illustrations of the Fourth Canto of Childe Harold," p. 35.

LXVII.

And on thy happy shore a temple[1] still,
Of small and delicate proportion, keeps,
Upon a mild declivity of hill,
Its memory of thee; beneath it sweeps
Thy current's calmness; oft from out it leaps
The finny darter with the glittering scales,
Who dwells and revels in thy glassy deeps;
While, chance, some scatter'd water-lily sails
Down where the shallower wave still tells its bubbling tales.

LXVIII.

Pass not unblest the Genius of the place!
If through the air a zephyr more serene
Win to the brow, 'tis his; and if ye trace
Along his margin a more eloquent green,
If on the heart the freshness of the scene
Sprinkle its coolness, and from the dry dust
Of weary life a moment lave it clean
With Nature's baptism,—'tis to him ye must
Pay orisons for this suspension of disgust.[2]

[1] ["This pretty little gem stands on the acclivity of a bank overlooking its crystal waters, which have their source at the distance of some hundred yards towards Spoleto. The temple, fronting the river, is of an oblong form, in the Corinthian order. Four columns support the pediment, the shafts of which are covered in spiral lines, and in forms to represent the scales of fishes: the bases, too, are richly sculptured. Within the building is a chapel, the walls of which are covered with many hundred names; but we saw none which we could recognise as British. Can it be that this classical temple is seldom visited by our countrymen, though celebrated by Dryden and Addison? To future travellers from Britain it will surely be rendered interesting by the beautiful lines of Lord Byron, flowing as sweetly as the lovely stream which they describe."—H. W. WILLIAMS.]

[2] [Perhaps there are no verses in our language of happier descriptive power than the two stanzas which characterize the

LXIX.

The roar of waters!—from the headlong height
Velino cleaves the wave-worn precipice;
The fall of waters! rapid as the light
The flashing mass foams shaking the abyss;
The hell of waters! where they howl and hiss,
And boil in endless torture; while the sweat
Of their great agony, wrung out from this
Their Phlegethon, curls round the rocks of jet
That gird the gulf around, in pitiless horror set,

LXX.

And mounts in spray the skies, and thence again
Returns in an unceasing shower, which round,
With its unemptied cloud of gentle rain,
Is an eternal April to the ground,
Making it all one emerald:—how profound
The gulf! and how the giant element
From rock to rock leaps with delirious bound,
Crushing the cliffs, which, downward worn and rent
With his fierce footsteps, yield in chasms a fearful vent.

Clitumnus. In general poets find it so difficult to leave an interesting subject, that they injure the distinctness of the description by loading it so as to embarrass, rather than excite, the fancy of the reader; or else, to avoid that fault, they confine themselves to cold and abstract generalities. Byron has, in these stanzas, admirably steered his course betwixt these extremes: while they present the outlines of a picture as pure and as brilliant as those of Claude Lorraine, the task of filling up the more minute particulars is judiciously left to the imagination of the reader; and it must be dull indeed if it does not supply what the poet has left unsaid, or but generally and briefly intimated. While the eye glances over the lines, we seem to feel the refreshing coolness of the scene—we hear the bubbling tale of the more rapid streams, and see the slender proportions of the rural temple reflected in the crystal dept of the calm pool.—SIR WALTER SCOTT.]

LXXI.

To the broad column which rolls on, and shows
More like the fountain of an infant sea
Torn from the womb of mountains by the throes
Of a new world, than only thus to be
Parent of rivers, which flow gushingly, [back!
With many windings, through the vale:—Look
Lo! where it comes like an eternity,
As if to sweep down all things in its track,
Charming the eye with dread,—a matchless cataract,[1]

LXXII.

Horribly beautiful! but on the verge,
From side to side, beneath the glittering morn,
An Iris sits, amidst the infernal surge,[2]
Like Hope upon a death-bed, and, unworn
Its steady dyes, while all around is torn
By the distracted waters, bears serene
Its brilliant hues with all their beams unshorn:
Resembling, mid the torture of the scene,
Love watching Madness with unalterable mien.

[1] I saw the Cascata del Marmore of Terni twice, at different periods; once from the summit of the precipice, and again from the valley below. The lower view is far to be preferred, if the traveller has time for one only; but in any point of view, either from above or below, it is worth all the cascades and torrents of Switzerland put together: the Staubach, Reichenbach, Pisse Vache, fall of Arpenaz, &c. are rills in comparative appearance. Of the fall of Schaffhausen I cannot speak, not yet having seen it. ["The stunning sound, the mist, uncertainty, and tremendous depth, bewildered the senses for a time, and the eye had little rest from the impetuous and hurrying waters, to search into the mysterious and whitened gulf, which presented, through a cloud of spray, the apparitions, as it were, of rocks and overhanging wood. The wind, however, would sometimes remove for an instant this misty veil, and display such a scene of havoc as appalled the soul." —H. W. WILLIAMS.]

[2] Of the time, place, and qualities of this kind of iris, the reader will see a short account, in a note to *Manfred*. The fall looks so

LXXIII.

Once more upon the woody Apennine
The infant Alps, which—had I not before
Gazed on their mightier parents, where the pine
Sits on more shaggy summits, and where roar[1]
The thundering lauwine—might be worshipp'd more;
But I have seen the soaring Jungfrau rear
Her never-trodden snow, and seen the hoar
Glaciers of bleak Mont Blanc both far and near,
And in Chimari heard the thunder-hills of fear,

LXXIV.

Th' Acroceraunian mountains of old name;
And on Parnassus seen the eagles fly
Like spirits of the spot, as 'twere for fame,
For still they soar'd unutterably high:
I've look'd on Ida with a Trojan's eye;
Athos, Olympus, Ætna, Atlas, made
These hills seem things of lesser dignity,
All, save the lone Soracte's height, display'd
Not *now* in snow, which asks the lyric Roman's aid

much like "the hell of waters," that Addison thought the descent alluded to by the gulf in which Alecto plunged into the infernal regions. It is singular enough, that two of the finest cascades in Europe should be artificial—this of the Velino, and the one at Tivoli. The traveller is strongly recommended to trace the Velino, at least as high as the little lake, called *Pie' di Lup.* The Reatine territory was the Italian Tempe, (Cicer. Epist. ad Attic. xv. lib. iv.,) and the ancient naturalists, (Plin. Hist. Nat. lib. ii. cap. lxii.,) amongst other beautiful varieties, remarked the daily rainbows of the lake Velinus. A scholar of great name has devoted a treatise to this district alone. See Ald. Manut. de Reatina Urbe Agroque, ap. Sallengre, Thesaur. tom. i. p. 773.

[1] In the greater part of Switzerland, the avalanches are known by the name of lauwine.

LXXV.

For our remembrance, and from out the plain
Heaves like a long-swept wave about to break,
And on the curl hangs pausing: not in vain
May he, who will, his recollections rake,
And quote in classic raptures, and awake
The hills with Latian echoes; I abhorr'd
Too much, to conquer for the poet's sake,
The drill'd dull lesson, forced down word by word[1]
In my repugnant youth, with pleasure to record

[1] These stanzas may probably remind the reader of Ensign Northerton's remarks, "D—n Homo," &c.; but the reasons for our dislike are not exactly the same. I wish to express, that we become tired of the task before we can comprehend the beauty; that we learn by rote before we can get by heart; that the freshness is worn away, and the future pleasure and advantage deadened and destroyed, by the didactic anticipation, at an age when we can neither feel nor understand the power of compositions which it requires an acquaintance with life, as well as Latin and Greek, to relish, or to reason upon. For the same reason, we never can be aware of the fulness of some of the finest passages of Shakspeare ("To be, or not to be," for instance,) from the habit of having them hammered into us at eight years old, as an exercise, not of mind, but of memory; so that when we are old enough to enjoy them, the taste is gone, and the appetite palled. In some parts of the continent young persons are taught from more common authors, and do not read the best classics till their maturity. I certainly do not speak on this point from any pique or aversion towards the place of my education. I was not a slow, though an idle boy; and I believe no one could, or can be, more attached to Harrow than I have always been, and with reason;—a part of the time passed there was the happiest of my life; and my preceptor, the Rev. Dr. Joseph Drury, was the best and worthiest friend I ever possessed, whose warnings I have remembered but too well, though too late when I have erred,—and whose counsels I have but followed when I have done well or wisely. If ever this imperfect record of my feelings towards him should reach his eyes, let it remind him of one who never thinks of him but with gratitude and veneration—of one who would more gladly boast of having been his pupil, if, by more closely following his injunctions, he could reflect any honour upon his instructer.

LXXVI.

Aught that recalls the daily drug which turn'd
My sickening memory; and, though time hath taught
My mind to meditate what then it learn'd,
Yet such the fix'd inveteracy wrought
By the impatience of my early thought,
That, with the freshness wearing out before
My mind could relish what it might have sought,
If free to choose, I cannot now restore
Its health; but what it then detested, still abhor.

LXXVII.

Then farewell, Horace; whom I hated so,[1]
Not for thy faults, but mine: it is a curse
To understand, not feel thy lyric flow,
To comprehend, but never love thy verse,
Although no deeper moralist rehearse
Our little life, nor bard prescribe his art,
Nor livelier satirist the conscience pierce,
Awakening without wounding the touch'd heart,
Yet fare thee well—upon Soracte's ridge we part.

LXXVIII.

Oh Rome! my country! city of the soul!
The orphans of the heart must turn to thee,
Lone mother of dead empires! and control
In their shut breasts their petty misery.
What are our woes and sufferance? Come and see
The cypress, hear the owl, and plod your way
O'er steps of broken thrones and temples, Ye!
Whose agonies are evils of a day—
A world is at our feet as fragile as our clay.

[1] [Lord Byron's prepossession against Horace is not without a parallel. It was not till released from the duty of reading Virgil as a task, that Gray could feel himself capable of enjoying the beauties of that poet.—Moore.]

LXXIX.

The Niobe of nations! there she stands,[1]
Childless and crownless, in her voiceless woe;
An empty urn within her wither'd hands,
Whose holy dust was scatter'd long ago;
The Scipios' tomb contains no ashes now;[2]
The very sepulchres lie tenantless
Of their heroic dwellers: dost thou flow,
Old Tiber! through a marble wilderness?
Rise, with thy yellow waves, and mantle her distress.

LXXX.

The Goth, the Christian, Time, War, Flood, and Fire
Have dealt upon the seven-hill'd city's pride;
She saw her glories star by star expire,
And up the steep barbarian monarchs ride,
Where the car climb'd the capitol; far and wide
Temple and tower went down, nor left a site:—
Chaos of ruins! who shall trace the void,
O'er the dim fragments cast a lunar light,
And say, "here was or is," where all is doubly night?

[1] ["I have been some days in Rome the Wonderful. I am delighted with Rome. As a whole,—ancient and modern,—it beats Greece, Constantinople, every thing—at least that I have ever seen. But I can't describe, because my first impressions are always strong and confused, and my memory *selects* and reduces them to order, like distance in the landscape, and blends them better, although they may be less distinct. I have been on horseback most of the day, all days since my arrival. I have been to Albano, its lakes, and to the top of the Alban Mount, and to Frescati, Aricia, &c. As for the Coliseum, Pantheon, St. Peter's, the Vatican, Palatine, &c. &c.—they are quite inconceivable, and must be *seen*."—*Byron Letters*, May, 1817.]

[2] For a comment on this and the two following stanzas, the reader may consult "Historical Illustrations," p. 46.

LXXXI.

The double night of ages, and of her,
Night's daughter, Ignorance, hath wrapt and wrap
All round us; we but feel our way to err:
The ocean hath his chart, the stars their map,
And Knowledge spreads them on her ample lap:
But Rome is as the desert, where we steer
Stumbling o'er recollections; now we clap
Our hands, and cry "Eureka!" it is clear—
When but some false mirage of ruin rises near.

LXXXII.

Alas! the lofty city! and alas!
The trebly hundred triumphs![1] and the day
When Brutus made the dagger's edge surpass
The conqueror's sword in bearing fame away!
Alas, for Tully's voice, and Virgil's lay,
And Livy's pictured page!—but these shall be
Her resurrection! all beside—decay.
Alas, for Earth, for never shall we see
That brightness in her eye she bore when Rome was free!

LXXXIII.

Oh thou, whose chariot roll'd on Fortune's wheel,
Triumphant Sylla! Thou, who didst subdue
Thy country's foes ere thou wouldst pause to feel
The wrath of thy own wrongs, or reap the due
Of hoarded vengeance till thine eagles flew
O'er prostrate Asia;—thou who with thy frown
Annihilated senates—Roman, too,
With all thy vices, for thou didst lay down
With an atoning smile a more than earthly crown—

[1] Orosius gives 320 for the number of triumphs. He is followed by Panvinius; and Panvinius by Mr. Gibbon and the modern writers.

LXXXIV.

The dictatorial wreath,[1]—couldst thou divine
To what would one day dwindle that which made
Thee more than mortal? and that so supine
By aught than Romans Rome should thus be laid?
She who was named Eternal, and array'd
Her warriors but to conquer—she who veil'd
Earth with her haughty shadow, and display'd,
Until the o'er-canopied horizon fail'd,
Her rushing wings—Oh! she who was Almighty hail'd!

LXXXV.

Sylla was first of victors; but our own,
The sagest of usurpers, Cromwell; he
Too swept off senates while he hew'd the throne
Down to a block—immortal rebel! See
What crimes it costs to be a moment free
And famous through all ages! but beneath
His fate the moral lurks of destiny:
His day of double victory and death
Beheld him win two realms, and, happier, yield his [breath.[2]

[1] Certainly were it not for these two traits in the life of Sylla, alluded to in this stanza, we should regard him as a monster unredeemed by any admirable quality. The *atonement* of his voluntary resignation of empire may perhaps be accepted by us, as it seems to have satisfied the Romans, who if they had not respected must have destroyed him. There could be no mean, no division of opinion; they must have all thought, like Eucrates, that what had appeared ambition was a love of glory, and that what had been mistaken for pride was a real grandeur of soul.—("Seigneur, vous changez toutes mes idées de la façon dont je vous vois agir. Je croyais que vous aviez de l'ambition, mais aucune amour pour la gloire: je voyais bien que votre âme était haute; mais je ne soupçonnais pas qu'elle fut grande."—*Dialogues de Sylla et d'Eucrate.*)

[2] On the 3d of September Cromwell gained the victory of Dunbar: a year afterwards he obtained "his crowning mercy" of Worcester; and a few years after, on the same day, which he had ever esteemed the most fortunate for him, died.

LXXXVI.

The third of the same moon whose former course
Had all but crown'd him, on the selfsame day
Deposed him gently from his throne of force,
And laid him with the earth's preceding clay.
And show'd not Fortune thus how fame and sway
And all we deem delightful, and consume
Our souls to compass through each arduous way,
Are in her eyes less happy than the tomb?
Were they but so in man's, how different were his
doom!

LXXXVII.

And thou, dread statue! yet existent in[1]
The austerest form of naked majesty,
Thou who beheldest, mid the assassins' din,
At thy bathed base the bloody Cæsar lie,
Folding his robe in dying dignity,
An offering to thine altar from the queen
Of gods and men, great Nemesis! did he die,
And thou, too, perish, Pompey? have ye been
Victors of countless kings, or puppets of a scene?

LXXXVIII.

And thou, the thunder-stricken nurse of Rome![2]
She-wolf! whose brazen-imaged dugs impart
The milk of conquest yet within the dome
Where, as a monument of antique art,
Thou standest:—Mother of the mighty heart,
Which the great founder suck'd from thy wild teat,
Scorch'd by the Roman Jove's ethereal dart,
And thy limbs black with lightning—dost thou
yet
Guard thine immortal cubs, nor thy fond charge
forget?

[1], [2] See Appendix, "Historical Notes," Nos. XXIV. XXV

LXXXIX.

Thou dost;—but all thy foster-babes are dead—
The men of iron; and the world hath rear'd
Cities from out their sepulchres: men bled
In imitation of the things they fear'd,
And fought and conquer'd, and the same course steer'd,
At apish distance; but as yet none have,
Nor could, the same supremacy have near'd,
Save one vain man, who is not in the grave,
But, vanquish'd by himself, to his own slaves a slave—

XC.

The fool of false dominion—and a kind
Of bastard Cæsar, following him of old
With steps unequal; for the Roman's mind
Was modell'd in a less terrestrial mould,[1]
With passions fiercer, yet a judgment cold,
And an immortal instinct which redeem'd
The frailties of a heart so soft, yet bold,
Alcides with the distaff now he seem'd
At Cleopatra's feet,—and now himself he beam'd,

XCI.

And came—and saw—and conquer'd! But the man
Who would have tamed his eagles down to flee,
Like a train'd falcon, in the Gallic van,
Which he, in sooth, long led to victory,
With a deaf heart which never seem'd to be
A listener to itself, was strangely framed;
With but one weakest weakness—vanity,
Coquettish in ambition—still he aim'd—
At what? can he avouch—or answer what he claim'd?

[1] See Appendix, "Historical Notes," No. XXVI

XCII.

And would be all or nothing—nor could wait
For the sure grave to level him; few years
Had fix'd him with the Cæsars in his fate,
On whom we tread: For *this* the conqueror rears
The arch of triumph! and for this the tears
And blood of earth flow on as they have flow'd,
An universal deluge, which appears
Without an ark for wretched man's abode,
And ebbs but to reflow!—Renew thy rainbow, God!

XCIII.

What from this barren being do we reap?
Our senses narrow, and our reason frail,[1]
Life short, and truth a gem which loves the deep,
And all things weigh'd in custom's falsest scale;
Opinion an omnipotence,—whose veil
Mantles the earth with darkness, until right
And wrong are accidents, and men grow pale
Lest their own judgments should become too bright,
And their free thoughts be crimes, and earth have too much light.

XCIV.

And thus they plod in sluggish misery,
Rotting from sire to son, and age to age,
Proud of their trampled nature, and so die,
Bequeathing their hereditary rage

[1] ——"Omnes pene veteres; qui nihil cognosci, nihil percepi, nihil sciri posse dixerunt; angustos sensus; imbecillos animos, brevia curricula vitæ; in profundo veritatem demersam; opinionibus et institutis omnia teneri; nihil veritati relinqui: deinceps omnia tenebris circumfusa esse dixerunt."—Academ. l. 13. The eighteen hundred years which have elapsed since Cicero wrote this, have not removed any of the imperfections of humanity: and the complaints of the ancient philosophers may, without injustice or affectation, be transcribed in a poem written yesterday.

To the new race of inborn slaves, who wage
War for their chains, and, rather than be free,
Bleed gladiator-like, and still engage
Within the same arena where they see
Their fellows fall before, like leaves of the same tree.

XCV.

I speak not of men's creeds—they rest between
Man and his Maker—but of things allow'd,
Averr'd, and known,—and daily, hourly seen—
The yoke that is upon us doubly bow'd,
And the intent of tyranny avow'd,
The edict of earth's rulers, who are grown
The apes of him who humbled once the proud,
And shook them from their slumbers on the throne;
Too glorious, were this all his mighty arm had
done.

XCVI.

Can tyrants but by tyrants conquer'd be,
And Freedom find no champion and no child
Such as Columbia saw arise when she
Sprung forth a Pallas, arm'd and undefiled?
Or must such minds be nourish'd in the wild,
Deep in the unpruned forest, midst the roar
Of cataracts, where nursing Nature smiled
On infant Washington? Has earth no more
Such seeds within her breast, or Europe no such
shore?

XCVII.

But France got drunk with blood to vomit crime;
And fatal have her Saturnalia been
To Freedom's cause, in every age and clime;
Because the deadly days which we have seen,
And vile Ambition, that built up between

Man and his hopes an adamantine wall,
And the base pageant last upon the scene,
Are grown the pretext for the eternal thrall
Which nips life's tree, and dooms man's worst—his
second fall.

XCVIII.

Yet, Freedom! yet thy banner, torn, but flying,
Streams like the thunder-storm *against* the wind;
Thy trumpet voice, though broken now and dying,
The loudest still the tempest leaves behind;
Thy tree hath lost its blossoms, and the rind,
Chopp'd by the axe, looks rough and little worth,
But the sap lasts,—and still the seed we find
Sown deep, even in the bosom of the North;
So shall a better spring less bitter fruit bring forth.

XCIX

There is a stern round tower of other days,[1]
Firm as a fortress, with its fence of stone,
Such as an army's baffled strength delays,
Standing with half its battlements alone,
And with two thousand years of ivy grown,
The garland of eternity, where wave
The green leaves over all by time o'erthrown;—
What was this tower of strength? within its cave
What treasure lay so lock'd, so hid?—A woman's grave.

C.

But who was she, the lady of the dead,
Tomb'd in a palace? Was she chaste and fair?
Worthy a king's—or more—a Roman's bed?
What race of chiefs and heroes did she bear?
What daughter of her beauties was the heir?

[1] Alluding to the tomb of Cecilia Metella, called Capo di Bove. See "Historical Illustrations," p. 200.

How lived—how loved--how died she? Was she [not
So honour'd—and conspicuously there,
Where meaner relics must not dare to rot,
Placed to commemorate a more than mortal lot?

CI.

Was she as those who love their lords, or they
Who love the lords of others? such have been
Even in the olden time, Rome's annals say.
Was she the matron of Cornelia's mien,
Or the light air of Egypt's graceful queen,
Profuse of joy—or 'gainst it did she war,
Inveterate in virtue? Did she lean
To the soft side of the heart, or wisely bar
Love from amongst her griefs?—for such the affections are.

CII.

Perchance she died in youth: it may be, bow'd
With woes far heavier than the ponderous tomb
That weigh'd upon her gentle dust, a cloud
Might gather o'er her beauty, and a gloom
In her dark eye, prophetic of the doom
Heaven gives its favourites—early death; yet shed[1]
A sunset charm around her, and illume
With hectic light, the Hesperus of the dead,
Of her consuming cheek the autumnal leaf-like red.

CIII.

Perchance she died in age—surviving all,
Charms, kindred, children—with the silver gray
On her long tresses, which might yet recall,
It may be, still a something of the day
When they were braided, and her proud array

[1] Ὃν οἱ θεοὶ φιλοῦσιν, ἀποθνήσκει νέος·
Τὸ γὰρ θανεῖν οὐκ αἰσχρὸν, ἀλλ' αἰσχρῶς θανεῖν·
Rich. Franc. Phil. Brunck. Poetæ Gnomici. p. 231. edit. 1784.

And lovely form were envied, praised, and eyed
By Rome—But whither would Conjecture stray?
Thus much alone we know—Metella died,
The wealthiest Roman's wife: Behold his love or pride.

CIV.

I know not why—but standing thus by thee,
It seems as if I had thine inmate known,
Thou tomb! and other days come back on me
With recollected music, though the tone
Is changed and solemn, like the cloudy groan
Of dying thunder on the distant wind;
Yet could I seat me by this ivied stone
Till I had bodied forth the heated mind, [behind;[1]
Forms from the floating wreck which Ruin leaves

CV.

And from the planks, far shatter'd o'er the rocks,
Built me a little bark of hope, once more
To battle with the ocean and the shocks
Of the loud breakers, and the ceaseless roar
Which rushes on the solitary shore
Where all lies founder'd that was ever dear:
But could I gather from the wave-worn store
Enough for my rude boat, where should I steer?
There woos no home, nor hope, nor life, save what is here.

[1] [Four words, and two initials, compose the whole of the inscription, which, whatever was its ancient position, is now placed in front of this towering sepulchre: CÆCILIÆ . Q . CRETICI . F . METELLÆ . CRASSI. It is more likely to have been the pride than the love of Crassus, which raised so superb a memorial to a wife whose name is not mentioned in history, unless she be supposed to be that lady whose intimacy with Dolabella was so offensive to Tullia, the daughter of Cicero; or she who was divorced by Lentulus Spinther; or she, perhaps the same person, from whose ear the son of Æsopus transferred a precious jewel to enrich his daughter.—HOBHOUSE.]

CVI.

Then let the winds howl on! their harmony
Shall henceforth be my music, and the night
The sound shall temper with the owlet's cry,
As I now hear them, in the fading light
Dim o'er the bird of darkness' native site,
Answering each other on the Palatine,
With their large eyes, all glistening gray and bright.
And sailing pinions.—Upon such a shrine
What are our petty griefs?—let me not number mine.

CVII.

Cypress and ivy, weed and wallflower grown
Matted and mass'd together, hillocks heap'd
On what were chambers, arch crush'd column strown
In fragments, choked up vaults, and frescos steep'd
In subterranean damps, where the owl peep'd,
Deeming it midnight:—Temples, baths, or halls?
Pronounce who can; for all that Learning reap'd
From her research hath been, that these are walls—
Behold the Imperial Mount! 'tis thus the mighty falls.[1]

CVIII.

There is the moral of all human tales;[2]
'Tis but the same rehearsal of the past,
First Freedom, and then Glory—when that fails,
Wealth, vice, corruption,—barbarism at last.

[1] The Palatine is one mass of ruins, particularly on the side towards the Circus Maximus. The very soil is formed of crumbled brickwork. Nothing has been told, nothing can be told, to satisfy the belief of any but a Roman antiquary. See "Historical Illustrations," p. 206.—["The voice of Marius could not sound more deep and solemn among the ruined arches of Carthage, than the strains of the Pilgrim amid the broken shrines and fallen statues of her subduer."—Sir Walter Scott.]

[2] The author of the life of Cicero, speaking of the opinion entertained of Britain by that orator and his contemporary Romans,

And History, with all her volumes vast,
Hath but *one* page,—'tis better written here,
Where gorgeous Tyranny hath thus amass'd
All treasures, all delights, that eye or ear,
Heart, soul could seek, tongue ask—Away with words! draw near,

CIX.

Admire, exult—despise—laugh, weep,—for here
There is such matter for all feeling:—Man!
Thou pendulum betwixt a smile and tear,
Ages and realms are crowded in this span,
This mountain, whose obliterated plan
The pyramid of empires pinnacled,
Of Glory's gewgaws shining in the van
Till the sun's rays with added flame were fill'd!
Where are its golden roofs? where those who dared to build?

has the following eloquent passage:—"From their railleries of this kind, on the barbarity and misery of our island, one cannot help reflecting on the surprising fate and revolutions of kingdoms; how Rome, once the mistress of the world, the seat of arts, empire, and glory, now lies sunk in sloth, ignorance, and poverty, enslaved to the most cruel as well as to the most contemptible of tyrants, superstition and religious imposture: while this remote country, anciently the jest and contempt of the polite Romans, is become the happy seat of liberty, plenty, and letters; flourishing in all the arts and refinements of civil life; yet, running, perhaps, the same course which Rome itself had run before it, from virtuous industry to wealth; from wealth to luxury; from luxury to an impatience of discipline, and corruption of morals: till, by a total degeneracy and loss of virtue, being grown ripe for destruction, it fall a prey at last to some hardy oppressor, and, with the loss of liberty, losing every thing that is valuable, sinks gradually again into its original barbarism." (See History of the Life of M Tullius Cicero, sect. vi. vol. ii. p. 102.)

CX.

Tully was not so eloquent as thou,
Thou nameless column with the buried base!
What are the laurels of the Cæsar's brow?
Crown me with ivy from his dwelling-place.
Whose arch or pillar meets me in the face,
Titus or Trajan's? No—'tis that of Time:
Triumph, arch, pillar, all he doth displace
Scoffing; and apostolic statues climb
To crush the imperial urn, whose ashes slept sublime,[1]

CXI.

Buried in air, the deep blue sky of Rome,
And looking to the stars: they had contain'd
A spirit which with these would find a home,
The last of those who o'er the whole earth reign'd,
The Roman globe, for after none sustain'd,
But yielded back his conquest:—he was more
Than a mere Alexander, and, unstain'd
With household blood and wine, serenely wore
His sovereign virtues—still we Trajan's name adore.[2]

[1] The column of Trajan is surmounted by St. Peter; that of Aurelius by St. Paul. See "Historical Illustrations," p. 214.

[2] Trajan was *proverbially* the best of the Roman princes; and it would be easier to find a sovereign uniting exactly the opposite characteristics, than one possessed of all the happy qualities ascribed to this emperor. "When he mounted the throne," says the historian Dion, "he was strong in body, he was vigorous in mind; age had impaired none of his faculties; he was altogether free from envy and from detraction; he honoured all the good, and he advanced them; and on this account they could not be the objects of his fear, or of his hate; he never listened to informers; he gave not way to his anger; he abstained equally from unfair exactions and unjust punishments; he had rather be loved as a man than honoured as a sovereign; he was affable with his people, respectful to the senate, and universally beloved by both; he inspired none with dread but the enemies of his country." See Eutrop. Brev. Hist. Rom. lib. viii. c. 5. Dion. Hist. Rom. lib. lxiii. c. 6, 7.

CXII.

Where is the rock of Triumph, the high place
Where Rome embraced her heroes? where the steep
Tarpeian? fittest goal for Treason's race,
The promontory whence the Traitor's Leap
Cured al ambition. Did the conquerors heap
Their spoils here? Yes; and in yon field below,
A thousand years of silenced factions sleep—
The Forum, where the immortal accents glow,
And still the eloquent air breathes—burns with Cicero!

CXIII.

The field of freedom, faction, fame, and blood:
Here a proud people's passions were exhaled,
From the first hour of empire in the bud
To that when further worlds to conquer failed;
But long before had Freedom's face been veil'd,
And Anarchy assumed her attributes;
Till every lawless soldier who assail'd
Trod on the trembling senate's slavish mutes,
Or raised the venal voice of baser prostitutes.

CXIV.

Then turn we to her latest tribune's name,
From her ten thousand tyrants turn to thee,
Redeemer of dark centuries of shame—
The friend of Petrarch—hope of Italy—
Rienzi! last of Romans?[1] While the tree
Of freedom's wither'd trunk puts forth a leaf,
Even for thy tomb a garland let it be—
The forum's champion, and the people's chief—
Her new-born Numa thou—with reign, alas! too brief.

[1] The name and exploits of Rienzi must be familiar to the reader of Gibbon. Some details and inedited manuscripts, relative to this unhappy hero, will be seen in the "Historical Illustrations of the Fourth Canto," p. 248

CXV.

Egeria! sweet creation of some heart[1]
Which found no mortal resting-place so fair
As thine ideal breast; whate'er thou art
Or wert,—a young Aurora of the air,
The nympholepsy of some fond despair;
Or, it might be, a beauty of the earth,
Who found a more than common votary there
Too much adoring; whatsoe'er thy birth,
Thou wert a beautiful thought, and softly bodied forth.

CXVI.

The mosses of thy fountain still are sprinkled
With thine Elysian water-drops; the face
Of thy cave-guarded spring, with years unwrinkled,
Reflects the meek-eyed genius of the place,
Whose green, wild margin now no more erase
Art's works; nor must the delicate waters sleep,
Prison'd in marble, bubbling from the base
Of the cleft statue, with a gentle leap
The rill runs o'er, and round, fern, flowers, and ivy, creep,

CXVII.

Fantastically tangled: the green hills
Are clothed with early blossoms, through the grass
The quick-eyed lizard rustles, and the bills
Of summer-birds sing welcome as ye pass;
Flowers fresh in hue, and many in their class,
Implore the pausing step, and with their dyes
Dance in the soft breeze in a fairy mass;
The sweetness of the violet's deep blue eyes,
Kiss'd by the breath of heaven, seems colour'd by its skies.

[1] See Appendix, "Historical Notes," No. XXVII.

CXVIII.

Here didst thou dwell, in this enchanted cover,
Egeria! thy all heavenly bosom beating
For the far footsteps of thy mortal lover;
The purple Midnight veil'd that mystic meeting
With her most starry canopy, and seating
Thyself by thine adorer, what befell?
This cave was surely shaped out for the greeting
Of an enamour'd goddess, and the cell
Haunted by holy Love—the earliest oracle!

CXIX.

And didst thou not, thy breast to his replying,
Blend a celestial with a human heart;
And Love, which dies as it was born, in sighing,
Share with immortal transports? could thine art
Make them indeed immortal, and impart
The purity of heaven to earthly joys,
Expel the venom and not blunt the dart—
The dull satiety which all destroys—
And root from out the soul the deadly weed which cloys?

CXX.

Alas! our young affections run to waste,
Or water but the desert; whence arise
But weeds of dark luxuriance, tares of haste,
Rank at the core, though tempting to the eyes,
Flowers whose wild odours breathe but agonies,
And trees whose gums are poison: such the plants
Which spring beneath her steps as Passion flies
O'er the world's wilderness, and vainly pants
For some celestial fruit forbidden to our wants

CXXI.

Oh Love! no habitant of earth art thou—
An unseen seraph, we believe in thee,
A faith whose martyrs are the broken heart,
But never yet hath seen, nor e'er shall see
The naked eye, thy form, as it should be;
The mind hath made thee, as it peopled heaven,
Even with its own desiring fantasy,
And to a thought such shape and image given,
As haunts the unquench'd soul—parch'd—wearied—
wrung—and riven.

CXXII.

Of its own beauty is the mind diseased,
And fevers into false creation:—where,
Where are the forms the sculptor's soul hath seized?
In him alone. Can Nature show so fair?
Where are the charms and virtues which we dare
Conceive in boyhood and pursue as men,
The unreach'd Paradise of our despair,
Which o'er-informs the pencil and the pen,
And overpowers the page where it would bloom
again?

CXXIII.

Who loves, raves—'tis youth's frenzy—but the
cure
Is bitterer still; as charm by charm unwinds
Which robed our idols, and we see too sure
Nor worth nor beauty dwells from out the mind's
Ideal shape of such; yet still it binds
The fatal spell, and still it draws us on,
Reaping the whirlwind from the oft-sown winds;
The stubborn heart, its alchymy begun,
Seems ever near the prize—wealthiest when most
undone.

CXXIV.

We wither from our youth, we gasp away—
Sick—sick; unfound the boon—unslaked the thirst,
Though to the last, in verge of our decay,
Some phantom lures, such as we sought at first—
But all too late,—so are we doubly curst.
Love, fame, ambition, avarice—'tis the same,
Each idle—and all ill—and none the worst—
For all are meteors with a different name,
And Death the sable smoke where vanishes the flame.

CXXV.

Few—none—find what they love or could have loved,
Though accident, blind contact, and the strong
Necessity of loving, have removed
Antipathies—but to recur, ere long,
Envenom'd with irrevocable wrong;
And Circumstance, that unspiritual god
And miscreator, makes and helps along
Our coming evils with a crutch-like rod,
Whose touch turns Hope to dust,—the dust we all have trod.

CXXVI.

Our life is a false nature—'tis not in
The harmony of things,—this hard decree,
This uneradicable taint of sin,
This boundless upas, this all-blasting tree,
Whose root is earth, whose leaves and branches be
The skies which rain their plagues on men like dew—
Disease, death, bondage—all the woes we see—
And worse, the woes we see not—which throb through
The immedicable soul, with heartaches ever new

CXXVII.

Yet let us ponder boldly—'tis a base[1]
Abandonment of reason to resign
Our right of thought—our last and only place
Of refuge; this, at least, shall still be mine:
Though from our birth the faculty divine
Is chain'd and tortured—cabin'd, cribb'd, confined
And bred in darkness, lest the truth should shine
Too brightly on the unprepared mind,
The beam pours in, for time and skill will couch
the blind.

CXXVIII.

Arches on arches! as it were that Rome,
Collecting the chief trophies of her line,
Would build up all her triumphs in one dome,
Her Coliseum stands; the moonbeams shine
As 'twere its natural torches, for divine
Should be the light which streams here, to illume
This long-explored but still exhaustless mine
Of contemplation; and the azure gloom
Of an Italian night, where the deep skies assume

[1] "At all events," says the author of the Academical Questions, "I trust, whatever may be the fate of my own speculations, that philosophy will regain that estimation which it ought to possess. The free and philosophic spirit of our nation has been the theme of admiration to the world. This was the proud distinction of Englishmen, and the luminous source of all their glory. Shall we then forget the manly and dignified sentiments of our ancestors, to prate in the language of the mother or the nurse about our good old prejudices? This is not the way to defend the cause of truth. It was not thus that our fathers maintained it in the brilliant periods of our history. Prejudice may be trusted to guard the outworks for a short space of time, while reason slumbers in the citadel; but if the latter sink into a lethargy, the former will quickly erect a standard for herself. Philosophy, wisdom, and liberty support each other; he who will not reason is a bigot; he who cannot, is a fool; and he who dares not, is a slave."—Vol. pref. p. 14, 15.

CXXIX.

Hues which have words, and speak to ye of heaven,
Floats o'er this vast and wondrous monument,
And shadows forth its glory. There is given
Unto the things of earth, which Time hath bent,
A spirit's feeling, and where he hath leant
His hand, but broke his scythe, there is a power
And magic in the ruin'd battlement,
For which the palace of the present hour
Must yield its pomp, and wait till ages are its dower.

CXXX.

Oh Time! the beautifier of the dead,
Adorner of the ruin, comforter
And only healer when the heart hath bled—
Time! the corrector where our judgments err,
The test of truth, love,—sole philosopher,
For all besides are sophists, from thy thrift,
Which never loses though it doth defer—
Time, the avenger! unto thee I lift
My hands, and eyes, and heart, and crave of thee a gift:

CXXXI.

Amidst this wreck, where thou hast made a shrine
And temple more divinely desolate,
Among thy mightier offerings here are mine,
Ruins of years—though few, yet full of fate:—
If thou hast ever seen me too elate,
Hear me not; but if calmly I have borne
Good, and reserved my pride, against the hate
Which shall not whelm me, let me not have worn
This iron in my soul in vain—shall *they* not mourn?

CXXXII.

And thou, who never yet of human wrong
Left the unbalanced scale, great Nemesis![1]
Here, where the ancient paid thee homage long—
Thou, who didst call the Furies from the abyss,
And round Orestes bade them howl and hiss
For that unnatural retribution—just,
Had it not been from hands less near—in this
Thy former realm, I call thee from the dust!
Dost thou not hear my heart?—Awake! thou shalt,
and must.

CXXXIII.

It is not that I may not have incurr'd
For my ancestral faults or mine the wound
I bleed withal, and, had it been conferr'd
With a just weapon, it had flown unbound;
But now my blood shall not sink in the ground;
To thee I do devote it—*thou* shalt take
The vengeance, which shall yet be sought and
found,
Which if *I* have not taken for the sake——
But let that pass—I sleep, but thou shalt yet awake.

CXXXIV.

And if my voice break forth, 'tis not that now
I shrink from what is suffer'd: let him speak
Who hath beheld decline upon my brow,
Or seen my mind's convulsion leave it weak;
But in this page a record will I seek.
Not in the air shall these my words disperse,
Though I be ashes; a far hour shall wreak
The deep prophetic fulness of this verse,
And pile on human heads the mountain of my
curse!

[1] See Appendix, "Historical Notes," No. XXVIII.

CXXXV.

That curse shall be forgiveness.—Have I not—
Hear me, my mother earth! behold it, Hea
ven—
Have I not had to wrestle with my lot?
Have I not suffer'd things to be forgiven?
Have I not had my brain sear'd, my heart riven,
Hopes sapp'd, name blighted, Life's life lied
away?
And only not to desperation driven,
Because not altogether of such clay
As rots into the souls of those whom I survey.

CXXXVI.

From mighty wrongs to petty perfidy
Have I not seen what human things could do?
From the loud roar of foaming calumny
To the small whisper of the as paltry few,
And subtler venom of the reptile crew,
The Janus glance of whose significant eye,
Learning to lie with silence, would *seem* true,
And without utterance, save the shrug or sigh,
Deal round to happy fools its speechless obloquy.[1]

[1] [Between stanzas CXXXV. and CXXXVI. we find in the original MS. the following:—
"If to forgive be heaping coals of fire—
As God hath spoken—on the heads of foes,
Mine should be a volcano, and rise higher
Than, o'er the Titans crush'd, Olympus rose,
Or Athos soars, or blazing Etna glows:—
True, they who stung were creeping things; but what
Than serpents' teeth inflicts with deadlier throes?
The lion may be goaded by the gnat.—
Who sucks the slumberer's blood?—The eagle?—No: the
bat."]

CXXXVII.

But I have lived, and have not lived in vain:
My mind may lose its force, my blood its fire,
And my frame perish even in conquering pain;
But there is that within me which shall tire
Torture and Time, and breathe when I expire;
Something unearthly, which they deem not of,
Like the remember'd tone of a mute lyre,
Shall on their soften'd spirits sink, and move
In hearts all rocky now the late remorse of love.

CXXXVIII.

The seal is set.—Now welcome, thou dread power!
Nameless, yet thus omnipotent, which here
Walk'st in the shadow of the midnight hour
With a deep awe, yet all distinct from fear;
Thy haunts are ever where the dead walls rear
Their ivy mantles, and the solemn scene
Derives from thee a sense so deep and clear,
That we become a part of what has been,
And grow unto the spot, all-seeing but unseen.

CXXXIX.

And here the buzz of eager nations ran,
In murmur'd pity, or loud-roar'd applause,
As man was slaughter'd by his fellow man.
And wherefore slaughter'd? wherefore, but because
Such were the bloody Circus' genial laws,
And the imperial pleasure.—Wherefore not?
What matters where we fall to fill the maws
Of worms—on battle-plains or listed spot?
Both are but theatres where the chief actors rot.

CXL.

I see before me the Gladiator lie:
He leans upon his hand—his manly brow
Consents to death, but conquers agony,
And his droop'd head sinks gradually low—
And through his side the last drops, ebbing slow
From the red gash, fall heavy, one by one,
Like the first of a thunder-shower; and now
The arena swims around him—he is gone,
Ere ceased the inhuman shout which hail'd the wretch
who won.

CXLI.

He heard it, but he heeded not—his eyes
Were with his heart, and that was far away;[1]
He reck'd not of the life he lost nor prize,
But where his rude hut by the Danube lay,
There were his young barbarians all at play,

[1] Whether the wonderful statue which suggested this image be a laquearian gladiator, which, in spite of Winkelmann's criticism, has been stoutly maintained; or whether it be a Greek herald, as that great antiquary positively asserted;* or whether it is to be thought a Spartan or barbarian shield-bearer, according to the opinion of his Italian editor; it must assuredly seem *a copy* of that masterpiece of Ctesilaus which represented "a wounded man dying, who perfectly expressed what there remained of life in him." Montfauçon and Maffei thought it the identical statue; but that statue was of bronze. The Gladiator was once in the Villa Ludovizi, and was bought by Clement XII. The right arm is an entire restoration of Michael Angelo.

---

* Either Polifontes, herald of Laius, killed by Œdipus; or Cepreas, herald of Euritheus, killed by the Athenians when he endeavoured to drag the Heraclidæ from the altar of mercy, and in whose honour they instituted annual games, continued to the time of Hadrian; or Anthemocritus, the Athenian herald, killed by the Megarenses, who never recovered the impiety. See Storia delle Arti. &c. tom. ii. pag. 203—207, lib. ix. cap. ii.

There was their Dacian mother—he, their sire,
Butcher'd to make a Roman holiday—[1]
All this rush'd with his blood—Shall he expire
And unavenged?—Arise! ye Goths, and glut your
ire!

CXLII.

But here, where Murder breathed her bloody steam;
And here, where buzzing nations choked the ways,
And roar'd or murmur'd like a mountain stream
Dashing or winding as its torrent strays;
Here, where the Roman million's blame or praise
Was death or life, the playthings of a crowd,[2]
My voice sounds much—and fall the stars' faint rays
On the arena void—seats crush'd—walls bow'd—
And galleries, where my steps seem echoes strangely
loud.

CXLIII.

A ruin—yet what ruin! from its mass
Walls, palaces, half-cities, have been rear'd;
Yet oft the enormous skeleton ye pass,
And marvel where the spoil could have appear'd.
Hath it indeed been plunder'd, or but clear'd?
Alas! developed, opens the decay,
When the colossal fabric's form is near'd:
It will not bear the brightness of the day, [away.
Which streams too much on all years, man, have reft

CXLIV.

But when the rising moon begins to climb
Its topmost arch, and gently pauses there;
When the stars twinkle through the loops of time,
And the low night-breeze waves along the air
The garland-forest, which the gray walls wear,

[1], [2] See Appendix, "Historical Notes," Nos. XXIX. XXX

Like laurels on the bald first Cæsar's head;[1]
When the light shines serene, but doth not glare,
Then in this magic circle raise the dead:
Heroes have trod this spot—'tis on their dust ye tread.

CXLV.

"While stands the Coliseum, Rome shall stand;[2]
When falls the Coliseum, Rome shall fall; [land
And when Rome falls—the world." From our own
Thus spake the pilgrims o'er this mighty wall
In Saxon times, which we are wont to call
Ancient; and these three mortal things are still
On their foundations, and unalter'd all;
Rome and her ruin past Redemption's skill, [will.
The world, the same wide den—of thieves, or what ye

CXLVI.

Simple, erect, severe, austere, sublime—
Shrine of all saints and temple of all gods,
From Jove to Jesus—spared and blest by time;[3]
Looking tranquillity, while falls or nods
Arch, empire, each thing round thee, and man plods

[1] Suetonius informs us that Julius Cæsar was particularly gratified by that decree of the senate which enabled him to wear a wreath of laurel on all occasions. He was anxious, not to show that he was the conqueror of the world, but to hide that he was bald. A stranger at Rome would hardly have guessed at the motive, nor should we without the help of the historian.

[2] This is quoted in the "Decline and Fall of the Roman Empire," as a proof that the Coliseum was entire, when seen by the Anglo-Saxon pilgrims at the end of the seventh, or the beginning of the eighth century. A notice on the Coliseum may be seen in the "Historical Illustrations," p. 263.

[3] "Though plundered of all its brass, except the ring which was necessary to preserve the aperture above; though exposed to repeated fires; though sometimes flooded by the river, and always open to the rain, no monument of equal antiquity is so well preserved as this rotunda. It passed with little alteration from the pagan into the present worship; and so convenient were its niches for the Christian altar, that Michael Angelo, ever studious

His way through thorns to ashes—glorious dome!
Shalt thou not last? Time's scythe and tyrants' rods
Shiver upon thee—sanctuary and home
Of art and piety—Pantheon!—pride of Rome!

CXLVII.

Relic of nobler days, and noblest arts!
Despoil'd yet perfect, with thy circle spreads
A holiness appealing to all hearts—
To art a model; and to him who treads
Rome for the sake of ages, Glory sheds
Her light through thy sole aperture; to those
Who worship, here are altars for their beads;
And they who feel for genius may repose [close.[1]
Their eyes on honour'd forms, whose busts around them

CXLVIII.

There is a dungeon, in whose dim drear light[2]
What do I gaze on? Nothing: Look again!
Two forms are slowly shadow'd on my sight—
Two insulated phantoms of the brain:
It is not so; I see them full and plain—
An old man, and a female young and fair,
Fresh as a nursing mother, in whose vein
The blood is nectar:—but what doth she there,
With her unmantled neck, and bosom white and bare?

of ancient beauty, introduced their design as a model in the Catholic church."—FORSYTH'S *Italy*, p. 137, 2d edit.

[1] The Pantheon has been made a receptacle for the busts of modern great or, at least, distinguished men. The flood of light which once fell through the large orb above on the whole circle of divinities, now shines on a numerous assemblage of mortals, some one or two of whom have been almost deified by the veneration of their countrymen. For a notice of the Pantheon, see "Historical Illustrations," p. 287.

[2] This and the three next stanzas allude to the story of the Roman daughter, which is recalled to the traveller by the site, or pretended site, of that adventure, now shown at the church of St. Nicholas *in Carcere*. The difficulties attending the full belief of the tale are stated in "Historical Illustrations," p. 295.

CXLIX.

Full swells the deep pure fountain of young life,
Where *on* the heart and *from* the heart we took
Our first and sweetest nurture, when the wife,
Blest into mother, in the innocent look,
Or even the piping cry of lips that brook
No pain and small suspense, a joy perceives
Man knows not, when from out its cradled nook
She sees her little bud put forth its leaves—
What may the fruit be yet?—I know not—Cain was Eve's.

CL.

But here youth offers to old age the food,
The milk of his own gift:—it is her sire
To whom she renders back the debt of blood
Born with her birth. No; he shall not expire
While in those warm and lovely veins the fire
Of health and holy feeling can provide
Great Nature's Nile, whose deep stream rises higher
Than Egypt's river:—from that gentle side
Drink, drink and live, old man! Heaven's realm holds no such tide.

CLI.

The starry fable of the milky way
Has not thy story's purity; it is
A constellation of a sweeter ray,
And sacred Nature triumphs more in this
Reverse of her decree, than in the abyss
Where sparkle distant worlds:—Oh, holiest nurse!
No drop of that clear stream its way shall miss
To thy sire's heart, replenishing its source
With life as our freed souls rejoin the universe.

CLII.

Turn to the mole which Hadrian rear'd on high,[1]
Imperial mimic of old Egypt's piles,
Colossal copyist of deformity,
Whose travell'd fantasy from the far Nile's
Enormous model, doom'd the artist's toils
To build for giants, and for his vain earth,
His shrunken ashes, raise this dome: How smiles
The gazer's eye with philosophic mirth,
To view the huge design which sprung from such a birth!

CLIII.

But lo! the dome—the vast and wondrous dome,[2]
To which Diana's marvel was a cell—
Christ's mighty shrine above his martyr's tomb!
I have beheld the Ephesian's miracle—
Its columns strew the wilderness, and dwell
The hyæna and the jackal in their shade;
I have beheld Sophia's bright roofs swell
Their glittering mass i' the sun, and have survey'd
Its sanctuary the while the usurping Moslem pray'd;

CLIV.

But thou, of temples old, or altars new,
Standest alone—with nothing like to thee—
Worthiest of God, the holy and the true.
Since Zion's desolation, when that He
Forsook his former city, what could be,

[1] The castle of St. Angelo. See "Historical Illustrations."

[2] This and the six next stanzas have a reference to the church of St. Peter's. For a measurement of the comparative length of this basilica and the other great churches of Europe, see the pavement of St. Peter's, and the Classical Tour through Italy, vol. ii. p. 125, et seq. ch. iv.

Of earthly structures, in his honour piled,
Of a sublimer aspect? Majesty,
Power, Glory, Strength, and Beauty, all are aisled
In this eternal ark of worship undefiled.

CLV.

Enter: its grandeur overwhelms thee not;
And why? it is not lessen'd; but thy mind,
Expanded by the genius of the spot,
Has grown colossal, and can only find
A fit abode wherein appear enshrined
Thy hopes of immortality; and thou
Shalt one day, if found worthy, so defined,
See thy God face to face, as thou dost now
His Holy of Holies, nor be blasted by his brow.

[1] ["I remember very well," says Sir Joshua Reynolds, "my own disappointment when I first visited the Vatican; but on confessing my feelings to a brother student, of whose ingenuousness I had a high opinion, he acknowledged that the works of Raphael had the same effect on him, or rather that they did not produce the effect which he expected. This was a great relief to my mind; and, on inquiring further of other students, I found that those persons only who, from natural imbecility, appeared to be incapable of relishing those divine performances, made pretensions to instantaneous raptures on first beholding them.—My not relishing them as I was conscious I ought to have done, was one of the most humiliating circumstances that ever happened to me; I found myself in the midst of works executed upon principles with which I was unacquainted: I felt my ignorance, and stood abashed. All the undigested notions of painting which I had brought with me from England, where the art was in the lowest state it had ever been in, were to be totally done away and eradicated from my mind. It was necessary, as it is expressed on a very solemn occasion, that I should become *as a little child.* Notwithstanding my disappointment, I proceeded to copy some of those excellent works. I viewed them again and again; I even affected to feel their merit and admire them more than I really did. In a short time, a new taste and a new perception began to dawn upon me, and I was convinced that I had originally formed a false opinion of the perfection of the art, and that this great painter was well entitled to the high rank which he holds in the admiration of the world."]

CLVI.

Thou movest—but increasing with the advance,
Like climbing some great Alp, which still doth
rise,
Deceived by its gigantic elegance;
Vastness which grows—but grows to harmonize—
All musical in its immensities;
Rich marbles—richer painting—shrines where
flame
The lamps of gold—and haughty dome which vies
In air with earth's chief structures, though their
frame
Sits on the firm-set ground—and this the clouds must
claim.

CLVII.

Thou seest not all; but piecemeal thou must break,
To separate contemplation, the great whole;
And as the ocean many bays will make,
That ask the eye—so here condense thy soul
To more immediate objects, and control
Thy thoughts until thy mind hath got by heart
Its eloquent proportions, and unroll
In mighty graduations, part by part,
The glory which at once upon thee did not dart,

CLVIII.

Not by its fault—but thine: Our outward sense
Is but of gradual grasp—and as it is
That what we have of feeling most intense
Outstrips our faint expression; even so this
Outshining and o'erwhelming edifice
Fools our fond gaze, and, greatest of the great,
Defies at first our nature's littleness,
Till, growing with its growth, we thus dilate
Our spirits to the size of that they contemplate

CLIX.

Then pause, and be enlighten'd; there is more
In such a survey than the sating gaze
Of wonder pleased, or awe which would adore
The worship of the place, or the mere praise
Of art and its great masters, who could raise
What former time, nor skill, nor thought could plan;
The fountain of sublimity displays
Its depth, and thence may draw the mind of man
Its golden sands, and learn what great conceptions can.

CLX.

Or, turning to the Vatican, go see
Laocoon's torture dignifying pain—
A father's love and mortal's agony
With an immortal's patience blending:—Vain
The struggle; vain, against the coiling strain
And gripe, and deepening of the dragon's grasp,
The old man's clench; the long envenom'd chain
Rivets the living links,—the enormous asp
Enforces pang on pang, and stifles gasp on gasp.

CLXI.

Or view the lord of the unerring bow,
The god of life, and poesy, and light—
The sun in human limbs array'd, and brow
All radiant from his triumph in the fight;
The shaft hath just been shot—the arrow bright
With an immortal's vengeance; in his eye
And nostril beautiful disdain, and might
And majesty, flash their full lightnings by,
Developing in that one glance the deity.

CLXII.

But in his delicate form—a dream of Love,
Shaped by some solitary nymph, whose breast
Long'd for a deathless lover from above,
And madden'd in that vision—are exprest
All that ideal beauty ever blest
The mind with in its most unearthly mood,
When each conception was a heavenly guest
A ray of immortality—and stood,
Starlike, around, until they gather'd to a god!

CLXIII.

And if it be Prometheus stole from Heaven
The fire which we endure, it was repaid
By him to whom the energy was given
Which this poetic marble hath array'd
With an eternal glory—which, if made
By human hands, is not of human thought;
And Time himself hath hallow'd it, nor laid
One ringlet in the dust—nor hath it caught
A tinge of years, but breathes the flame with which
'twas wrought.

CLXIV.

But where is he, the Pilgrim of my song,
The being who upheld it through the past?
Methinks he cometh late and tarries long.
He is no more—these breathings are his last;
His wanderings done, his visions ebbing fast,
And he himself as nothing:—if he was
Aught but a fantasy, and could be class'd
With forms which live and suffer—let that
pass—
His shadow fades away into Destruction's mass,

CLXV.

Which gathers shadow, substance, life, and all
That we inherit in its mortal shroud,
And spreads the dim and universal pall
Through which all things grow phantoms; and the
cloud
Between us sinks and all which ever glow'd,
Till Glory's self is twilight, and displays
A melancholy halo scarce allow'd
To hover on the verge of darkness; rays
Sadder than saddest night, for they distract the
gaze,

CLXVI.

And send us prying into the abyss,
To gather what we shall be when the frame
Shall be resolved to something less than this
Its wretched essence; and to dream of fame,
And wipe the dust from off the idle name
We never more shall hear,—but never more,
Oh, happier thought! can we be made the same:
It is enough in sooth that *once* we bore
These fardels of the heart—the heart whose sweat
was gore.

CLXVII.

Hark! forth from the abyss a voice proceeds,
A long low distant murmur of dread sound,
Such as arises when a nation bleeds
With some deep and immedicable wound;
Through storm and darkness yawns the rending
ground,
The gulf is thick with phantoms, but the chief
Seems royal still, though with her head discrown'd
And pale, but lovely, with maternal grief
She clasps a babe, to whom her breast yields no relief

CLXVIII.

Scion of chiefs and monarchs, where art thou.
Fond hope of many nations, art thou dead?
Could not thy grave forget thee, and lay low
Some less majestic, less beloved head?
In the sad midnight, while thy heart still bled,
The mother of a moment, o'er thy boy,
Death hush'd that pang for ever: with thee fled
The present happiness and promised joy
Which fill'd the imperial isles so full it seem'd to cloy.

CLXIX.

Peasants bring forth in safety.—Can it be,
Oh thou that wert so happy, so adored!
Those who weep not for kings shall weep for thee,
And Freedom's heart, grown heavy, cease to hoard
Her many griefs for ONE; for she had pour'd
Her orison for thee, and o'er thy head
Beheld her Iris.—Thou, too, lonely lord,
And desolate consort—vainly wert thou wed!
The husband of a year! the father of the dead!

CLXX.

Of sackcloth was thy wedding garment made;
Thy bridal's fruit is ashes: in the dust
The fair-hair'd Daughter of the Isles is laid,
The love of millions! How we did intrust
Futurity to her! and, though it must
Darken above our bones, yet fondly deem'd
Our children should obey her child, and bless'd
Her and her hoped-for seed, whose promise seem'd
Like stars to shepherds' eyes:—'twas but a meteor beam'd.

CLXXI.

Woe unto us, not her;[1] for she sleeps well:
The fickle reek of popular breath, the tongue
Of hollow counsel, the false oracle,
Which from the birth of monarchy hath rung
Its knell in princely ears, till the o'erstung
Nations have arm'd in madness, the strange fate[2]
Which tumbles mightiest sovereigns, and hath flung
Against their blind omnipotence a weight
Within the opposing scale, which crushes soon or late,—

CLXXII.

These might have been her destiny; but no,
Our hearts deny it: and so young, so fair,
Good without effort, great without a foe:
But now a bride and mother—and now *there!*
How many ties did that stern moment tear!
From thy sire's to his humblest subject's breast
Is link'd the electric chain of that despair,
Whose shock was as an earthquake's, and opprest
The land which loved thee so that none could love thee best.

[1] ["The death of the Princess Charlotte has been a shock even here, (Venice,) and must have been an earthquake at home. The fate of this poor girl is melancholy in every respect; dying at twenty or so, in childbed—of a boy too, a present princess and future queen, and just as she began to be happy, and to enjoy herself, and the hopes which she inspired. I feel sorry in every respect."—*Byron Letters.*]

[2] Mary died on the scaffold; Elizabeth of a broken heart; Charles V. a hermit; Louis XIV. a bankrupt in means and glory; Cromwell of anxiety; and, "the greatest is behind," Napoleon lives a prisoner. To these sovereigns a long but superfluous list might be added of names equally illustrious and unhappy.

CLXXIII.

Lo, Nemi![1] navell'd in the woody hills
So far, that the uprooting wind which tears
The oak from his foundation, and which spills
The ocean o'er its boundary, and bears
Its form against the skies, reluctant spares
The oval mirror of thy glassy lake;
And, calm as cherish'd hate, its surface wears
A deep cold settled aspect naught can shake,
All coil'd into itself and round, as sleeps the snake.

CLXXIV.

And near Albano's scarce divided waves
Shine from a sister valley;—and afar
The Tiber winds, and the broad ocean laves
The Latian coast where sprung the Epic war,
"Arms and the Man," whose reascending star
Rose o'er an empire:—but beneath thy right
Tully reposed from Rome;—and where yon bar
Of girdling mountains intercepts the sight,
The Sabine farm was till'd, the weary bard's de light.[2]

[1] The village of Nemi was near the Arician retreat of Egeria, and, from the shades which embosomed the temple of Diana, has preserved to this day its distinctive appellation of *The Grove.* Nemi is but an evening's ride from the comfortable inn of Albano.

[2] The whole declivity of the Alban hill is of unrivalled beauty, and from the convent on the highest point, which has succeeded to the temple of the Latian Jupiter, the prospect embraces all the objects alluded to in this stanza; the Mediterranean; the whole scene of the latter half of the Æneid, and the coast from beyond the mouth of the Tiber to the headland of Circæum and the Cape of Terracina.—See Appendix, "Historical Notes," No. XXXI

CLXXV.

But I forget.—My Pilgrim's shrine is won,
And he and I must part,—so let it be,—
His task and mine alike are nearly done;
Yet once more let us look upon the sea;
The midland ocean breaks on him and me,
And from the Alban Mount we now behold
Our friend of youth, that ocean, which when we
Beheld it last by Calpe's rock unfold
Those waves, we follow'd on till the dark Euxine roll'd

CLXXVI.

Upon the blue Symplegades: long years—
Long, though not very many, since have done
Their work on both; some suffering and some tears
Have left us nearly where we had begun:
Yet not in vain our mortal race hath run,
We have had our reward—and it is here;
That we can yet feel gladden'd by the sun,
And reap from earth, sea, joy almost as dear
As if there were no man to trouble what is clear.

CLXXVII.

Oh! that the desert were my dwelling-place,
With one fair spirit for my minister,
That I might all forget the human race,
And, hating no one, love but only her!
Ye elements!—in whose ennobling stir
I feel myself exalted—Can ye not
Accord me such a being? Do I err
In deeming such inhabit many a spot?
Though with them to converse can rarely be our lot.

CLXXVIII.

There is a pleasure in the pathless woods,
There is a rapture on the lonely shore,
There is society, where none intrudes.
By the deep sea, and music in its roar:
I love not man the less, but nature more,
From these our interviews, in which I steal
From all I may be, or have been before,
To mingle with the universe, and feel
What I can ne'er express, yet cannot all conceal.

CLXXIX.

Roll on, thou deep and dark-blue ocean—roll!
Ten thousand fleets sweep over thee in vain;
Man marks the earth with ruin—his control
Stops with the shore;—upon the watery plain
The wrecks are all thy deed, nor doth remain
A shadow of man's ravage, save his own,
When, for a moment, like a drop of rain,
He sinks into thy depths with bubbling groan,
Without a grave, unknell'd, uncoffin'd, and unknown.

CLXXX.

His steps are not upon thy paths,—thy fields
Are not a spoil for him,—thou dost arise
And shake him from thee; the vile strength he wields
For earth's destruction thou dost all despise,
Spurning him from thy bosom to the skies,
And send'st him, shivering in thy playful spray
And howling, to his gods, where haply lies
His petty hope in some near port or bay,
And dashest him again to earth:—there let him lay.

CLXXXI.

The armaments which thunderstrike the walls
Of rock-built cities, bidding nations quake,
And monarchs tremble in their capitals,
The oak leviathans, whose huge ribs make
Their clay creator the vain title take
Of lord of thee, and arbiter of war;
These are thy toys, and, as the snowy flake,
They melt into thy yeast of waves, which mar
Alike the Armada's pride, or spoils of Trafalgar.

CLXXXII.

Thy shores are empires, changed in all save thee—
Assyria, Greece, Rome, Carthage, what are they?[1]
Thy waters wasted them while they were free,
And many a tyrant since; their shores obey
The stranger, slave, or savage; their decay
Has dried up realms to deserts:—not so thou,
Unchangeable save to thy wild waves' play—
Time writes no wrinkle on thine azure brow—
Such as creation's dawn beheld, thou rollest now.

[1] [When Lord Byron wrote this stanza, he had, no doubt, the following passage in Boswell's Johnson floating on his mind:—"Dining one day with General Paoli, and talking of his projected journey to Italy,—'A man,' said Johnson, 'who has not been in Italy, is always conscious of an inferiority, from his not having seen what it is expected a man should see. The grand object of all travelling is to see the shores of the Mediterranean. On those shores were the four great empires of the world; the Assyrian, the Persian, the Grecian, and the Roman. All our religion, almost all our law, almost all our arts, almost all that sets us above savages, has come to us from the shores of the Mediterranean.' The general observed, that 'The Mediterranean' would be a noble subject for a poem."—*Life of Johnson*, vol. v. p. 154. ed. 1835.]

CLXXXIII.

Thou glorious mirror, where the Almighty's form
Glasses itself in tempests; in all time,
Calm or convulsed—in breeze, or gale, or storm,
Icing the pole, or in the torrid clime
Dark-heaving; boundless, endless, and sublime—
The image of Eternity—the throne
Of the Invisible; even from out thy slime
The monsters of the deep are made; each zone
Obeys thee; thou goest forth, dread, fathomless, alone.

CLXXXIV.

And I have loved thee, ocean![1] and my joy
Of youthful sports was on thy breast to be
Borne, like thy bubbles, onward: from a boy
I wanton'd with thy breakers—they to me
Were a delight; and if the freshening sea
Made them a terror—'twas a pleasing fear,
For I was as it were a child of thee,
And trusted to thy billows far and near,
And laid my hand upon thy mane—as I do here.

[1] ["This passage would, perhaps, be read without emotion, if we did not know that Lord Byron was here describing his actual feelings and habits, and that this was an unaffected picture of his propensities and amusements even from childhood,—when he listened to the roar, and watched the bursts of the northern ocean on the tempestuous shores of Aberdeenshire. It was a fearful and violent change at the age of ten years to be separated from this congenial solitude,—this independence so suited to his haughty and contemplative spirit,—this rude grandeur of nature,—and thrown among the mere worldly-minded and selfish ferocity, the affected polish and repelling coxcombry, of a great public school. How many thousand times did the moody, sullen, and indignant boy wish himself back to the keen air and boisterous billows that broke lonely upon the simple and soul-invigorating haunts of his childhood! How did he prefer some ghost-story; some tale of second-sight; some relation of Robin Hood's feats; some harrow-

CLXXXV.

My task is done[1]—my song hath ceased—my theme
Has died into an echo; it is fit
The spell should break of this protracted dream.
The torch shall be extinguish'd which hath lit
My midnight lamp—and what is writ, is writ:—

ing narrative of buccaneer-exploits, to all of Horace, and Virgil, and Homer, that was dinned into his repulsive spirit! To the shock of this change is, I suspect, to be traced much of the eccentricity of Lord Byron's future life. This fourth Canto is the fruit of a mind which had stored itself with great care and toil, and had digested with profound reflection and intense vigour what it had learned: the sentiments are not such as lie on the surface, but could only be awakened by long meditation. Whoever reads it, and is not impressed with the many grand virtues as well as gigantic powers of the mind that wrote it, seems to me to afford a proof both of insensibility of heart, and great stupidity of intellect." —SIR E. BRYDGES.]

1 ["It was a thought worthy of the great spirit of Byron, after exhibiting to us his Pilgrim amidst all the most striking scenes of earthly grandeur and earthly decay,—after teaching us, like him, to sicken over the mutability, and vanity, and emptiness of human greatness, to conduct him and us at last to the borders of "the Great Deep." It is there that we may perceive an image of the awful and unchangeable abyss of eternity, into whose bosom so much has sunk, and all shall one day sink,—of that eternity wherein the scorn and contempt of man, and the melancholy of great, and the fretting of little minds, shall be at rest for ever. No one, but a true poet of man and of nature, would have dared to frame such a termination for such a Pilgrimage. The image of the wanderer may well be associated, for a time, with the rock of Calpe, the shattered temples of Athens, or the gigantic fragments of Rome; but when we wish to think of this dark personification as of a thing which is, where can we so well imagine him to have his daily haunt as by the roaring of the waves? It was thus that Homer represented Achilles in his moments of ungovernable and inconsolable grief for the loss of Patroclus. It was thus he chose to depict the paternal despair of Chriseus—

Βῆ δ' ἀκέων παρὰ θῖνα πολυφλοίσβοιο θαλάσσης."

—WILSON.]

Would it were worthier! but I am not now
That which I have been — and my visions flit
Less palpably before me — and the glow
Which in my spirit dwelt is fluttering, faint, and low.

CLXXXVI.

Farewell! a word that must be, and hath been —
A sound which makes us linger; — yet — farewell
Ye! who have traced the Pilgrim to the scene
Which is his last, if in your memories dwell
A thought which once was his, if on ye swell
A single recollection, not in vain
He wore his sandal-shoon, and scallop-shell;
Farewell! with *him* alone may rest the pain,
If such there were — with *you*, the moral of his strain.

APPENDIX.

APPENDIX.

NOTES TO CANTO II.

Note [A].—Removal of the Works of Art from Athens. See p. 75.

"*To rive what Goth, and Turk, and Time hath spared.*"
Stanza xii. line 2.

At this moment, (January 3, 1810,) besides what has been already deposited in London, a Hydriot vessel is in the Pyræus to receive every portable relic. Thus, as I heard a young Greek observe, in common with many of his countrymen—for, lost as they are, they yet feel on this occasion—thus may Lord Elgin boast of having ruined Athens. An Italian painter of the first eminence, named Lusieri, is the agent of devastation; and like the Greek *finder* of Verres in Sicily, who followed the same profession, he has proved the able instrument of plunder. Between this artist and the French Consul Fauvel, who wishes to rescue the remains for his own government, there is now a violent dispute concerning a car employed in their conveyance, the wheel of which—I wish they were both broken upon it!—has been locked up by the consul, and Lusieri has laid his complaint before the waywode. Lord Elgin has been extremely happy in his choice of Signor Lusieri. During a residence of ten years in Athens, he never had the curiosity to proceed as far as Sunium, (now Cape Colonna,) till he accompanied us in our second excursion. However, his works, as far as they go, are most beautiful: but they are almost all unfinished. While he and his patrons confine themselves to tasting medals, appreciating cameos, sketching columns, and cheapening gems, their little absurdities are as harmless as insect or fox-hunting, maiden speechifying, barouche-driving, or any such pastime; but when they carry away three or four shiploads of the most valuable and massy relics that time and barbarism have left to the most injured and most celebrated of cities; when they destroy, in a vain attempt to tear down, those works which have been the admiration of ages, I know no motive which can excuse, no name which can designate, the perpetrators of this dastardly devastation. It was not the least of the crimes laid to the charge of Verres, that he had plundered Sicily, in the manner since imitated at Athens. The most unblushing impudence could hardly go farther than to affix the name of its plunderer to the walls of the Acropolis; while the wanton and useless defacement of the whole range of the basso-relievos, in one compartment of the temple, will never permit that name to be pronounced by an observer without execration.

On this occasion I speak impartially: I am not a collector or admirer of collections, consequently no rival; but I have some early prepossession in favour of Greece, and do not think the honour of England advanced by plunder, whether of India or Attica.

Another noble lord has done better, because he has done less: but some others, more or less noble, yet "all honourable men," have done *best*, because, after a deal of excavation and execration, bribery to the waywode, mining and countermining, they have done nothing at all. We had such ink-shed, and wine-shed, which almost ended in bloodshed! Lord E.'s "prig"—see Jonathan Wild for the definition of "priggism"—quarrelled with another, *Gropius** by name, (a very good name too for his business,) and muttered something about satisfaction, in a verbal answer to a note of the poor Prussian: this was stated at table to Gropius, who laughed, but could eat no dinner afterwards. The rivals were not reconciled when I left Greece. I have reason to remember their squabble, for they wanted to make me their arbitrator.

---

* This Sr. Gropius was employed by a noble lord for the sole purpose of sketching, in which he excels; but I am sorry to say, that he has, through the abused sanction of that most respectable name, been treading at humble distance in the steps of Sr. Lusieri.—A shipful of his trophies was detained, and I believe confiscated, at Constantinople, in 1810. I am most happy to be now enabled to state, that "this was not in his bond;" that he was employed solely as a painter, and that his noble patron disavows all connection with him, except as an artist. If the error in the first and second edition of this poem has given the noble lord a moment's pain, I am very sorry for it: Sr. Gropius has assumed for years the name of his agent; and though I cannot much condemn myself for sharing in the mistake of so many, I am happy in being one of the first to be undeceived. Indeed, I have as much pleasure in contradicting this as I felt regret in stating it.—*Note to third edition.*

Note [B].—ALBANIA AND THE ALBANIANS. See p. 85.

"*Land of Albania! let me bend mine eyes*
On thee, thou rugged nurse of savage men!"
Stanza xxxvii. lines 5 and 6.

Albania comprises part of Macedonia, Illyria, Chaonia, and Epirus. Iskander is the Turkish word for Alexander; and the celebrated Scanderbeg (Lord Alexander) is alluded to in the third and fourth lines of the thirty-eighth stanza. I do not know whether I am correct in making Scanderbeg the countryman of Alexander, who was born at Pella in Macedon, but Mr. Gibbon terms him so, and adds Pyrrhus to the list, in speaking of his exploits.

Of Albania, Gibbon remarks, that a country "within sight of Italy is less known than the interior of America." Circumstances, of little consequence to mention, led Mr. Hobhouse and myself into that country before we visited any other part of the Ottoman dominions; and with the exception of Major Leake, then officially resident at Joannina, no other Englishmen have ever advanced beyond the capital into the interior, as that gentleman very lately assured me. Ali Pasha was at that time (October, 1809) carrying on war against Ibrahim Pasha, whom he had driven to Berat, a strong fortress, which he was then besieging: on our arrival at Joannina we were invited to Tepaleni, his highness's birth-place, and favourite serai, only one day's distance from Berat; at this juncture the vizier had made it his head-quarters. After some stay in the capital, we accordingly followed; but though furnished with every accommodation, and escorted by one of the vizier's secretaries, we were nine days (on account of the rains) in accomplishing a journey which, on our return, barely occupied four. On our route we passed two cities, Argyrocastro and Libochabo, apparently little inferior to Yanina in size; and no pencil or pen can ever do justice to the scenery in the vicinity of Zitza and Delvinachi, the frontier village of Epirus and Albania Proper.

On Albania and its inhabitants I am unwilling to descant, because this will be done so much better by my fellow-traveller, in a work which may probably precede this in publication, that I as little wish to follow as I would to anticipate him. But some few observations are necessary to the text. The Arnaouts, or Albanese, struck me forcibly by their resemblance to the Highlanders of Scotland, in dress, figure, and manner of living. Their very mountains seemed Caledonian, with a kinder climate.

The kilt, though white; the spare, active form; their dialect, Celtic in its sound, and their hardy habits, all carried me back to Morven. No nation are so detested and dreaded by their neighbours as the Albanese; the Greeks hardly regard them as Christians, or the Turks as Moslems; and in fact they are a mixture of both, and sometimes neither. Their habits are predatory—all are armed; and the red-shawled Arnaouts, the Montenegrins, Chimariots, and Gegdes, are treacherous; the others differ somewhat in garb, and essentially in character. As far as my own experience goes, I can speak favourably. I was attended by two, an Infidel and a Mussulman, to Constantinople and every other part of Turkey which came within my observation; and more faithful in peril, or indefatigable in service, are rarely to be found. The Infidel was named Basilius, the Moslem, Dervish Tahiri; the former a man of middle age, and the latter about my own. Basili was strictly charged by Ali Pasha in person to attend us; and Dervish was one of fifty who accompanied us through the forests of Acarnania to the banks of Achelous, and onward to Messalonghi in Ætolia. There I took him into my own service, and never had occasion to repent it till the moment of my departure.

When, in 1810, after the departure of my friend Mr. Hobhouse for England, I was seized with a severe fever in the Morea, these men saved my life by frightening away my physician, whose throat they threatened to cut if I was not cured within a given time. To this consolatory assurance of posthumous retribution, and a resolute refusal of Dr. Romanelli's prescriptions, I attributed my recovery. I had left my last remaining English servant at Athens; my dragoman was as ill as myself, and my poor Arnaouts nursed me with an attention which would have done honour to civilization. They had a variety of adventures, for the Moslem, Dervish, being a remarkably handsome man, was always squabbling with the husbands of Athens; insomuch that four of the principal Turks paid me a visit of remonstrance at the convent, on the subject of his having taken a woman from the bath—whom he had lawfully bought, however—a thing quite contrary to etiquette. Basili also was extremely gallant amongst his own persuasion, and had the greatest veneration for the church, mixed with the highest contempt of churchmen, whom he cuffed upon occasion in a most heterodox manner. Yet he never passed a church without crossing himself; and I remember the risk he ran in entering St. Sophia, in Stambol, because it had once been a place of his worship. On remonstrat ing with him on his inconsistent proceedings, he invariably answered, "Our church is holy, our priests are thieves:" and then he crossed himself as usual, and boxed the ears of the first "papas" who refused to assist in any required operation, as was always found to be necessary where a priest had any influence with the Cogia Bashi of his village. Indeed, a more abandoned race of miscreants cannot exist than the lower orders of the Greek clergy.

When preparations were made for my return, my Albanians were summoned to receive their pay. Basili took his with an awkward show of regret at my intended departure, and marched away to his quarters with his bag of piastres. I sent for Dervish, but for some time he was not to be found; at last he entered, just as Signor Logotheti, father to the ci-devant Anglo-consul of Athens, and some other of my Greek acquaintances, paid me a visit. Dervish took the money, but on a sudden dashed it to the ground; and clasping his hands, which he raised to his forehead, rushed out of the room weeping bitterly. From that moment to the hour of my embarkation, he continued his lamentations, and all our efforts to console him only producd this answer, "Μ' αφέινει," "He leaves me." Signor Logotheti, who never wept before for any thing less than the loss of a para, (about the fourth of a farthing,) melted; the padre of the convent, my attendants, my visiters—and I verily believe that even Sterne's "foolish fat scullion" would have left her "fish-kettle" to sympathize with the unaffected and unexpected sorrow of this barbarian.

For my own part, when I remembered that, a short time before my departure from England, a noble and most intimate associate had excused himself from taking leave of me because he had to attend a relation "to a milliner's," I felt no less surprised than humiliated by the present occurrence and the past recollection. That Dervish would leave me with some regret was to be expected: when master and man have been scrambling over the mountains of a dozen provinces together, they are unwilling to separate; but his present feelings, contrasted with his native ferocity, improved my opinion of the human heart. I believe this almost feudal fidelity is frequent amongst them One day, on our journey over Parnassus, an Englishman in my service gave him a push in some dispute about the baggage, which he unluckily mistook for a blow; he spoke not, but sat down leaning his head upon his hands. Foreseeing the consequences, we endeavoured to explain away the affront, which produced the following answer:—"I *have been* a robber; I *am* a soldier; no captain ever struck me; *you* are my master, I have eaten your bread, but by *that* bread! (an usual oath) had it been otherwise, I would have stabbed the dog your servant, and gone to the mountains." So the affair ended, but from that day forward he never thoroughly forgave the thoughtless fellow who insulted him. Dervish excelled in the dance of his country, conjectured to be a remnant of the ancient Pyrrhic: be that as it may, it is manly, and requires wonderful agility. It is very distinct from the stupid Romaika, the dull round-about of the Greeks, of which our Athenian party had so many specimens.

The Albanians in general (I do not mean the cultivators of the earth in the provinces, who have also that appellation, but the mountaineers) have a fine cast of countenance; and the most beautiful women I ever beheld, in stature and in features, we saw *levelling* the *road* broken down by the torrents between Delvinachi and Libochabo. Their manner of walking is truly theatrical; but this strut is probably the effect of the capote, or cloak, depending from one shoulder. Their long hair reminds you of the Spartans, and their courage in desultory warfare is unquestionable. Though they have some cavalry amongst the Gegdes, I never saw a good Arnaout horseman; my own preferred the English saddles, which, however, they could never keep. But on foot they are not to be subdued by fatigue.

Note [C.]—Specimen of the Albanian or Arnaout Dialect of the Illyric. See p. 100.

"*While thus in concert,*" *&c.*

Stanza lxxii.

As a specimen of the Albanian or Arnaout dialect of the Illyric, I here insert two of their most popular choral songs, which are generally chanted in dancing by men or women indiscriminately. The first words are merely a kind of chorus without meaning, like some in our own and all other languages.

1. Bo, Bo, Bo, Bo, Bo, Bo, Naciarura, popuso.	1. Lo, Lo, I come, I come: be thou silent.
2. Naciarura na civin Ha pen derini ti hin	2. I come, I run; open the door that I may enter.

3. Ha pe uderi escrotini Ti vin ti mar servetini.	3. Open the door by halves, that I may take my turban.
4. Caliriote me surme Ea ha pe pse dua tive.	4. Caliriotes* with the dark eyes, open the gate that I may enter.
5. Buo, Bo, Bo, Bo, Bo, Gi egem spirta esimiro.	5. Lo, Lo, I hear thee, my soul.
6. Caliriote vu le funde Ede vete tunde tunde.	6. An Arnaout girl, in costly garb, walks with graceful pride.
7. Caliriote me surme Ti mi put e poi mi le.	7. Caliriot maid of the dark eyes, give me a kiss.
8. Se ti puta citi mora Si mi ri ni veti udo gia.	8. If I have kissed thee, what hast thou gained? My soul is consumed with fire.
9. Va le ni il che cadale Celo more, more celo.	9. Dance lightly, more gently, and gently still.
10. Plu hari ti tirete Plu huron cai pra seti.	10. Make not so much dust to destroy your embroidered hose.

The last stanza would puzzle a commentator: the men have certainly buskins of the most beautiful texture, but the ladies (to whom the above is supposed to be addressed) have nothing under their little yellow boots and slippers but a well-turned and sometimes very white ankle. The Arnaout girls are much handsomer than the Greeks, and their dress is far more picturesque. They preserve their shape much longer also, from being always in the open air. It is to be observed, that the Arnaout is not a *written* language: the words of this song, therefore, as well as the one which follows, are spelt according to their pronunciation. They are copied by one who speaks and understands the dialect perfectly, and who is a native of Athens.

1. Ndi sefda tinde ulavossa Vettimi upri vi lofsa.	1. I am wounded by thy love, and have loved but to scorch myself.
2. Ah vaisisso mi privo lofse Si mi rini mi la vosse.	2. Thou hast consumed me! Ah, maid! thou hast struck me to the heart.

---

* The Albanese, particularly the women, are frequently termed "Caliriotes;" for what reason I inquired in vain.

3. Uti tasa roba stua Sitti eve tulati dua.	3. I have said I wish no dowry but thine eyes and eyelashes
4. Roba stinori ssidua Qu mi sini vetti dua.	4. The accursed dowry I want not, but thee only.
5. Qurmini dua civileni Roba ti siarmi tildi eni.	5. Give me thy charms, and let the portion feed the flames
6. Utara pisa vaisisso me simi rin ti hapti Eti mi bire a piste si gui dendroi tiltati.	6. I have loved thee, maid, with a sincere soul, but thou hast left me like a withered tree.
7. Udi vura udorini udiri cicova cilti mora Udorini talti hollna u ede caimoni mora.	7. If I have placed my hand on thy bosom, what have I gained? my hand is withdrawn, but retains the flame.

I believe the two last stanzas, as they are in a different measure, ought to belong to another ballad. An idea something similar to the thought in the last lines was expressed by Socrates, whose arm having come in contact with one of his "ὑποκολπιοι," Critobulus or Cleobulus, the philosopher complained of a shooting pain as far as his shoulder for some days after, and therefore very properly resolved to teach his disciples in future without touching them.

Note [D.]—Thoughts on the Present State of Greece.

See p. 103.

"*Fair Greece! sad relic of departed worth!*
Immortal, though no more; though fallen, great!"
Stanza lxxiii.

I.

Before I say any thing about a city of which everybody, traveller or not, has thought it necessary to say something, I will request Miss Owenson, when she next borrows an Athenian heroine for her four volumes, to have the goodness to marry her to somebody more of a gentleman than a "Disdar Aga," (who, by-the-by, is not an Aga,) the most impolite of petty officers, the greatest patron of larceny Athens ever saw, (except Lord E.,) and the unworthy occupant of the Acropolis, on a handsome annual stipend of 150 piastres, (eight pounds sterling,) out of which he has only to pay his garrison, the most ill-regulated corps in the ill-regulated Ottoman Empire. I speak it tenderly, seeing I was once the cause of the husband of "Ida of Athens" nearly suffering the bastinado; and because the said "Disdar" is a turbulent husband, and beats his wife; so that I exhort and beseech Miss Owenson to sue for a separate maintenance in behalf of "Ida." Having premised thus much, on a matter of such import to the readers of romances, I may now leave Ida, to mention her birthplace.

Setting aside the magic of the name, and all those associations which it would be pedantic and superfluous to recapitulate, the very situation of Athens would render it the favourite of all who have eyes for art or nature. The climate, to me at least, appeared a perpetual spring; during eight months I never passed a day without being as many hours on horseback: rain is extremely rare, snow never lies in the plains, and a cloudy day is an agreeable rarity. In Spain, Portugal, and every part of the East which I visited, except Ionia and Attica, I perceived no such superiority of climate to our own; and at Constantinople, where I passed May, June, and part of July, (1810,) you might "damn the climate, and complain of spleen," five days out of seven.

The air of the Morea is heavy and unwholesome, but the moment you pass the isthmus in the direction of Megara, the change is strikingly perceptible. But I fear Hesiod will still be found correct in his description of a Bœotian winter.

We found at Livadia an "esprit fort" in a Greek bishop, of all freethinkers! This worthy hypocrite rallied his own religion with great intrepidity, (but not before his flock,) and talked of a mass as a "coglioneria." It was impossible to think better of him for this; but, for a Bœotian, he was brisk with all his absurdity. This phenomenon (with the exception indeed of Thebes, the remains of Chæronea, the plain of Platea, Orchomenus, Livadia, and its nominal cave of Trophonius) was the only remarkable thing we saw before we passed Mount Cithæron.

The fountain of Dirce turns a mill: at least my companion (who, resolving to be at once cleanly and classical, bathed in it) pronounced it to be the fountain of Dirce, and anybody who thinks it worth while may contradict him. At Castri we drank of half a dozen streamlets, some none of the purest, before we decided to our satisfaction which was the true Castalian, and even that had a villanous twang, probably from the snow, though it did not throw us into an epic fever, like poor Dr. Chandler.

From Fort Phyle, of which large remains still exist, the Plain of Athens, Pentelicus, Hymettus, the Ægean, and the Acropolis burst upon the eye at once; in my opinion, a more glorious prospect than even Cintra or Istambol. Not the view from the Troad, with Ida, the Hellespont, and the more distant Mount Athos, can equal it, though so superior in extent.

I heard much of the beauty of Arcadia, but excepting the view from the monastery of Megaspelion, (which is inferior to Zitza in a command of country,) and the descent from the mountains on the way from Tripolitza to Argos, Arcadia has little to recommend it beyond the name.

"Sternitur, et *dulces* moriens reminiscitur Argos."

Virgil could have put this into the mouth of none but an Argive, and (with reverence be it spoken,) it does not deserve the epithet. And if the Polynices of Statius, "In mediis audit duo litora campis," did actually hear both shores in crossing the isthmus of Corinth, he had better ears than have ever been worn in such a journey since.

"Athens," says a celebrated topographer, "is still the most polished city of Greece." Perhaps it may of *Greece*, but not of the *Greeks*; for Joannina in Epirus is universally allowed, amongst themselves, to be superior in the wealth, refinement, learning, and dialect of its inhabitants. The Athenians are remarkable for their cunning; and the lower orders are not improperly characterized in that proverb, which classes them with "the Jews of Salonica, and the Turks of the Negropont."

Among the various foreigners resident in Athens, French, Italians, Germans, Ragusans, &c., there was never a difference of opinion in their estimate of the Greek character, though on all other topics they disputed with great acrimony.

M. Fauvel, the French consul, who has passed thirty years principally at Athens, and to whose talents as an artist, and manners as a gentleman, none who have known him can refuse their testimony, has frequently declared in my hearing, that the Greeks do not deserve to be emancipated; reasoning on the grounds of their "national and individual depravity!" while he forgot that such depravity is to be attributed to causes which can only be removed by the measure he reprobates.

M. Roque, a French merchant of respectability long settled in Athens, asserted with the most amusing gravity, "Sir, they are the same *canaille* that existed *in the days of Themistocles!*" an alarming remark to the "Laudator temporis acti." The ancients banished Themistocles; the moderns cheat Monsieur Roque: thus great men have ever been treated!

In short, all the Franks who are fixtures, and most of the Englishmen, Germans, Danes, &c. of passage, came over by degrees to their opinion, on much the same grounds that a Turk in England would condemn the nation by wholesale, because he was wronged by his lacquey, and overcharged by his washerwoman.

Certainly it was not a little staggering when the Sieurs Fauvel and Lusiera, the two greatest demagogues of the day, who divide between them the power of Pericles and the popularity of Cleon, and puzzle the poor waywode with perpetual differences agreed in the utter condemnation, "nulla virtute redemptum," of the Greeks in general, and of the Athenians in particular.

For my own humble opinion, I am loath to hazard it, knowing, as I do, that there be now in MS. no less than five tours of the first magnitude and of the most threatening aspect, all in typographical array, by persons of wit, and honour, and regular commonplace books: but, if I may say this without offence, it seems to me rather hard to declare so positively and pertinaciously, as almost everybody has declared, that the Greeks, because they are very bad, will never be better.

Eton and Sonnini have led us astray by their panegyrics and projects; but, on the other hand, De Pauw and Thornton have debased the Greeks beyond their demerits.

The Greeks will never be independent; they will never be sovereigns as heretofore, and God forbid they ever should! but they may be subjects without being slaves. Our colonies are not independent, but they are free and industrious, and such may Greece be hereafter.

At present, like the Catholics of Ireland and the Jews throughout the world, and such other cudgelled and heterodox people, they suffer all the moral and physical ills that can afflict humanity. Their life is a struggle against truth; they are vicious in their own defence. They are so unused to kindness, that when they occasionally meet with it they look upon it with suspicion, as a dog often beaten snaps at your fingers if you attempt to caress him. "They are ungrateful, notoriously, abominably ungrateful!"—this is the general cry. Now, in the name of Nemesis! for what are they to be grateful! Where is the human being that ever conferred a benefit on Greek or Greeks? They are to be grateful to the Turks for their fetters, and to the Franks for their broken promises and lying counsels. They are to be grateful to the artist who engraves their ruins, and to the antiquary who carries them away; to the traveller whose janissary flogs them, and to the scribbler whose journal abuses them! This is he amount of their obligations to foreigners.

II.

Franciscan Convent, Athens, January 23, 1811.

Amongst the remnants of the barbarous policy of the earlier ages, are the traces of bondage which yet exist in different countries; whose inhabitants, however divided in religion and manners, almost all agree in oppression.

The English have at last compassionated their negroes, and under a less bigoted government, may probably one day release their Catholic brethren: but the interposition of foreigners alone can emancipate the Greeks, who otherwise, appear to have as small a chance of redemption from the Turks, as the Jews have from mankind in general.

Of the ancient Greeks we know more than enough; at least the younger men of Europe devote much of their time to the study of the Greek writers and history, which would be more usefully spent in mastering their own. Of the moderns, we are perhaps more neglectful than they deserve; and while every man of any pretensions to learning is tiring out his youth, and often his age, in the study of the language and of the harangues of the Athenian demagogues in favour of freedom, the real or supposed descendants of these sturdy republicans are left to the actual tyranny of their masters, although a very slight effort is required to strike off their chains.

To talk, as the Greeks themselves do, of their rising again to their pristine superiority, would be ridiculous: as the rest of the world must resume its barbarism, after reasserting the sovereignty of Greece: but there seems to be no very great obstacle, except in the apathy of the Franks, to their becoming a useful dependency, or even a free state with a proper guarantee;—under correction, however, be it spoken, for many and well informed men doubt the practicability even of this.

The Greeks have never lost their hope, though they are now more divided in opinion on the subject of their probable deliverers. Religion recommends the Russians; but they have twice been deceived and abandoned by that power, and the dreadful lesson they received after the Muscovite desertion in the Morea has never been forgotten. The French they dislike; although the subjugation of the rest of Europe will, probably, be attended by the deliverance of continental Greece. The islanders look to the English for succour, as they have very lately possessed themselves of the Ionian republic, Corfu excepted. But whoever appear with arms in their hands will be welcome; and when that day arrives, Heaven have mercy on the Ottomans, they cannot expect it from the Giaours.

But instead of considering what they have been, and speculating on what they may be, let us look at them as they are.

And here it is impossible to reconcile the contrariety of opinions; some, particularly the merchants, decrying the Greeks in the strongest language; others, generally travellers, turning periods in their eulogy, and publishing very curious speculations grafted on their former state, which can have no more effect on their present lot, than the existence of the Incas on the future fortunes of Peru.

One very ingenious person terms them the "natural allies of Englishmen;" another, no less ingenious, will not allow them to be the allies of anybody, and denies their very descent from the ancients; a third, more ingenious than either, builds a Greek empire on a Russian foundation, and realizes (on paper) all the chimeras of Catharine II. As to the question of their descent, what can it import whether the Mainotes are the lineal Laconians or not? or the present Athenians as indigenous as the bees of Hymettus or as the grasshoppers, to which they once likened themselves? What Englishman cares if he be of a Danish, Saxon, Norman, or Trojan blood? or who, except a Welshman, is afflicted with a desire of being descended from Caractacus?

The poor Greeks do not so much abound in the good things of this world, as to render even their claims to antiquity an object of envy; it is very cruel, then, in Mr. Thornton to disturb them in the possession of all that time has left them; viz. their pedigree, of which they are the more tenacious, as it is all they can call their own. It would be worth while to publish together, and compare, the works of Messrs. Thornton and De Pauw, Eton and Sonnini; paradox on one side, and prejudice on the other. Mr. Thornton conceives himself to have claims to public confidence from a fourteen years' residence at Pera; perhaps he may on the subject of the Turks, but this can give him no more insight into the real state of Greece and her inhabitants, than as many years spent in Wapping into that of the Western Highlands.

The Greeks of Constantinople live in Fanal; and if Mr. Thornton did not oftener cross the Golden Horn than his brother merchants are accustomed to do, I should place no great reliance on his information. I actually heard one of these gentlemen boast of their little general intercourse with the city, and assert of himself, with an air of triumph, that he had been but four times at Constantinople in as many years.

As to Mr. Thornton's voyages in the Black Sea with Greek vessels, they gave him the same idea of Greece as a cruise to Berwick in a Scotch smack would of Johnny Grot's house. Upon what grounds then does he arrogate the right of condemning by wholesale a body of men, of whom he can know little? It is rather a curious circumstance that Mr. Thornton, who so lavishly dispraises Pouqueville on every occasion of mentioning the Turks, has yet recourse to him as authority on the Greeks, and terms him an impartial observer. Now, Dr. Pouqueville is as little entitled to that appellation, as Mr. Thornton to confer it on him.

The fact is, we are deplorably in want of information on the subject of the Greeks, and in particular their literature; nor is there any probability of our being better acquainted, till our intercourse becomes more intimate, or their independence confirmed: the relations of passing travellers are as little to be depended on as the invectives of angry factors; but till something more can be attained, we must be content with the little to be acquired from similar sources.*

However defective these may be, they are preferable to the paradoxes of men who have read superficially of the ancients, and

---

* A word, *en passant*, with Mr. Thornton and Dr. Pouqueville, who have been guilty between them of sadly clipping the Sultan's Turkish.

Dr. Pouqueville tells a long story of a Moslem who swallowed corrosive sublimate in such quantities, that he acquired the name of "*Suleyman Yeyen*," i. e. quoth the doctor, "*Suleyman, the eater of corrosive sublimate.*" "Aha!" thinks Mr. Thornton, (angry with the doctor for the fiftieth time,) "have I caught you!"—Then, in a note twice the thickness of the doctor's anecdote, he questions the doctor's proficiency in the Turkish tongue, and his veracity in his own.—"For," observes Mr. Thornton, (after inflicting on us the tough participle of a Turkish verb,) "it means nothing more than *Suleyman the eater*," and quite cashiers the supplementary "*sublimate*." Now, both are right, and both are wrong. If Mr. Thornton, when he next resides "fourteen years in the factory," will consult his Turkish dictionary, or ask any of his Stamboline acquaintance, he will discover that "*Suleyma'n yeyen*," put together discreetly, mean the "*Swallower of sublimate*," without any "*Suleyman*" in the case: "*Suleyma*" signifying "*corrosive sublimate*," and not being a proper name on this occasion, although it be an orthodox name enough with the addition of *n*. After Mr. Thornton's frequent hints of profound Orientalism, he might have found this out before he sang such pæans over Dr. Pouqueville.

After this, I think "Travellers *versus* Factors" shall be our motto, though the above Mr. Thornton has condemned "hoc genus omne," for mistake and misrepresentation "Ne Sutor ultra crepidam," "No merchant beyond his bales." N.B. For the benefit of Mr. Thornton, "Sutor" is not a proper name

seen nothing of the moderns, such as De Pauw; who, when he asserts that the British breed of horses is ruined by Newmarket, and that the Spartans were cowards in the field, betrays an equal knowledge of English horses and Spartan men. His "philosophical observations" have a much better claim to the title of "poetical." It could not be expected that he who so liberally condemns some of the most celebrated institutions of the ancient, should have mercy on the modern Greeks; and it fortunately happens, that the absurdity of his hypothesis on their forefathers refutes his sentence on themselves.

Let us trust, then, that, in spite of the prophecies of De Pauw, and the doubts of Mr. Thornton, there is a reasonable hope of the redemption of a race of men, who, whatever may be the errors of their religion and policy, have been amply punished by three centuries and a half of captivity.

III.

Athens, Franciscan Convent, March 17, 1811.

"I must have some talk with this learned Theban."

Some time after my return from Constantinople to this city, I received the thirty-first number of the Edinburgh Review as a great favour, and certainly at this distance an acceptable one, from the captain of an English frigate off Salamis. In that number, Art. 3., containing the review of a French translation of Strabo, there are introduced some remarks on the modern Greeks and their literature, with a short account of Coray, a co-translator in the French version. On those remarks I mean to ground a few observations; and the spot where I now write will, I hope, be sufficient excuse for introducing them in a work in some degree connected with the subject. Coray, the most celebrated of living Greeks, at least among the Franks, was born at Scio, (in the Review, Smyrna is stated, I have reason to think, incorrectly,) and besides the translation of Beccaria and other works mentioned by the Reviewer, has published a lexicon in Romaic and French, if I may trust the assurance of some Danish travellers lately arrived from Paris; but the latest we have seen here in French and Greek is that of Gregory Zolikogloou.* Coray has recently been

* I have in my possession an excellent lexicon "*τριγλωσσον*," which I received in exchange from S. G—, Esq., for a small gem: my antiquarian friends have never forgotten it, or forgiven me.

involved in an unpleasant controversy with M. Gail,* a Parisian commentator and editor of some translations from the Greek poets, in consequence of the Institute having awarded him the prize for his version of Hippocrates "Περὶ ὑδάτων," &c. to the disparagement, and consequently displeasure, of the said Gail. To his exertions, literary and patriotic, great praise is undoubtedly due; but a part of that praise ought not to be withheld from the two brothers Zosimado, (merchants settled in Leghorn,) who sent him to Paris, and maintained him, for the express purpose of elucidating the ancient, and adding to the modern, researches of his countrymen. Coray, however, is not considered by his countrymen equal to some who lived in the two last centuries; more particularly Dorotheus of Mitylene, whose Hellenic writings are so much esteemed by the Greeks, that Meletius terms him "Μετὰ τὸν Θουκυδίδην καὶ Ξενοφῶντα ἄριστος Ἑλλήνων." (P. 224. Ecclesiastical History, vol. iv.)

Panagiotes Kodrikas, the translator of Fontenelle, and Kamarases, who translated Ocellus Lucanus on the Universe into French, Christodoulus, and more particularly Psalida, whom I have conversed with in Joannina, are also in high repute among their literati. The last-mentioned has published in Romaic and Latin a work on "True Happiness," dedicated to Catherine II. But Polyzois, who is stated by the Reviewer to be the only modern except Coray who has distinguished himself by a knowledge of Hellenic, if he be the Polyzois Lampanitziotes of Yanina, who has published a number of editions in Romaic, was neither more nor less than an itinerant vender of books; with the contents of which he had no concern beyond his name on the titlepage, placed there to secure his property in the publication; and he was, moreover, a man utterly destitute of scholastic acquirements. As the name, however, is not uncommon, some other Polyzois may have edited the Epistles of Aristænetus.

It is to be regretted that the system of continental blockade has closed the few channels through which the Greeks received their publications, particularly Venice and Trieste. Even the common grammars for children are become too dear for the lower

---

* In Gail's pamphlet against Coray, he talks of "throwing the insolent Hellenist out of the windows." On this a French critic exclaims, "Ah, my God throw an Hellenist out of the window! what sacrilege!" It certainly would be a serious business for those authors who dwell in the attics: but I have quoted the passage merely to prove the similarity of style among the controversialists of all polished countries; London or Edinburgh could hardly parallel this Parisian ebullition

orders. Amongst their original works the Geography of Meletius, Archbishop of Athens, and a multitude of theological quartos and poetical pamphlets, are to be met with; their grammars and lexicons of two, three, and four languages, are numerous and excellent. Their poetry is in rhyme. The most singular piece I have lately seen is a satire in dialogue between a Russian, English, and French traveller, and the Waywode of Wallachia, (or Blackbey, as they term him,) an archbishop, a merchant, and Cogia Bachi, (or primate,) in succession; to all of whom under the Turks the writer attributes their present degeneracy. Their songs are sometimes pretty and pathetic, but their tunes generally unpleasing to the ear of a Frank; the best is the famous "Δεῦτε παῖδες τῶν 'Ελλήνων," by the unfortunate Riga. But from a catalogue of more than sixty authors, now before me, only fifteen can be found who have touched on any theme except theology.

I am intrusted with a commission by a Greek of Athens named Marmarotouri to make arrangements, if possible, for printing in London a translation of Barthelemi's Anacharsis in Romaic, as he has no other opportunity, unless he despatches the MS. to Vienna by the Black Sea and Danube.

The Reviewer mentions a school established at Hecatonesi, and suppressed at the instigation of Sebastiani: he means Cidonies, or, in Turkish, Haivali; a town on the continent, where that institution for a hundred students and three professors still exists. It is true that this establishment was disturbed by the Porte, under the ridiculous pretext that the Greeks were constructing a fortress instead of a college: but on investigation, and the payment of some purses to the Divan, it has been permitted to continue. The principal professor, named Ueniamin, (i. e. Benjamin,) is stated to be a man of talent, but a freethinker. He was born in Lesbos, studied in Italy, and is master of Hellenic, Latin, and some Frank languages; besides a smattering of the sciences.

Though it is not my intention to enter farther on this topic than may allude to the article in question, I cannot but observe that the Reviewer's lamentation over the fall of the Greeks appears singular, when he closes it with these words: "*The change is to be attributed to their misfortunes rather than to any 'physical degradation.'*" It may be true that the Greeks are not physically degenerated, and that Constantinople contained on the day when it changed masters as many men of six feet and upwards as in the hour of prosperity; but ancient history and modern politics instruct us that something more than physical perfection is necessary to preserve a state in vigour and independence; and the Greeks, in particular, are a melancholy example of the near connection between moral degradation and national decay.

The Reviewer mentions a plan, "*we believe*" by Potemkin, for the purification of the Romaic; and I have endeavoured in vain to procure any tidings or traces of its existence. There was an academy at St. Petersburg for the Greeks; but it was suppressed by Paul, and has not been revived by his successor.

There is a slip of the pen, and it can only be a slip of the pen, in p. 58, No. 31, of the Edinburgh Review, where these words occur:—"We are told that when the capital of the East yielded to *Solyman.*"—It may be presumed that this last word will, in a future edition, be altered to Mahomet II.* The "ladies of Constantinople," it seems, at that period spoke a dialect, "which would not have disgraced the lips of an Athenian." I do not know how that might be, but am sorry to say the ladies in general, and the Athenians in particular, are much altered; being far from choice either in their dialect or expression, as the whole Attic race are barbarous to a proverb:—

"Ω Αθηνα, προτη χωρα,
Τι γαιδαρους τρεφεις τωρα."

In Gibbon, vol. x. p. 161, is the following sentence:—"The vulgar dialect of the city was gross and barbarous, though the compositions of the church and palace sometimes affected to copy the purity of the Attic models." Whatever may be asserted on the subject, it is difficult to conceive that the "ladies of

---

* In a former number of the Edinburgh Review, 1808, it is observed, "Lord Byron passed some of his early years in Scotland, where he might have learned that *pibroch* does not mean a *bagpipe*, any more than *duet* means a *fiddle*." Query,—Was it in Scotland that the young gentlemen of the Edinburgh Review *learned* that *Solyman* means *Mahomet II.*, any more than *criticism* means *infallibility?*—but thus it is,

"Cædimus inque vicem præbemus crura sagittis."

The mistake seemed so completely a lapse of the pen, (from the great *similarity* of the two words, and the *total absence of error* from the former pages of the literary leviathan,) that I should have passed it over as in the text, had I not perceived in the Edinburgh Review much facetious exultation on all such detections, particularly a recent one, where words and syllables are subjects of disquisition and transposition; and the above-mentioned parallel passage in my own case irresistibly propelled me to hint how much easier it is to be critical than correct. The *gentlemen*, having enjoyed many a *triumph* on such victories, will hardly begrudge me a slight *ovation* for the present.

Constantinople," in the reign of the last Cæsar, spoke a purer dialect than Anna Comnena wrote three centuries before: and those royal pages are not esteemed the best models of composition, although the princess γλωτταν ειχεν ΑΚΡΙΒΩΣ Αττικιζουσαν. In the Fanal, and in Yanina, the best Greek is spoken: in the latter there is a flourishing school under the direction of Psalida.

There is now in Athens a pupil of Psalida's, who is making a tour of observation through Greece: he is intelligent, and better educated than a fellow-commoner of most colleges. I mention this as a proof that the spirit of inquiry is not dormant among the Greeks.

The Reviewer mentions Mr. Wright, the author of the beautiful poem "Horæ Ionicæ," as qualified to give details of these nominal Romans and degenerate Greeks; and also of their language: but Mr. Wright, though a good poet and an able man, has made a mistake where he states the Albanian dialect of the Romaic to approximate nearest to the Hellenic; for the Albanians speak a Romaic as notoriously corrupt as the Scotch of Aberdeenshire, or the Italian of Naples. Yanina, (where, next to the Fanal, the Greek is purest,) although the capital of Ali Pasha's dominions, is not in Albania but Epirus; and beyond Delvinachi in Albania Proper up to Argyrocastro and Tepaleen, (beyond which I did not advance,) they speak worse Greek than even the Athenians. I was attended for a year and a half by two of these singular mountaineers, whose mother tongue is Illyric, and I never heard them or their countrymen (whom I have seen, not only at home, but to the amount of twenty thousand in the army of Vely Pasha) praised for their Greek, but often laughed at for their provincial barbarisms.

I have in my possession about twenty-five letters, amongst which some from the Bey of Corinth, written to me by Notarus, the Cogia Bachi, and others by the dragoman of the Caimacam of the Morea, (which last governs in Vely Pasha's absence,) are said to be favourable specimens of their epistolary style. I also received some at Constantinople from private persons, written in a most hyperbolical style, but in the true antique character.

The Reviewer proceeds, after some remarks on the tongue in its past and present state, to a paradox (page 59) on the great mischief the knowledge of his own language has done to Coray, who, it seems, is less likely to understand the ancient Greek, because he is perfect master of the modern! This observation follows a paragraph, recommending, in explicit terms, the study of the Romaic, as "a powerful auxiliary," not only to the traveller and foreign merchant, but also to the classical scholar; in short, to everybody except the only person who can be thoroughly acquainted with its uses; and, by a parity of reasoning, our old language is conjectured to be probably more attainable by "foreigners" than by ourselves! Now, I am inclined to think, that a Dutch tyro in our tongue (albeit himself of Saxon blood) would be sadly perplexed with "Sir Tristram," or any other given "Auchinleck MS.," with or without a grammar or glossary; and to most apprehensions it seems evident, that none but a native can acquire a competent, far less complete, knowledge of our obsolete idioms. We may give the critic credit for his ingenuity, but no more believe him than we do Smollett's Lismahago, who maintains that the purest English is spoken in Edinburgh. That Coray may err is very possible; but if he does, the fault is in the man rather than in his mother tongue, which is, as it ought to be, of the greatest aid to the native student.—Here the Reviewer proceeds to business on Strabo's translators, and here I close my remarks.

Sir W. Drummond, Mr. Hamilton, Lord Aberdeen, Dr. Clarke, Captain Leake, Mr. Gell, Mr. Walpole, and many others now in England, have all the requisites to furnish details of this fallen people. The few observations I have offered I should have left where I made them, had not the article in question, and, above all, the spot where I read it, induced me to advert to those pages, which the advantage of my present situation enabled me to clear, or at least to make the attempt.

I have endeavoured to waive the personal feelings, which rise in despite of me in touching upon any part of the Edinburgh Review; not from a wish to conciliate the favour of its writers, or to cancel the remembrance of a syllable I have formerly published, but simply from a sense of the impropriety of mixing up private resentments with a disquisition of the present kind, and more particularly at this distance of time and place.

Note [E.]—On the present State of Turkey and the Turks. See p. 103.

The difficulties of travelling in Turkey have been much exaggerated, or rather have considerably diminished, of late years The Mussulmans have been beaten into a kind of sullen civility very comfortable to voyagers.

It is hazardous to say much on the subject of Turks and Turkey; since it is possible to live amongst them twenty years without acquiring information, at least from themselves. As far as my own slight experience carried me, I have no complaint tc make; but am indebted for many civilities (I might almost say for friendship) and much hospitality, to Ali Pasha, his son Veli Pasha of the Morea, and several others of high rank in the provinces. Suleyman Aga, late Governor of Athens, and now of Thebes, was a *bon vivant*, and as social a being as ever sat cross-legged at a tray or a table. During the carnival, when our English party were masquerading, both himself and his successor were more happy to "receive masks," than any dowager in Grosvenor-square.

On one occasion of his supping at the convent, his friend and visiter, the Cadi of Thebes, was carried from table perfectly qualified for any club in Christendom; while the worthy way-wode himself triumphed in his fall.

In all money transactions with the Moslems, I ever found the strictest honour, the highest disinterestedness. In transacting business with them, there are none of those dirty peculations, under the name of interest, difference of exchange, commission, &c. &c. uniformly found in applying to a Greek consul to cash bills, even on the first houses in Pera.

With regard to presents, an established custom in the East, you will rarely find yourself a loser; as one worth acceptance is generally returned by another of similar value—a horse, or a shawl.

In the capital and at court the citizens and courtiers are formed in the same school with those of Christianity; but there does not exist a more honourable, friendly, and high-spirited character than the true Turkish provincial aga, or Moslem country gentleman. It is not meant here to designate the governors of towns, but those agas who, by a kind of feudal tenure, possess lands and houses, of more or less extent, in Greece and Asia Minor.

The lower orders are in as tolerable discipline as the rabble in countries with greater pretensions to civilization. A Moslem, in walking the streets of our country towns, would be more incommoded in England than a Frank in a similar situation in Turkey. Regimentals are the best travelling dress.

The best accounts of the religion and different sects of Islamism, may be found in D'Ohsson's French; of their manners, &c. perhaps in Thornton's English. The Ottomans, with all their defects, are not a people to be despised. Equal, at least, to the Spaniards, they are superior to the Portuguese. If it be diffi cult to pronounce what they are, we can at least say what they are *not*: they are *not* treacherous, they are *not* cowardly, they do *not* burn heretics, they are *not* assassins, nor has an enemy advanced to *their* capital. They are faithful to their sultan till he becomes unfit to govern, and devout to their God without an inquisition. Were they driven from St. Sophia to-morrow, and the French or Russians enthroned in their stead, it would become a question whether Europe would gain by the exchange. England would certainly be the loser.

With regard to that ignorance of which they are so generally, and sometimes justly accused, it may be doubted, always excepting France and England, in what useful points of knowledge they are excelled by other nations. Is it in the common arts of life? In their manufactures? Is a Turkish sabre inferior to a Toledo? or is a Turk worse clothed or lodged, or fed and taught, than a Spaniard? Are their pashas worse educated than a grandee? or an effendi than a Knight of St. Jago? I think not.

I remember Mahmout, the grandson of Ali Pasha, asking whether my fellow-traveller and myself were in the upper or lower House of Parliament. Now, this question from a boy of ten years old proved that his education had not been neglected. It may be doubted if an English boy at that age knows the difference of the Divan from a College of Dervises; but I am very sure a Spaniard does not. How little Mahmout, surrounded, as he had been, entirely by his Turkish tutors, had learned that there was such a thing as a Parliament, it were useless to conjecture, unless we suppose that his instructors did not confine his studies to the Koran.

In all the mosques there are schools established, which are very regularly attended; and the poor are taught without the church of Turkey being put into peril. I believe the system is not yet printed; (though there is such a thing as a Turkish press, and books printed on the late military institution of the Nizam Gedidd;) nor have I heard whether the Mufti and the Mollas have subscribed, or the Caimacam and the Tefterdar taken the alarm, for fear the ingenuous youth of the turban should be taught not to "pray to God their way." The Greeks also—a kind of Eastern Irish Papists—have a college of their own at Maynooth,—no, at Haivali; where the heterodox receive much the same kind of countenance from the Ottoman as the Catholic college from the English legislature. Who shall then affirm that the Turks are ignorant bigots, when they thus evince the exact proportion of Christian charity which is tolerated in the most prosperous and orthodox of all possible kingdoms? But though they allow all this, they will not suffer the Greeks to participate in their privileges: no, let them fight their battles, and pay their haratch, (taxes,) be drubbed in this world, and damned in the next. And shall we then emancipate our Irish Helots? Mahomet forbid! We should then be bad Mussulmans, and worse Christians: at present we unite the best of both—jesuitical faith, and something not much inferior to Turkish toleration.

NOTES TO CANTO III.

Note [F.]

> "*Not vainly did the early Persian make*
> *His altar the high places and the peak*
> *Of earth o'ergazing mountains, &c.*"—Stanza xci.

It is to be recollected, that the most beautiful and impressive doctrines of the divine Founder of Christianity were delivered, not in the *Temple*, but on the *Mount*. To waive the question of devotion, and turn to human eloquence,—the most effectual and splendid specimens were not pronounced within walls. Demosthenes addressed the public and popular assemblies. Cicero spoke in the forum. That this added to their effect on the mind of both orators and hearers, may be conceived from the difference between what we read of the emotions then and there produced, and those we ourselves experience in the perusal in the closet. It is one thing to read the Iliad at Sigæum, and on the tumuli, or by the springs with Mount Ida above, and the plain and rivers and Archipelago around you; and another to trim your taper over it in a snug library—*this* I know. Were the early and rapid progress of what is called Methodism to be attributed to any cause beyond the enthusiasm excited by its vehement faith and doctrines, (the truth or error of which I presume neither to canvass nor to question,) I should venture to ascribe it to the practice of preaching in the *fields*, and the unstudied and extemporaneous effusions of its teachers.—The Mussulmans, whose erroneous devotion (at least in the lower orders) is most sincere, and therefore impressive, are accustomed to repeat their prescribed orisons and prayers, wherever they may be, at the stated hours—of course, frequently in the open air, kneeling upon a light mat, (which they carry for the purpose of a bed or cushion as required;) the cere mony lasts some minutes, during which they are totally absorbed, and only living in their supplication: nothing can disturb them. On me the simple and entire sincerity of these men, and the spirit which appeared to be within and upon them, made a far greater impression than any general rite which was ever performed in places of worship, of which I have seen those of almost every persuasion under the sun, including most of our own sectaries, and the Greek, the Catholic, the Armenian, the Lutheran, the Jewish, and the Mahometan. Many of the negroes, of whom there are numbers in the Turkish empire, are idolaters, and have free exercise of their belief and its rites: some of these I had a distant view of at Patras; and, from what I could make out of them, they appeared to be of a truly pagan description, and not very agreeable to a spectator.

Note [G.]

"*Clarens! by heavenly feet thy paths are trod,—*
Undying Love's, who here ascends a throne
To which the steps are mountains; where the god
Is a pervading life and light," *&c.*—Stanza c. See p. 161.

Rousseau's Héloïse, Lettre 17, part. 4, note. "Ces montagnes sont si hautes qu'une demi-heure après le soleil couche, leurs sommets sont éclairés de ses rayons; dont le rouge forme sur ces cimes blanches *une belle couleur de rose*, qu'on aperçoit de fort loin."—This applies more particularly to the heights over Meillerie.—"J'allai à Vevay loger à la Clef, et pendant deux jours que j'y restai sans voir personne, je pris pour cette ville un amour qui m'a suivi dans tous mes voyages, et qui m'y a fait établir enfin les héros de mon roman. Je dirais volontiers à ceux qui ont du goût et qui sont sensibles: Allez à Vevay—visitez le pays, examinez les sites, promenez-vous sur le lac, et dites si la Nature n'a pas fait ce beau pays pour une Julie, pour une Claire, et pour un St. Preux; mais ne les y cherchez pas." *Les Confessions*, livre iv. p. 306. Lyon, ed. 1796.—In July, 1816, I made a voyage round the Lake of Geneva; and, as far as my own observations have led me in a not uninteresting nor inattentive survey of all the scenes most celebrated by Rousseau in his "Héloïse," I can safely say, that in this there is no exaggeration. It would be difficult to see Clarens (with the scenes around it, Vevay, Chillon, Bôveret, St. Gingo, Meillerie, Eivan, and the entrances of the Rhone) without being forcibly struck with its peculiar adaptation to the persons and events with which it has been peopled. But this is not all: the feeling with which all around Clarens, and the opposite rocks of Meillerie, is invested, is of a still higher and more comprehensive order than the mere sympathy with individual passion; it is a sense of the existence of love in its most extended and sublime capacity, and of our own participation of its good and of its glory: it is the great principle of the universe, which is there more condensed, but not less manifested; and of which, though knowing ourselves a part, we lose our individuality, and mingle in the beauty of the whole.—If Rousseau had never written, nor lived, the same associations would not less have belonged to such scenes. He has added to the interest of his works by their adoption; he has shown his sense of their beauty by the selection; but they have done that for him which no human being could do for them.—I had the fortune (good or evil as it might be) to sail from Meillerie (where we landed for some time) to St. Gingo during a lake storm, which added to the magnificence of all around, although occasionally accompanied by danger to the boat, which was small and overloaded. It was over this very part of the lake that Rousseau has driven the boat of St. Preux and Madame Wolmar to Meillerie for shelter during a tempest. On gaining the shore at St. Gingo, I found that the wind had been sufficiently strong to blow down some fine old chestnut trees on the lower part of the mountains. On the opposite height of Clarens is a château. The hills are covered with vineyards, and interspersed with some small but beautiful woods; one of these was named the "Bosquet de Julie;" and it is remarkable that, though long ago cut down by the brutal selfishness of the monks of St. Bernard, (to whom the land appertained,) that the ground might be enclosed into a vineyard for the miserable drones of an execrable superstition, the inhabitants of Clarens still point out the spot where its trees stood, calling it by the name which consecrated and survived them. Rousseau has not been particularly fortunate in the preservation of the "local habitations" he has given to "airy nothings." The Prior of Great St. Bernard has cut down some of his woods for the sake of a few casks of wine, and Bonaparte has levelled part of the rocks of Meillerie in improving the road to the Simplon. The road is an excellent one; but I cannot quite agree with the remark which I heard made, that "La route vaut mieux que les souvenirs."

HISTORICAL NOTES TO CANTO IV

No. I.—State Dungeons of Venice.

"*I stood in Venice, on the Bridge of Sighs;*
A palace and a prison on each hand."—Stanza i

The communication between the ducal palace and the prisons of Venice is by a gloomy bridge, or covered gallery, high above the water, and divided by a stone wall into a passage and a cell. The state dungeons, called *pozzi*, or wells, were sunk in the thick walls of the palace; and the prisoner when taken out to die was conducted across the gallery to the other side, and being then led back into the other compartment, or cell, upon the bridge, was there strangled. The low portal through which the criminal was taken into this cell is now walled up; but the passage is still open, and is still known by the name of the Bridge of Sighs. The pozzi are under the flooring of the chamber at the foot of the bridge. They were formerly twelve; but on the first arrival of the French, the Venetians hastily blocked or broke up the deeper of these dungeons. You may still, however, descend by a trap-door, and crawl down through holes, half choked by rubbish, to the depth of two stories below the first range. If you are in want of consolation for the extinction of patrician power, perhaps you may find it there; scarcely a ray of light glimmers into the narrow gallery which leads to the cells, and the places of confinement themselves are totally dark. A small hole in the wall admitted the damp air of the passages, and served for the introduction of the prisoner's food. A wooden pallet, raised a foot from the ground, was the only furniture. The conductors tell you that a light was not allowed. The cells are about five paces in length, two and a half in width, and seven feet in height. They are directly beneath one another, and respiration is somewhat difficult in the lower holes. Only one prisoner was found when the republicans descended into these hideous recesses, and he is said to have been confined sixteen years. But the inmates of the dungeons beneath had left traces of their repentance, or of their despair, which are still visible, and may, perhaps, owe something to recent ingenuity. Some of the detained appear to have offended against, and others to have belonged to, the sacred body, not only from their signatures, but from the churches and belfries which they have scratched upon the walls. The reader may not object to see a specimen of the records prompted by so terrific a solitude. As nearly as they could be copied by more than one pencil, three of them are as follows:—

1. NON TI FIDAR AD ALCUNO PENSA e TACI
SE FUGIR VUOI DE SPIONI INSIDIE e LACCI
IL PENTIRTI PENTIRTI NULLA GIOVA
MA BEN DI VALOR TUO LA VERA PROVA
1607. ADI 2. GENARO. FUI RE-
TENTO P' LA BESTIEMMA P' AVER DATO
DA MANZAR A UN MORTO
IACOMO . GRITTI . SCRISSE.

2. UN PARLAR POCHO et
NEGARE PRONTO et
UN PENSAR AL FINE PUO DARE LA VITA
A NOI ALTRI MESCHINI
1605.
EGO IOHN BAPTISTA AD
ECCLESIAM CORTELLARIUS.

3. DE CHI MI FIDO GUARDAMI DIO
DE CHI NON MI FIDO MI GUARDARO IO
A TA H A NA
V . LA S . C . K . R .

The copyist has followed, not corrected, the solecisms; some of which are, however, not quite so decided, since the letters were evidently scratched in the dark. It only need be observed, that *bestemmia* and *mangiar* may be read in the first inscription, which was probably written by a prisoner confined for some act of impiety committed at a funeral; that *Cortellarius* is the name of a parish on terra firma, near the sea; and that the last initials evidently are put for *Viva la santa Chiesa Kattolica Romana.*

No. II.—Songs of the Gondoliers.

"*In Venice Tasso's echoes are no more.*"—Stanza iii.

The well known song of the gondoliers, of alternate stanza from Tasso's Jerusalem, has died with the independence of

Venice. Editions of the poem, with the original in one column, and the Venetian variations on the other, as sung by the boatmen, were once common, and are still to be found. The following extract will serve to show the difference between the Tuscan epic and the "Canta alla Barcariola."

ORIGINAL.

Canto l' arme pietose, e 'l capitano
Che 'l gran Sepolcro liberò di Cristo.
Molto egli oprò col senno, e con la mano
Molto soffri nei glorioso acquisto;
E in van l' Inferno a lui s' oppose, e in vano
S' armò d' Asia, e di Libia il popol misto,
Che il Ciel gli diè favore, e sotto a i Santi
Segni ridusse i suoi compagni erranti.

VENETIAN.

L' arme pietose de cantar gho vogia,
E de Goffredo la immortal braura
Che al fin l' ha libera co strassia, e dogia
Del nostro buon Gesú la Sepoltura
De mezo mondo unito, e de quel Bogia
Missier Pluton non l' ha bu mai paura
Dio l' ha agiutá, e i compagni sparpagnai
Tutti 'l gh' i ha messi insieme i di del Dai.

Some of the elder gondoliers will, however, take up and continue a stanza of their once familiar bard.

On the 7th of last January, the author of Childe Harold, and another Englishman, the writer of this notice, rowed to the Lido with two singers, one of whom was a carpenter, and the other a gondolier. The former placed himself at the prow, the latter at the stern of the boat. A little after leaving the quay of the Piazzetta, they began to sing, and continued their exercise until they arrived at the island. They gave us, amongst other essays, the death of Clorinda, and the palace of Armida; and did not sing the Venetian, but the Tuscan verses. The carpenter, however, who was the cleverer of the two, and was frequently obliged to prompt his companion, told us that he could *translate* the original. He added, that he could sing almost three hundred stanzas, but had not spirits (*morbin* was the word he used) to learn any more, or to sing what he already knew; a man must have idle time on his hands to acquire, or to repeat, and, said the poor fellow, "look at my clothes and at me; I am starving."

This speech was more affecting than his performance, which habit alone can make attractive. The recitative was shrill, screaming, and monotonous; and the gondolier behind assisted his voice by holding his hand to one side of his mouth. The carpenter used a quiet action, which he evidently endeavoured to restrain; but was too much interested in his subject altogether to repress. From these men we learned that singing is not confined to the gondoliers, and that, although the chant is seldom, if ever, voluntary, there are still several amongst the lower classes who are acquainted with a few stanzas.

It does not appear that it is usual for the performers to row and sing at the same time. Although the verses of the Jerusalem are no longer casually heard, there is yet much music upon the Venetian canals; and upon holidays, those strangers who are not near or informed enough to distinguish the words, may fancy that many of the gondolas still resound with the strains of Tasso. The writer of some remarks which appeared in the "Curiosities of Literature," must excuse his being twice quoted; for, with the exception of some phrases a little too ambitious and extravagant, he has furnished a very exact, as well as agreeable, description:—

"In Venice the gondoliers know by heart long passages from Ariosto and Tasso, and often chant them with a peculiar melody. But this talent seems at present on the decline:—at least, after taking some pains, I could find no more than two persons who delivered to me in this way a passage from Tasso. I must add, that the late Mr. Berry once chanted to me a passage in Tasso in the manner, as he assured me, of the gondoliers.

"There are always two concerned, who alternately sing the strophes. We know the melody eventually by Rousseau, to whose songs it is printed; it has properly no melodious movement, and is a sort of medium between the canto fermo and the canto figurato; it approaches to the former by recitativical declamation, and to the latter by passages and course, by which one syllable is detained and embellished.

"I entered a gondola by moonlight; one singer placed himself forward and the other aft, and thus proceeded to St. Georgio. One began the song: when he had ended his strophe, the other took up the lay, and so continued the song alternately. Throughout the whole of it, the same notes invariably returned; but, according to the subject matter of the strope, they laid a greater or a smaller stress, sometimes on one, and sometimes on another note, and indeed changed the enunciation of the whole strophe as the object of the poem altered.

"On the whole, however, the sounds were hoarse and screaming: they seemed, in the manner of all rude, uncivilized men, to make the excellency of their singing in the force of their voice: one seemed desirous of conquering the other by the strength of his lungs; and so far from receiving delight from this scene, (shut up as I was in the box of the gondola,) I found myself in a very unpleasant situation.

"My companion, to whom I communicated this circumstance, being very desirous to keep up the credit of his countrymen, assured me that this singing was very delightful when heard at a distance. Accordingly we got out upon the shore, leaving one of the singers in the gondola, while the other went to the distance of some hundred paces. They now began to sing against one another, and I kept walking up and down between them both, so as always to leave him who was to begin his part. I frequently stood still and hearkened to the one and to the other.

"Here the scene was properly introduced. The strong declamatory, and, as it were, shrieking sound, met the ear from far, and called forth the attention; the quickly succeeding transitions, which necessarily required to be sung in a lower tone, seemed like plaintive strains succeeding the vociferations of emotion or of pain. The other, who listened attentively, immediately began where the former left off, answering him in the milder or more vehement notes, according as the purport of the strophe required. The sleepy canals, the lofty buildings, the splendour of the moon, the deep shadows of the few gondolas that moved like spirits hither and thither, increased the striking peculiarity of the scene; and amidst all these circumstances, it was easy to confess the character of this wonderful harmony.

"It suits perfectly well with an idle solitary mariner, lying at length in his vessel at rest on one of these canals, waiting for his company, or for a fare, the tiresomeness of which situation is somewhat alleviated by the songs and poetical stories he has in memory. He often raises his voice as loud as he can, which extends itself to a vast distance over the tranquil mirror; and as all is still around, he is, as it were, in a solitude in the midst of a large and populous town. Here is no rattling of carriages, no noise of foot passengers; a silent gondola glides now and then by him, of which the splashings of the oars are scarcely to be heard.

"At a distance he hears another, perhaps utterly unknown to him. Melody and verse immediately attach the two strangers; he becomes the responsive echo to the former, and exerts himself to be heard as he had heard the other. By a tacit convention they alternate verse for verse; though the song should last the whole night through, they entertain themselves without fatigue: the hearers, who are passing between the two, take part in the amusement.

"This vocal performance sounds best at a great distance, and is then inexpressibly charming, as it only fulfils its design in the sentiment of remoteness. It is plaintive, but not dismal in its sound, and at times it is scarcely possible to refrain from tears. My companion, who otherwise was not a very delicately organized person, said quite unexpectedly:—E singolare come quel canto intenerisce, e molto più quando lo cantano meglio.

"I was told that the women of Libo, the long row of islands that divides the Adriatic from the Lagoons,* particularly the women of the extreme districts of Malamocco and Palestrina, sing in like manner the works of Tasso to these and similar tunes.

"They have the custom, when their husbands are fishing out at sea, to sit along the shore in the evenings and vociferate these songs, and continue to do so with great violence, till each of them can distinguish the responses of her own husband at a distance."†

The love of music and of poetry distinguishes all classes of Venetians, even amongst the tuneful sons of Italy. The city itself can occasionally furnish respectable audiences for two and even three opera-houses at a time; and there are few events in private life that do not call forth a printed and circulated sonnet. Does a physician or a lawyer take his degree, or a clergyman preach his maiden sermon, has a surgeon performed an operation, would a harlequin announce his departure or his benefit, are you to be congratulated on a marriage, or a birth, or a lawsuit, the muses are invoked to furnish the same number of syllables, and the individual triumphs blaze abroad in virgin white or party-coloured placards on half the corners of the capital. The last courtesy of a favourite "prima donna" brings down a shower of these poetical tributes from those upper regions, from which, in our theatres, nothing but cupids and snow-storms are accustomed to descend. There is a poetry in the very life of a Venetian, which, in its common course, is varied with those surprises and

* The writer meant *Lido*, which is not a long row of islands, but a long island: *littus*, the shore.

† Curiosities of Literature, vol. ii. p. 156, edit. 1807; and Appendix xxix. to Black's Life of Tasso.

changes so recommendable in fiction, but so different from the sober monotony of northern existence; amusements are raised into duties, duties are softened into amusements, and every object being considered as equally making a part of the business of life, is announced and performed with the same earnest indifference and gay assiduity. The Venetian gazette constantly closes its columns with the following triple advertisement:—

Charade.

Exposition of the most Holy Sacrament in the church of St. ——

Theatres.

St. Moses, opera.
St. Benedict, a comedy of characters.
St. Luke, repose.

When it is recollected what the Catholics believe their consecrated wafer to be, we may perhaps think it worthy of a more respectable niche than between poetry and the playhouse.

No. III.—The Lion and Horses of St. Mark's.

"*St. Mark yet sees his lion where he stood*
Stand,"——Stanza xi.

The lion has lost nothing by his journey to the Invalides, but the gospel which supported the paw that is now on a level with the other foot. The horses also are returned to the ill-chosen spot whence they set out, and are, as before, half-hidden, under the porch window of St. Mark's church. Their history, after a desperate struggle, has been satisfactorily explored. The decisions and doubts of Erizzo and Zanetti, and, lastly, of the Count Leopold Cicognara, would have given them a Roman extraction, and a pedigree not more ancient than the reign of Nero. But M. de Schlegel stepped in to teach the Venetians the value of their own treasures, and a Greek vindicated, at last and forever, the pretension of his countrymen to this noble production.* M. Mustoxidi has not been left without a reply; but, as yet, he has received no

* Sui quattro cavalli della Basilica di S. Marco in Venezia. Lettera di Andrea Mustoxidi Corcirese. Padua, 1816.

answer. It should seem that the horses are irrevocably Chian, and were transferred to Constantinople by Theodosius. Lapidary writing is a favourite play of the Italians, and has conferred reputation on more than one of their literary characters. One of the best specimens of Bodoni's typography is a respectable volume of inscriptions, all written by his friend Pacciaudi. Several were prepared for the recovered horses. It is to be hoped the best was not selected, when the following words were ranged in gold letters above the cathedral porch:—

QUATUOR · EQUORUM · SIGNA · A · VENETIS · BYZANTIO · CAPTA · AD · TEMP · D · MAR · A · R · S · MCCIV · POSITA · QUÆ · HOSTILIS · CUPIDITAS · A · MDCCIIIC · ABSTULERAT · FRANC · I · IMP · PACIS · ORBI · DATÆ · TROPHÆUM · A · MDCCCXV · VICTOR · REDUXIT.

Nothing shall be said of the Latin, but it may be permitted to observe, that the injustice of the Venetians in transporting the horses from Constantinople was at least equal to that of the French in carrying them to Paris, and that it would have been more prudent to have avoided all allusions to either robbery. An apostolic prince should, perhaps, have objected to affixing over the principal entrance of a metropolitan church an inscription having reference to any other triumphs than those of religion. Nothing less than the pacification of the world can excuse such a solecism.

No. IV.—Submission of Barbarossa to Pope Alexander III.

"*The Suabian sued, and now the Austrian reigns—*
An emperor tramples where an emperor knelt." Stanza xii.

After many vain efforts on the part of the Italians entirely to throw off the yoke of Frederic Barbarossa, and as fruitless attempts of the emperor to make himself absolute master throughout the whole of his Cisalpine dominions, the bloody struggles of four-and-twenty years were happily brought to a close in the city of Venice. The articles of a treaty had been previously agreed upon between Pope Alexander III. and Barbarossa; and the former having received a safe-conduct, had already arrived at Venice from Ferrara, in company with the ambassadors of the King of Sicily and the consuls of the Lombard league. There still remained, however, many points to adjust, and for several days the peace was believed to be impracticable. At this juncture it was suddenly reported that the emperor had arrived at

Chioza a town fifteen miles from the capital. The Venetians rose tumultuously, and insisted upon immediately conducting him to the city. The Lombards took the alarm, and departed towards Treviso. The pope himself was apprehensive of some disaster if Frederic should suddenly advance upon him, but was reassured by the prudence and address of Sebastiani Ziani, the doge. Several embassies passed between Chioza and the capital, until, at last, the emperor, relaxing somewhat of his pretensions, "laid aside his leonine ferocity, and put on the mildness of the lamb."*

On Saturday, the 23d of July, in the year 1177, six Venetian galleys transferred Frederic, in great pomp, from Chioza to the island of Lido, a mile from Venice. Early the next morning the pope, accompanied by the Sicilian ambassadors, and by the envoys of Lombardy, whom he had recalled from the main land, together with a great concourse of people, repaired from the patriarchal palace to St. Mark's church, and solemnly absolved the emperor and his partisans from the excommunication pronounced against him. The Chancellor of the Empire, on the part of his master, renounced the anti-popes and their schismatic adherents. Immediately the doge, with a great suite both of the clergy and laity, got on board the galleys, and, waiting on Frederic, rowed him in mighty state from the Lido to the capital. The emperor descended from the galley at the quay of the Piazzetta. The doge, the patriarch, his bishops and clergy, and the people of Venice with their crosses and their standards, marched in solemn procession before him to the church of St. Mark. Alexander was seated before the vestibule of the basilica, attended by his bishops and cardinals, by the patriarch of Aquileja, by the archbishops and bishops of Lombardy, all of them in state, and clothed in their church robes. Frederic approached —"moved by the Holy Spirit, venerating the Almighty in the person of Alexander, laying aside his imperial dignity, and throwing off his mantle, he prostrated himself at full length at the feet of the pope. Alexander, with tears in his eyes, raised him benignantly from the ground, kissed him, blessed him; and immediately the Germans of the train sang, with a loud voice, 'We praise thee, O Lord.' The emperor then taking the pope by the right hand, led him to the church, and having received

* "Quibus auditis, imperator, operante eo, qui corda principium sicut vult et quando vult humiliter inclinat, leonina feritate deposita, ovinam mansuetudinem induit."—Romualdi Salernitani Chronicon, apud Script. Rer. Ital. tom. vii. p. 229.

his benediction, returned to the ducal palace."* The cerem ny of humiliation was repeated the next day. The pope himself, at the request of Frederic, said mass at St. Mark's. The emperor again laid aside his imperial mantle, and, taking a wand in his hand, officiated as *verger*, driving the laity from the choir, and preceding the pontiff to the altar. Alexander, after reciting the gospel, preached to the people. The emperor put himself close to the pulpit, in the attitude of listening; and the pontiff, touched by this mark of his attention, (for he knew that Frederic did not understand a word he said,) commanded the patriarch of Aquileja to translate the Latin discourse into the German tongue. The creed was then chanted. Frederic made his oblation, and kissed the pope's feet, and, mass being over, led him by the hand to his white horse. He held the stirrup, and would have led the horse's rein to the water side, had not the pope accepted of the inclination for the performance, and affectionately dismissed him with his benediction. Such is the substance of the account left by the archbishop of Salerno, who was present at the ceremony, and whose story is confirmed by every subsequent narration. It would be not worth so minute a record, were it not the triumph of liberty as well as of superstition. The states of Lombardy owed to it the confirmation of their privileges; and Alexander had reason to thank the Almighty, who had enabled an infirm, unarmed old man to subdue a terrible and potent sovereign.†

No. V.—Henry Dandolo.

"*Oh, for one hour of blind old Dandolo!*
Th' octogenarian chief, Byzantium's conquering foe." Stanza xii.

The reader will recollect the exclamation of the highlander, *Oh for one hour of Dundee!* Henry Dandolo, when elected doge, in 1192, was eighty-five years of age. When he commanded the Venetians at the taking of Constantinople, he was consequently ninety-seven years old. At this age he annexed the fourth and a half of the whole empire of Romania,‡ for so the Roman empire

* Rer. Ital. tom. vii. p. 231.

† See the above-cited Romuald of Salerno. In a second sermon which Alexander preached, on the first day of August, before the emperor, he compared Frederic to the prodigal son, and himself to the forgiving father.

‡ Mr. Gibbon has omitted the important *æ*, and has written Romani instead of Romaniæ. Decline and Fall, chap. lxi. note 9. But the title acquired by

was then called, to the title and to the territories of the Venetian doge. The three-eighths of this empire were preserved in the diplomas until the dukedom of Giovanni Dolfino, who made use of the above designation in the year 1357.*

Dandolo led the attack on Constantinople in person; two ships, the Paradise and the Pilgrim. were tied together, and a drawbridge or ladder let down from their higher yards to the walls. The doge was one of the first to rush into the city. Then was completed, said the Venetians, the prophecy of the Erythræan sibyl:—"A gathering together of the powerful shall be made amidst the waves of the Adriatic, under a blind leader; they shall beset the goat—they shall profane Byzantium—they shall blacken her buildings—her spoils shall be dispersed; a new goat shall bleat until they have measured out and run over fifty-four feet, nine inches and a half."† Dandolo died on the first of June, 1205, having reigned thirteen years, six months and five days, and was buried in the church of St. Sophia, at Constantinople. Strangely enough it must sound, that the name of the rebel apothecary who received the doge's sword, and annihilated the ancient government, in 1796–7, was Dandolo.

No. VI.—The War of Chioza.

"*But is not Doria's menace come to pass;*
Are they not bridled?"—Stanza xiii.

After the loss of the battle of Pola, and the taking of Chioza on the 16th of August, 1379, by the united armament of the Genoese and Francesco da Carrara, Signor of Padua, the Venetians were reduced to the utmost despair. An embassy was sent to the conquerors with a blank sheet of paper, praying them to prescribe what terms they pleased, and leave to Venice only her independ-

Dandolo runs thus in the chronicle of his namesake, the Doge Andrew Dandolo. "Ducali titulo addidit, 'Quartæ partis et dimidiæ totius imperii Romaniæ,'" And. Dand. Chronicon, cap. iii. pars xxxvii. ap. Script. Rer. Ital. tom. xii. page 331. And the Romaniæ is observed in the subsequent acts of the doges. Indeed, the continental possessions of the Greek empire in Europe were then generally known by the name of Romania, and that appellation is still seen in the maps of Turkey as applied to Thrace.

* See the continuation of Dandolo's Chronicle, ibid. p. 498. Mr. Gibbon appears not to include Dolfino, following Sanudo, who says, "il qual titolo si usò fin al Doge Giovanni Dolfino." See Vite de' Duchi di Venezia, ap. Script. Rer. Ital. tom. xxii. 530. 641.

† Chronicon, ibid. pars xxxiv.

ence. The Prince of Padua was inclined to listen to these pro posals, but the Genoese, who, after the victory at Pola, had shouted, "To Venice, to Venice, and long live St. George!" determined to anhihilate their rival; and Peter Doria, their commander-in-chief, returned this answer to the suppliants: "On God's faith, gentlemen of Venice, ye shall have no peace from the Signor of Padua, nor from our commune of Genoa, until we have first put a rein upon those unbridled horses of yours, that are upon the porch of your evangelist St. Mark. When we have bridled them, we shall keep you quiet. And this is the pleasure of us and of our commune. As for these my brothers of Genoa, that you have brought with you to give up to us, I will not have them; take them back; for, in a few days hence, I shall come and let them out of prison myself, both these and all the others." In fact, the Genoese did advance as far as Malamocco, within five miles of the capital; but their own danger and the pride of their enemies gave courage to the Venetians, who made prodigious efforts, and many individual sacrifices, all of them carefully recorded by their historians. Vettor Pisani was put at the head of thirty-four galleys. The Genoese broke up from Malamocco, and retired to Chioza in October; but they again threatened Venice, which was reduced to extremities. At this time, the 1st of January, 1380, arrived Carlo Zeno, who had been cruising on the Genoese coast with fourteen galleys. The Venetians were now strong enough to besiege the Genoese. Doria was killed on the 22d of January, by a stone bullet 195 pounds weight, discharged from a bombard called the Trevisan. Chioza was then closely invested: 5000 auxiliaries, amongst whom were some English condottieri, commanded by one Captain Ceccho, joined the Venetians. The Genoese, in their turn, prayed for conditions, but none were granted, until, at last, they surrendered at discretion; and, on the 24th of June, 1380, the Doge Contarini made his triumphal entry into Chioza. Four thousand prisoners, nineteen galleys, many smaller vessels and barks, with all the ammunition and arms, and outfit of the expedition, fell into the hands of the conquerors, who, had it not been for the inexorable answer of Doria, would have gladly reduced their dominion to the city of Venice. An account of these transactions is found in a work called the War of Chioza, written by Daniel Chinazzo, who was in Venice at the time.

No. VII.—Venice under the Government of Austria.

"*Thin streets, and foreign aspects, such as must*
Too oft remind her who and what enthrals."—Stanza xv.

The population of Venice at the end of the seventeenth century amounted to nearly two hundred thousand souls. At the last census, taken two years ago, it was no more than about one hundred and three thousand: and it diminishes daily. The commerce and the official employments, which were to be the unexhausted source of Venetian grandeur, have both expired. Most of the patrician mansions are deserted, and would gradually disappear, had not the government, alarmed by the demolition of seventy-two, during the last two years, expressly forbidden this sad resource of poverty. Many remnants of the Venetian nobility are now scattered and confounded with the wealthier Jews upon the banks of the Brenta, whose Palladian palaces have sunk, or are sinking, in the general decay. Of the "gentiluomo Veneto," the name is still known, and that is all. He is but the shadow of his former self, but he is polite and kind. It surely may be pardoned to him if he is querulous. Whatever may have been the vices of the republic, and although the natural term of its existence may be thought by foreigners to have arrived in the due course of mortality, only one sentiment can be expected from the Venetians themselves. At no time were the subjects of the republic so unanimous in their resolution to rally round the standard of St. Mark, as when it was for the last time unfurled; and the cowardice and the treachery of the few patricians who recommended the fatal neutrality were confined to the persons of the traitors themselves. The present race cannot be thought to regret the loss of their aristocratical forms and too despotic government; they think only on their vanished independence. They pine away at the remembrance, and on this subject suspend for a moment their gay good humour. Venice may be said, in the words of the Scripture, "to die daily;" and so general and so apparent is the decline, as to become painful to a stranger, not reconciled to the sight of a whole nation expiring as it were before his eyes. So artificial a creation, having lost that principle which called it into life and supported its existence, must fall to pieces at once, and sink more rapidly than it rose. The abhorrence of slavery which drove the Venetians to the sea, has, since their disaster, forced them to the land, where they may be at least overlooked amongst the crowd of dependants, and not present the humiliating spectacle of a whole nation loaded with recent chains. Their liveliness, their affability, and that happy indifference which constitution alone can give, (for philosophy aspires to it in vain,) have not sunk under circumstances; but many peculiarities of costume and manner have by degrees been lost, and the nobles, with a pride common to all Italians who have been masters, have not been persuaded to parade their insignificance. That splendour which was a proof and a portion of their power, they would not degrade into the trappings of their subjection. They retired from the space which they had occupied in the eyes of their fellow-citizens; their continuance in which would have been a symptom of acquiescence, and an insult to those who suffered by the common misfortune. Those who remained in the degraded capital might be said rather to haunt the scenes of their departed power, than to live in them. The reflection, "who and what enthrals," will hardly bear a comment from one who is, nationally, the friend and the ally of the conqueror. It may, however, be allowed to say thus much, that to those who wish to recover their independence, any masters must be an object of detestation; and it may be safely foretold that this unprofitable aversion will not have been corrected before Venice shall have sunk into the slime of her choked canals.

No. VIII.—Laura.

> "*Watering the tree which bears his lady's name*
> *With his melodious tears, he gave himself to fame.*"
> Stanza xxv.

Thanks to the critical acumen of a Scotchman, we now know as little of Laura as ever.* The discoveries of the Abbé de Sade, his triumphs, his sneers, can no longer instruct or amuse. We must not, however, think that these memoirs are as much a romance as Belisarius or the Incas, although we are told so by Dr. Beattie, a great name, but a little authority.† His "labour' has not been in vain, notwithstanding his "love" has, like most

---

* See An Historical and Critical Essay on the Life and Character of Petrarch, and a Dissertation on an Historical Hypothesis of the Abbé de Sade.

† Life of Beattie, by Sir W. Forbes, vol. ii. p. 106.

other passions, made him ridiculous.* The hypothesis which overpowered the struggling Italians, and carried along less interested critics in its current, is run out. We have another proof that we can be never sure that the paradox, the most singular, and therefore having the most agreeable and authentic air, will not give place to the re-established ancient prejudice.

It seems, then, first, that Laura was born, lived, died, and was buried, not in Avignon, but in the country. The fountains of the Sorga, the thickets of Cabrieres, may resume their pretensions, and the exploded *de la Bastie* again be heard with complacency. The hypothesis of the Abbé had no stronger props than the parchment sonnet and medal found on the skeleton of the wife of Hugo de Sade, and the manuscript note to the Virgil of Petrarch, now in the Ambrosian library. If these proofs were both incontestable, the poetry was written, the medal composed, cast, and deposited within the space of twelve hours: and these deliberate duties were performed round the carcass of one who died of the plague, and was hurried to the grave on the day of her death. These documents, therefore, are too decisive: they prove not the fact, but the forgery. Either the sonnet or the Virgilian note must be a falsification. The Abbé cites both as incontestably true; the consequent deduction is inevitable—they are both evidently false.†

Secondly, Laura was never married, and was a haughty virgin rather than that *tender and prudent* wife who honoured Avignon, by making that town the theatre of an honest French passion, and played off for one-and-twenty years her *little machinery* of alternate favours and refusals‡ upon the first poet of the age. It was, indeed, rather too unfair that a female should be made responsible for eleven children upon the faith of a misinterpreted abbreviation, and the decision of a librarian.§ It is, however,

* Mr. Gibbon called his Memoirs "a labour of love," (see Decline and Fall, chap. lxx. note 1,) and followed him with confidence and delight. The compiler of a very voluminous work must take much criticism upon trust. Mr. Gibbon has done so, though not as readily as some other authors.

† The sonnet had before awakened the suspicions of Mr. Horace Walpole. See his letter to Warton in 1763.

‡ "Par ce petit manège, cette alternative de faveurs et de rigueurs bien ménagée, une femme tendre et sage amuse, pendant vingt et un ans, le plus grand poëte de son siècle, sans faire la moindre brèche à son honneur." Mém. pour la Vie de Pétrarque, Preface aux Français.

§ In a dialogue with St. Augustin, Petrarch has described Laura as having a body exhausted with repeated *ptubs.* The old editors read and printed *perturbationibus:* but M. Capperonier, librarian to the French king in 1762, who saw the MS. in the Paris library, made an attestation that "on lit et qu'on doit lire,

satisfactory to think that the love of Petrarch was not platonic. The happiness which he prayed to possess but once and for a moment was surely not of the mind,* and something so very real as a marriage project, with one who has been idly called a shadowy nymph, may be, perhaps, detected in at least six places of his own sonnets. The love of Petrarch was neither platonic nor poetical: and if in one passage of his works he calls it "amore veementeissimo ma unico ed onesto," he confesses, in a letter to a friend, that it was guilty and perverse, that it absorbed him quite, and mastered his heart.

In this case, however, he was perhaps alarmed for the culpability of his wishes; for the Abbé de Sade himself, who certainly would not have been scrupulously delicate if he could have proved his descent from Petrarch as well as Laura, is forced into a stout defence of his virtuous grandmother. As far as relates to the poet, we have no security for the innocence, except perhaps in the constancy of his pursuit. He assures us in his epistle to posterity, that, when arrived at his fortieth year, he not only had in horror, but had lost all recollection and image of any "irregularity." But the birth of his natural daughter cannot be assigned earlier than his thirty-ninth year; and either the memory or the morality of the poet must have failed him, when he forgot or was guilty of this *slip*.† The weakest argument for the purity of this love has been drawn from the permanence of its effects, which survived the object of his passion. The reflection of M. de la Bastie, that virtue alone is capable of making impressions which death cannot efface, is one of those which everybody applauds, and everybody finds not to be true, the moment he examines his own breast or the records of human feeling.‡ Such apophthegms can do nothing for Petrarch or for the cause of morality, except with the very weak and the very

---

partubus exhaustum." De Sade joined the names of Messrs. Boudot and Bejot with M. Capperonier, and, in the whole discussion on this *ptubs*, showed himself a downright literary rogue. See Riflessioni, &c. p. 267. Thomas Aquinas is called in to settle whether Petrarch's mistress was a *chaste* maid or a *continent* wife.

"Pigmalion, quanto lodar ti dei
Dell' imagine tua, se mille volte
N' avesti quel ch' i' sol una vorrei."

Sonetto 58. *quando giunse a Simon l'alto concetto.*
Le Rime, &c. par. i. pag. 189. edit. Ven. 1756.

† "A questa confessione cosi sincera diede forse occasione una nuova caduta ch' ei fece." Tiraboschi, Storia, &c. v. 492.

‡ M. de Bimard, Baron de la Bastie, in the Mémoires de l'Académie des Inscriptions et Belles Lettres for 1740 and 1751. See also Riflessioni, &c. p 295

young. He that has made even a little progress beyond ignorance and pupillage cannot be edified with any thing but truth What is called vindicating the honour of an individual or a nation, is the most futile, tedious, and uninstructive of all writing although it will always meet with more applause than that sober criticism, which is attributed to the malicious desire of reducing a great man to the common standard of humanity. It is, after all, not unlikely that our historian was right in retaining his favourite hypothetic salvo, which secures the author, although it scarcely saves the honour of the still unknown mistress of Petrarch.*

No. IX.—Petrarch.

"*They keep his dust in Arquà, where he died.*"—Stanza xxxi.

Petrarch retired to Arquà immediately on his return from the unsuccessful attempt to visit Urban V. at Rome, in the year 1370 and, with the exception of his celebrated visit to Venice in company with Francesco Novello da Carrara, he appears to have passed the four last years of his life between that charming solitude and Padua. For four months previous to his death he was in a state of continual languor, and in the morning of July the 19th, in the year 1374, was found dead in his library chair with his head resting upon a book. The chair is still shown amongst the precious relics of Arquà, which, from the uninterrupted veneration that has been attached to every thing relative to this great man from the moment of his death to the present hour, have, it may be hoped, a better chance of authenticity than the Shakspearian memorials of Stratford-upon-Avon.

Arquà (for the last syllable is accented in pronunciation, although the analogy of the English language has been observed in the verse) is twelve miles from Padua, and about three miles on the right of the high road to Rovigo, in the bosom of the Euganean hills. After a walk of twenty minutes across a flat well-wooded meadow, you come to a little blue lake, clear but fathomless, and to the foot of a succession of acclivities and hills, clothed with vineyards and orchards, rich with fir and pomegranate trees, and every sunny fruit shrub. From the banks of

* "And if the virtue or prudence of Laura was inexorable, he enjoyed, and might boast of enjoying, the nymph of poetry."—Decline and Fall, chap. lxx p. 327. vol. xii. 8vo. Perhaps the *if* is here meant for *although*.

the lake the road winds into the hills, and the church of Arqua is soon seen between a cleft where two ridges slope towards each other, and nearly enclose the village. The houses are scattered at intervals on the steep sides of these summits; and that of the poet is on the edge of a little knoll overlooking two descents, and commanding a view, not only of the glowing gardens in the dales immediately beneath, but of the wide plains, above whose low woods of mulberry and willow, thickened into a dark mass by festoons of vines, tall, single cypresses, and the spires of towns, are seen in the distance, which stretches to the mouths of the Po and the shores of the Adriatic. The climate of these volcanic hills is warmer, and the vintage begins a week sooner than in the plains of Padua. Petrarch is laid, for he cannot be said to be buried, in a sarcophagus of red marble, raised on four pilasters on an elevated base, and preserved from an association with meaner tombs. It stands conspicuously alone, but will be soon overshadowed by four lately planted laurels. Petrarch's Fountain, for here every thing is Petrarch's, springs and expands itself beneath an artificial arch, a little below the church, and abounds plentifully, in the driest season, with that soft water which was the ancient wealth of the Euganean hills. It would be more attractive, were it not, in some seasons, beset with hornets and wasps. No other coincidence could assimilate the tombs of Petrarch and Archilochus. The revolutions of centuries have spared these sequestered valleys, and the only violence which has been offered to the ashes of Petrarch was prompted, not by hate, but veneration. An attempt was made to rob the sarcophagus of its treasure, and one of the arms was stolen by a Florentine through a rent which is still visible. The injury is not forgotten, but has served to identify the poet with the country where he was born, but where he would not live. A peasant boy of Arquà being asked who Petrarch was, replied, "that the people of the parsonage knew all about him, but that he only knew that he was a Florentine."

Mr. Forsyth* was not quite correct in saying that Petrarch never returned to Tuscany after he had once quitted it when a boy. It appears he did pass through Florence on his way from Parma to Rome, and on his return in the year 1350, and remained there long enough to form some acquaintance with its most distinguished inhabitants. A Florentine gentleman, ashamed of the aversion of the poet for his native country, was

* Remarks, &c. on Italy, p. 95, note, 2d edit.

eager to point out this trivial error in our accomplished traveller, whom he knew and respected for an extraordinary capacity, extensive erudition, and refined taste, joined to that engaging simplicity of manners which has been so frequently recognised as the surest, though it is certainly not an indispensable trait of superior genius.

Every footstep of Laura's lover has been anxiously traced and recorded. The house in which he lodged is shown in Venice. The inhabitants of Arezzo, in order to decide the ancient controversy between their city and the neighbouring Ancisa, where Petrarch was carried when seven months old, and remained until his seventh year, have designated by a long inscription the spot where their great fellow-citizen was born. A tablet has been raised to him at Parma, in the chapel of St. Agatha, at the cathedral, because he was archdeacon of that society, and was only snatched from his intended sepulture in their church by a *foreign* death. Another tablet, with a bust, has been erected to him at Pavia, on account of his having passed the autumn of 1368 in that city, with his son-in-law Brossano. The political condition which has for ages precluded the Italians from the criticism of the living, has concentrated their attention to the illustration of the dead.

No. X.—Tasso.

"*In face of all his foes, the Cruscan quire;*
And Boileau, whose rash envy," *&c.*—Stanza xxxviii.

Perhaps the couplet in which Boileau depreciates Tasso may serve as well as any other specimen to justify the opinion given of the harmony of French verse:—

"A Malherbe, à Racan, préfère Théophile,
Et le clinquant du Tasse à tout l'or de Virgile."—Sat. ix.

The biographer Serassi,* out of tenderness to the reputation either of the Italian or the French poet, is eager to observe that the satirist recanted or explained away this censure, and subsequently allowed the author of the Jerusalem to be a "genius, sublime, vast, and happily born for the higher flights of poetry." To this we will add, that the recantation is far from satisfactory.

---

* La Vita del Tasso, lib. iii.

when we examine the whole anecdote as reported by Olivet.* The sentence pronounced against him by Bohours† is recorded only to the confusion of the critic, whose *palinodia* the Italian makes no effort to discover, and would not, perhaps, accept. As to the opposition which the Jerusalem encountered from the Cruscan academy, who degraded Tasso from all competition with Ariosto, below Bojardo and Pulci, the disgrace of such opposition must also in some measure be laid to the charge of Alfonso, and the court of Ferrara. For Leonard Salviati, the principal and nearly the sole origin of this attack, was, there can be no doubt,‡ influenced by a hope to acquire the favour of the House of Este: an object which he thought attainable by exalting the reputation of a native poet at the expense of a rival, then a *prisoner of state.* The hopes and efforts of Salviati must serve to show the contemporary opinion as to the nature of the poet's imprisonment; and will fill up the measure of our indignation at the tyrant jailer.§ In fact, the antagonist of Tasso was not disappointed in the reception given to his criticism; he was called to the court of Ferrara, where, having endeavoured to heighten his claims to favour, by panegyrics on the family of his sovereign,‖ he was in turn abandoned, and expired in neglected poverty. The opposition of the Cruscans was brought to a close in six years after the commencement of the controversy; and if the academy owed its first renown to having almost opened with such a paradox,¶ it is probable that, on the other hand, the care of his reputation alleviated rather than aggravated the imprisonment of the injured

---

* Histoire de l'Académie Française depuis 1652 jusqu'à 1700, par l'Abbé d'Olivet. "Mais, ensuite, venant à l'usage qu'il a fait de ses talens, j'aurais montré que le bon sens n'est pas toujours ce qui domine chez lui," p. 182. Boileau said, he had not changed his opinion. "J'en ai si peu changé, dit-il," &c. p. 181.

† La Manière de bien Penser. Philanthes is for Tasso, and says in the outset, "De tous les beaux esprits que l'Italie a portés, le Tasse est peut-être celui qui pense le plus noblement." But Bohours seems to speak in Eudoxus, who closes with the absurd comparison; "Faites valoir le Tasse tant qu'il vous plaira, je m'en tiens pour moi à Virgile," &c.

‡ La Vita, &c. lib. iii. p. 90, tom. ii. The English reader may see an account of the opposition of the Crusca to Tasso, in Dr. Black, Life, &c. chap. xvii. vol. ii.

§ For a further, and it is hoped, decisive proof, that Tasso was neither more nor less than a *prisoner of state*, the reader is referred to "Historical Illustrations of the IVth Canto of Childe Harold," page 5, and following.

‖ Orazioni funebri . . . delle lodi di Don Luigi, Cardinal d'Este . . . delle odi di Donno Alfonso d' Este. See La Vita, lib. iii. p. 117.

¶ It was founded in 1582, and the Cruscan answer to Pellegrino's *Caraffa, or epica poesia*, was published in 1584.

poet. The defence of his father and of himself, for both were involved in the censure of Salviati, found employment for many of his solitary hours, and the captive could have been but little embarrassed to reply to accusations, where, amongst other delinquencies, he was charged with invidiously omitting, in his comparison between France and Italy, to make any mention of the cupola of St. Maria del Fiore at Florence.* The late biographer of Ariosto seems as if willing to renew the controversy by doubting the interpretation of Tasso's self-estimation† related in Serassi's life of the poet. But Tiraboschi had before laid that rivalry at rest,‡ by showing, that between Ariosto and Tasso it is not a question of comparison, but of preference.

No. XI.—Ariosto.

"*The lightning rent from Ariosto's bust*
The iron crown of laurel's mimick'd leaves."—Stanza xli.

Before the remains of Ariosto were removed from the Benedictine church to the library of Ferrara, his bust, which surmounted the tomb, was struck by lightning, and a crown of iron laurels melted away. The event has been recorded by a writer of the last century.§ The transfer of these sacred ashes, on the 6th of June, 1801, was one of the most brilliant spectacles of the short-lived Italian Republic; and to consecrate the memory of the ceremony, the once famous fallen *Intrepidi* were revived and reformed into the Ariostean academy. The large public place through which the procession paraded was then for the first time called Ariosto Square. The author of the Orlando is jealously claimed as the Homer, not of Italy, but Ferrara.‖ The mother of Ariosto was of Reggio, and the house in which he was born is carefully distinguished by a tablet with these words: "Qui nacque Ludovico Ariosto il giorno 8. di Settembre dell' anno

---

* "Cotanto potè sempre in lui il veleno della sua pessima volontà contro alla nazion Fiorentina." La Vita, lib. iii. pp. 96. 98. tom. ii.

† La Vita di M. L. Ariosto, scritta dall' Abate Girolamo Baruffaldi Giuniore, &c. Ferrara, 1807, lib. iii. p. 262. See "Historical Illustrations," &c. p. 26.

‡ Storia della Lett. &c. lib. iii. tom. vii. par. iii. p. 1220. sect. 4.

§ Op. di Bianconi, vol. iii. p. 176, ed. Milano, 1802; lettera al Signor Guido Savini Arcifisiocritico, sull' indole di un fulmine caduto in Dresda l'anno 1759.

‖ "Appassionata ammiratore ed invitto apologista dell' *Omera Ferrarese*" The title was first given by Tasso, and is quoted to the confusion of the *Tassisti*, ib. iii. pp. 262. 265. La Vita di M. L. Ariosto, &c.

1474." But the Ferrarese make light of the accident by which their poet was born abroad, and claim him exclusively for their own. They possess his bones, they show his arm-chair, and his inkstand, and his autographs.

"...... Hic illius arma,
Hic currus fuit ......"

The house where he lived, the room where he died, are designated by his own replaced memorial,* and by a recent inscription. The Ferrarese are more jealous of their claims since the animosity of Denina, arising from a cause which their apologists mysteriously hint is not unknown to them, ventured to degrade their soil and climate to a Bœotian incapacity for all spiritual productions. A quarto volume has been called forth by the detraction, and this supplement to Barotti's Memoirs of the illustrious Ferrarese has been considered a triumphant reply to the 'Quadro Storico Statistico dell' Alta Italia."

No. XII.—Ancient Superstitions respecting Lightning.

"*For the true laurel-wreath which glory weaves
Is of the tree no bolt of thunder cleaves.*"—Stanza xli.

The eagle, the sea calf, the laurel, and the white vine, were amongst the most approved preservatives against lightning: Jupiter chose the first, Augustus Cæsar the second, and Tiberius never failed to wear a wreath of the third when the sky threatened a thunder-storm.† These superstitions may be received without a sneer in a country where the magical properties of the hazel twig have not lost all their credit; and perhaps the reader may not be much surprised to find that a commentator on Suetonius has taken upon himself gravely to disprove the imputed virtues of the crown of Tiberius, by mentioning that a few years before he wrote a laurel was actually struck by lightning at Rome.‡

---

* "Parva sed apta mihi, sed nulli obnoxia, sed non
Sordida, parta meo sed tamen ære domus."

† Plin. Nat. Hist. lib. ii. cap. 55 Columella, lib. x. Sueton. in Vit. August. cap. xc. et in Vit. Tiberii, cap. lxix.

‡ Note 2, p. 409, edit. Lugd. Bat. 1667.

No. XIII.

"*Know that the lightning sanctifies below.*"—Stanza xli.

The Curtian lake and the Ruminal fig-tree in the Forum, having been touched by lightning, were held sacred, and the memory of the accident was preserved by a *puteal*, or altar resembling the mouth of a well, with a little chapel covering the cavity supposed to be made by the thunderbolt. Bodies scathed and persons struck dead were thought to be incorruptible;* and a stroke not fatal conferred perpetual dignity upon the man so distinguished by Heaven.†

Those killed by lightning were wrapped in a white garment, and buried where they fell. The superstition was not confined to the worshippers of Jupiter: the Lombards believed in the omens furnished by lightning; and a Christian priest confesses that, by a diabolical skill in interpreting thunder, a seer foretold to Agilulf, duke of Turin, an event which came to pass, and gave him a queen and a crown.‡ There was, however, something equivocal in this sign, which the ancient inhabitants of Rome did not always consider propitious; and as the fears are likely to last longer than the consolations of superstition, it is not strange that the Romans of the age of Leo X. should have been so much terrified at some misinterpreted storms as to require the exhortations of a scholar, who arrayed all the learning on thunder and lightning to prove the omen favourable; beginning with the flash which struck the walls of Velitræ, and including that which played upon a gate at Florence, and foretold the pontificate of one of its citizens.§

No. XIV.—The Venus of Medicis.

"*There, too, the goddess loves in stone.*"—Stanza xlix.

The view of the Venus of Medicis instantly suggests the lines in the *Seasons*, and the comparison of the object with the descrip-

---

* Vid. J. C. Bullenger, de Terræ Motu et Fulminib. lib. v. cap. xi.

† *Οὐδεὶς κεραυνωθεὶς ἄτιμός ἐστι, ὅθεν καὶ ως Θεὸς τιμᾶται.* Plut. Sympos. vid. J. C. Bulleng. ut sup.

‡ Pauli Diaconi de Gestis Langobard. lib. iii. cap. xiv.

§ I. P. Valeriani de fulminum significationibus declamatio, ap. Græv. Antiq. Rom. tom. v. p. 593. The declamation is addressed to Julian of Medicis.

tion proves, not only the correctness of the portrait, but the peculiar turn of thought, and, if the term may be used, the sexual imagination of the descriptive poet. The same conclusion may be deduced from another hint in the same episode of Musidora; for Thomson's notion of the privileges of favoured love must have been either very primitive, or rather deficient in delicacy, when he made his grateful nymph inform her discreet Damon that in some happier moment he might perhaps be the companion of her bath :—

"The time may come you need not fly."

The reader will recollect the anecdote told in the Life of Dr. Johnson. We will not leave the Florentine gallery without a word on the *Whetter*. It seems strange that the character of that disputed statue should not be entirely decided, at least in the mind of any one who has seen a sarcophagus in the vestibule of the Basilica of St. Paul without the walls, at Rome, where the whole group of the fable of Marsyas is seen in tolerable preservation; and the Scythian slave whetting the knife is represented exactly in the same position as this celebrated masterpiece. The slave is not naked; but it is easier to get rid of this difficulty than to suppose the knife in the hand of the Florentine statue an instrument for shaving, which it must be, if, as Lanzi supposes, the man is no other than the barber of Julius Cæsar. Winkelmann, illustrating a bas-relief of the same subject, follows the opinion of Leonard Agostini, and his authority might have been thought conclusive, even if the resemblance did not strike the most careless observer.* Amongst the bronzes of the same princely collection is still to be seen the inscribed tablet copied and commented upon by Mr. Gibbon.† Our historian found some difficulties, but did not desist from his illustration: he might be vexed to hear that his criticism has been thrown away on an inscription now generally recognised to be a forgery.

No. XV.—Madame de Stael.

"*In Santa Croce's holy precincts lie.*"—Stanza liv.

This name will recall the memory, not only of those whose tombs have raised the Santa Croce into the centre of pilgrimage,

---

* See Monim. Ant. Ined. par. i. cap. xvii. n. xlii. pag. 50; and Storia dell' Arti, &c. lib. xi. cap. i. tom. ii. pag. 314, not. B.

† Nomina gentesque Antiquæ Italiæ, p. 204, edit. oct.

the Mecca of Italy, but of her whose eloquence was poured over the illustrious ashes, and whose voice is now as mute as those she sung. CORINNA is no more; and with her should expire the fear, the flattery, and the envy, which threw too dazzling or too dark a cloud round the march of genius, and forbade the steady gaze of disinterested criticism. We have her picture embellished or distorted, as friendship or detraction has held the pencil: the impartial portrait was hardly to be expected from a contemporary. The immediate voice of her survivors will, it is probable, be far from affording a just estimate of her singular capacity. The gallantry, the love of wonder, and the hope of associated fame, which blunted the edge of censure, must cease to exist.—The dead have no sex; they can surprise by no new miracles; they can confer no privilege: Corinna has ceased to be a woman—she is only an author: and it may be foreseen that many will repay themselves for former complaisance, by a severity to which the extravagance of previous praises may perhaps give the colour of truth. The latest posterity, for to the latest posterity they will assuredly descend, will have to pronounce upon her various productions; and the longer the vista through which they are seen, the more accurately minute will be the object, the more certain the justice, of the decision. She will enter into that existence in which the great writers of all ages and nations are, as it were, associated in a world of their own, and, from that superior sphere, shed their eternal influence for the control and consolation of mankind. But the individual will gradually disappear as the author is more distinctly seen: some one, therefore, of all those whom the charms of involuntary wit, and of easy hospitality, attracted within the friendly circles of Coppet, should rescue from oblivion those virtues which, although they are said to love the shade, are, in fact, more frequently chilled than excited by the domestic cares of private life. Some one should be found to portray the unaffected graces with which she adorned those dearer relationships, the performance of whose duties is rather discovered amongst the interior secrets, than seen in the outward management, of family intercourse; and which, indeed, it requires the delicacy of genuine affection to qualify for the eye of an indifferent spectator. Some one should be found, not to celebrate, but to describe, the amiable mistress of an open mansion, the centre of a society, ever varied, and always pleased, the creator of which, divested of the ambition and the arts of public rivalry, shone forth only to give fresh animation to those around her. The mother tenderly affectionate and tenderly beloved, the friend unboundedly generous, but still esteemed, the charitable patroness of all distress, cannot be forgotten by those whom she cherished, and protected, and fed. Her loss will be mourned the most where she was known the best; and, to the sorrows of very many friends, and more dependants, may be offered the disinterested regret of a stranger, who, amidst the sublimer scenes of the Leman lake, received his chief satisfaction from contemplating the engaging qualities of the incomparable Corinna.

No. XVI.—Alfieri.

"*Here repose*
Angelo's, Alfieri's bones."—Stanza liv.

Alfieri is the great name of this age. The Italians, without waiting for the hundred years, consider him as "a poet good in law."—His memory is the more dear to them because he is the bard of freedom; and because, as such, his tragedies can receive no countenance from any of their sovereigns. They are but very seldom, and but very few of them, allowed to be acted. It was observed by Cicero, that nowhere were the true opinions and feelings of the Romans so clearly shown as at the theatre.* In the autumn of 1816, a celebrated improvvisatore exhibited his talents at the Opera-house of Milan. The reading of the theses handed in for the subjects of his poetry was received by a very numerous audience, for the most part in silence, or with laughter; but when the assistant, unfolding one of the papers, exclaimed, *The apotheosis of Victor Alfieri*, the whole theatre burst into a shout, and the applause was continued for some moments. The lot did not fall on Alfieri; and the Signor Sgricci had to pour forth his extemporary commonplaces on the bombardment of Algiers. The

---

* The free expression of their honest sentiments survived their liberties. Titius, the friend of Antony, presented them with games in the theatre of Pompey. They did not suffer the brilliancy of the spectacle to efface from their memory that the man who furnished them with the entertainment had murdered the son of Pompey: they drove him from the theatre with curses. The moral sense of a populace, spontaneously expressed, is never wrong. Even the soldiers of the triumvirs joined in the execration of the citizens, by shouting round the chariots of Lepidus and Plancus, who had proscribed their brothers, *De Germanis non de Gallis duo triumphant Consules;* a saying worth a record, were it nothing but a good pun. [C. Vell. Paterculi Hist. lib. ii. cap. lxxix. pag 78. edit. Elzevir. 1639. Ibid. lib. ii. cap. lxxvii.]

choice, indeed, is not left to accident quite so much as might be thought from a first view of the ceremony; and the police not only takes care to look at the papers beforehand, but, in case of any prudential after-thought, steps in to correct the blindness of chance. The proposal for deifying Alfieri was received with immediate enthusiasm, the rather because it was conjectured here would be no opportunity of carrying it into effect.

No. XVII.—Machiavelli.

"*Here Machiavelli's earth return'd to whence it rose.*"—
Stanza liv.

The affectation of simplicity in sepulchral inscriptions, which so often leaves us uncertain whether the structure before us is an actual depository, or a cenotaph, or a simple memorial not of death but life, has given to the tomb of Machiavelli no information as to the place or time of the birth or death, the age or parentage, of the historian.

TANTO NOMINI NVLLVM PAR ELOGIVM
NICCOLAVS MACHIAVELLI.

There seems at least no reason why the name should not have been put above the sentence which alludes to it.

It will readily be imagined that the prejudices which have passed the name of Machiavelli into an epithet proverbial of iniquity exist no longer at Florence. His memory was persecuted, as his life had been, for an attachment to liberty incompatible with the new system of despotism which succeeded the fall of the free governments of Italy. He was put to the torture for being a "libertine," that is, for wishing to restore the republic of Florence; and such are the undying efforts of those who are interested in the perversion, not only of the nature of actions, but the meaning of words, that what was once *patriotism*, has by degrees come to signify *debauch*. We have ourselves outlived the old meaning of "liberality," which is now another word for treason in one country and for infatuation in all. It seems to have been a strange mistake to accuse the author of "The Prince," as being a pander to tyranny; and to think that the In quisition would condemn his work for such a delinquency. The fact is, that Machiavelli, as is usual with those against whom no crime can be proved, was suspected of and charged with atheism; and the first and last most violent opposers of "The

Prince" were both Jesuits, one of whom persuaded the Inquisition, "benchè fosse tardo," to prohibit the treatise, and the other qualified the secretary of the Florentine republic as no better than a fool. The father Possevin was proved never to have read the book, and the father Lucchesini not to have understood it. It is clear, however, that such critics must have objected not to the slavery of the doctrines, but to the supposed tendency of a lesson which shows how distinct are the interests of a monarch from the happiness of mankind. The Jesuits are re-established in Italy, and the last chapter of "The Prince" may again call forth a particular refutation from those who are employed once more in moulding the minds of the rising generation, so as to receive the impressions of despotism. The chapter bears for title, "Esortazione a liberare la Italia dai Barbari," and concludes with a *libertine* excitement to the future redemption of Italy. "Non si deve adunque lasciar passare questa occasione, acciocchè la Italia vegga dopo tanto tempo apparire un suo redentore. Nè posso esprimere con qual amore ei fusse ricevuto in tutte quelle provincie, che hanno patito per queste illuvioni esterne, con qual sete di vendetta, con che ostinata fede, con che lacrime. Quali porte se li serrerebeno? Quali popoli li negherebbono la obbedienza? Quale Italiano li negherebbe l'ossequio? AD OGNUNO PUZZA QUESTO BARBARO DOMINIO."*

No. XVIII.—Dante.

"*Ungrateful Florence! Dante sleeps afar.*"—Stanza lvii.

Dante was born in Florence, in the year 1261. He fought in two battles, was fourteen times ambassador, and once prior of the republic. When the party of Charles of Anjou triumphed over the Bianchi, he was absent on an embassy to Pope Boniface VIII., and was condemned to two years' banishment, and to a fine of 8000 lire; on the non-payment of which he was further punished by the sequestration of all his property. The republic, however, was not content with this satisfaction, for in 1772 was discovered in the archives at Florence a sentence in which Dante is the eleventh of a list of fifteen condemned in 1302 to be burnt alive; *Talis perveniens igne comburatur sic quoa*

---

* Il Principe di Niccolò Machiavelli, &c., con la prefazione e le note istoriche e politiche di M. Amelot de la Houssaye e l' esame e confutazione dell' opera . . Cosmopoli. 1769.

moriatur. The pretext for this judgment was a proof of unfair barter, extortions, and illicit gains. *Baracteriarum iniquarum, extorsionum et illicitorum lucrorum*,* and with such an accusation it is not strange that Dante should have always protested his innocence, and the injustice of his fellow-citizens. His appeal to Florence was accompanied by another to the Emperor Henry; and the death of that sovereign in 1313 was the signal for a sentence of irrevocable banishment. He had before lingered near Tuscany with hopes of recall; then travelled into the north of Italy, where Verona had to boast of his longest residence; and he finally settled at Ravenna, which was his ordinary but not constant abode until his death. The refusal of the Venetians to grant him a public audience, on the part of Guido Novello da Polenta, his protector, is said to have been the principal cause of this event, which happened in 1321. He was buried ("in sacra minorum æde") at Ravenna, in a handsome tomb, which was erected by Guido, restored by Bernardo Bembo in 1483, prætor for that republic which had refused to hear him; again restored by Cardinal Corsi, in 1692, and replaced by a more magnificent sepulchre, constructed in 1780 at the expense of the Cardinal Luigi Valenti Gonzaga. The offence or misfortune of Dante was an attachment to a defeated party, and, as his least favourable biographers allege against him, too great a freedom of speech and haughtiness of manner. But the next age paid honours almost divine to the exile. The Florentines, having in vain and frequently attempted to recover his body, crowned his image in a church,† and his picture is still one of the idols of their cathedral. They struck medals, they raised statues to him. The cities of Italy, not being able to dispute about his own birth, contended for that of his great poem; and the Florentines thought it for their honour to prove that he had finished the seventh canto before they drove him from his native city. Fifty-one years after his death, they endowed a professorial chair for the expounding of his verses, and Boccaccio was appointed to this patriotic employment. The example was imitated by Bologna and Pisa, and the commentators, if they performed but little service to literature, augmented the veneration which beheld a sacred or moral allegory in all the images of his mystic muse. His birth and his infancy were discovered to have been distin-

---

* Storia della Lett. Ital. tom. v. lib. iii. par. 2, p. 448. Tiraboschi is incorrect; the dates of the three decrees against Dante are A. D. 1302, 1314, and 1316.

† So relates Ficino, but some think his coronation only an allegory. See Storia, &c. ut sup. p. 453.

guished above those of ordinary men: the author of the Decameron, his earliest biographer, relates that his mother was warned in a dream of the importance of her pregnancy: and it was found, by others, that at ten years of age he had manifested his precocious passion for that wisdom or theology, which, under the name of Beatrice, had been mistaken for a substantial mistress. When the Divine Comedy had been recognised as a mere mortal production, and at the distance of two centuries, when criticism and competition had sobered the judgment of the Italians, Dante was seriously declared superior to Homer;* and though the preference appeared to some casuists "an heretical blasphemy worthy of the flames," the contest was vigorously maintained for nearly fifty years. In later times it was made a question which of the Lords of Verona could boast of having patronised him,† and the jealous skepticism of one writer would not allow Ravenna the undoubted possession of his bones. Even the critical Tiraboschi was inclined to believe that the poet had foreseen and foretold one of the discoveries of Galileo.—Like the great originals of other nations, his popularity has not always maintained the same level. The last age seemed inclined to undervalue him as a model and a study: and Bettinelli one day rebuked his pupil Monti, for poring over the harsh and obsolete extravagances of the Commedia. The present generation having recovered from the Gallic idolatries of Cesarotti, has returned to the ancient worship, and the *Danteggiare* of the northern Italians is thought even indiscreet by the more moderate Tuscans.

There is still much curious information relative to the life and writings of this great poet, which has not as yet been collected even by the Italians; but the celebrated Ugo Foscolo meditates to supply this defect, and it is not to be regretted that this national work has been reserved for one so devoted to his country and the cause of truth.

---

* By Varchi, in his Ercolano. The controversy continued from 1570 to 1616 See Storia, &c. tom. vii. lib. iii. par. iii. p. 1280.

† Gio. Jacopo Dionisi Canonico di Verona. Serie di Aneddoti, n. 2. See Storia, &c. tom. v lib. i. par. i. p. 24.

No. XIX.—Tomb of the Scipios.

"*Like Scipio, buried by the upbraiding shore;*
Thy factions, in their worse than civil war,
Proscribed," *&c.*—Stanza lvii.

The elder Scipio Africanus, had a tomb if he was not buried at Liternum, whither he had retired to voluntary banishment. This tomb was near the sea-shore, and the story of an inscription upon it, *Ingrata Patria*, having given a name to a modern tower, is, if not true, an agreeable fiction. If he was not buried, he certainly lived there.*

In così angusta e solitaria villa
Era 'l grand' uomo che d' Africa s' appella
Perchè prima col ferro al vivo aprilla.†

Ingratitude is generally supposed the vice peculiar to republics; and it seems to be forgotten that for one instance of popular inconstancy, we have a hundred examples of the fall of courtly favourites. Besides, a people have often repented—a monarch seldom or never. Leaving apart many familiar proofs of this fact, a short story may show the difference between even an aristocracy and the multitude.

Vettor Pisani, having been defeated in 1354 at Portolongo, and many years afterwards in the more decisive action of Pola, by the Genoese, was recalled by the Venetian government, and thrown into chains. The Avvogadori proposed to behead him, but the supreme tribunal was content with the sentence of imprisonment. Whilst Pisani was suffering this unmerited disgrace, Chioza, in the vicinity of the capital,‡ was, by the assistance of the *Signor of Padua*, delivered into the hands of Pietro Doria. At the intelligence of that disaster, the great bell of St. Mark's tower tolled to arms, and the people and the soldiery of the galleys were summoned to the repulse of the approaching enemy; but they protested they would not move a step, unless Pisani were liberated and placed at their head. The great council was instantly assembled: the prisoner was called before them, and the Doge, Andrea Contarini, informed him of the demands of the people, and the necessities of the state, whose only hope of safety was reposed in his efforts, and who

---

* Vitam Literni egit sine desiderio urbis. See T. Liv. Hist. lib. xxxviii. Livy reports that some said he was buried at Liternum, others at Rome. Ibid. cap. lv

† Trionfo della Castità.

‡ See Note VI. page 290.

implored him to forget the indignities he had endured in her service. "I have submitted," replied the magnanimous republican, "I have submitted to your deliberations without complaint; I have supported patiently the pains of imprisonment, for they were inflicted at your command: this is no time to inquire whether I deserved them—the good of the republic may have seemed to require it, and that which the republic resolves is always resolved wisely. Behold me ready to lay down my life for the preservation of my country." Pisani was appointed generalissimo, and by his exertions, in conjunction with those of Carlo Zeno, the Venetians soon recovered the ascendancy over their maritime rivals.

The Italian communities were no less unjust to their citizens than the Greek republics. Liberty, both with the one and the other, seems to have been a national, not an individual object: and, notwithstanding the boasted *equality before the laws*, which an ancient Greek writer* considered the great distinctive mark between his countrymen and the barbarians, the mutual rights of fellow-citizens seem never to have been the principal scope of the old democracies. The world may have not yet seen an essay by the author of the Italian Republics, in which the distinction between the liberty of former states and the signification attached to that word by the happier constitution of England, is ingeniously developed. The Italians, however, when they had ceased to be free, still looked back with a sigh upon those times of turbulence, when every citizen might rise to a share of sovereign power, and have never been taught fully to appreciate the repose of a monarchy. Sperone Speroni, when Francis Maria II. Duke of Rovere proposed the question, "Which was preferable, the republic or the principality—the perfect and not durable, or the less perfect and not so liable to change," replied, "That our happiness is to be measured by its quality, not by its duration; and that he preferred to live for one day like a man, than for a hundred years like a brute, a stock, or a stone." This was thought, and called, a *magnificent* answer, down to the last days of Italian servitude.†

---

* The Greek boasted that he was ἰσονόμος. See the last chapter of the first book of Dionysius of Halicarnassus.

† "E intorno *alla magnifica risposta*," &c. Serassi, Vita del Tasso, lib. iii. pag 149, tom. ii. edit. 3, Bergamo.

No. XX.—Petrarch's Crown.

"*And the crown*
Which Petrarch's laureate brow supremely wore,
Upon a far and foreign soil had grown."—Stanza lvii.

The Florentines did not take the opportunity of Petrarch' short visit to their city in 1350, to revoke the decree which confiscated the property of his father, who had been banished shortly after the exile of Dante. His crown did not dazzle them; but when in the next year they were in want of his assistance in the formation of their university, they repented of their injustice, and Boccaccio was sent to Padua to entreat the laureate to conclude his wanderings in the bosom of his native country, where he might finish his *immortal Africa*, and enjoy, with his recovered possessions, the esteem of all classes of his fellow-citizens. They gave him the option of the book and the science he might condescend to expound: they called him the glory of his country, who was dear, and who would be dearer to them; and they added, that if there was any thing unpleasing in their letter, he ought to return amongst them, were it only to correct their style.* Petrarch seemed at first to listen to the flattery and to the entreaties of his friend, but he did not return to Florence, and preferred a pilgrimage to the tomb of Laura and the shades of Vaucluse.

No. XXI.—Boccaccio.

"*Boccaccio to his parent earth bequeathed*
His dust."—Stanza lviii.

Boccaccio was buried in the church of St. Michael and St. James, at Certaldo, a small town in the Valdelsa, which was by some supposed the place of his birth. There he passed the latter part of his life in a course of laborious study, which shortened his existence; and there might his ashes have been secure, if not of honour at least of repose. But the "hyena bigots" of Certaldo

* "Accingiti innoltre, se ci è lecito ancor l' esortarti, a compire l' immortal ua Africa . . . Se ti avviene d' incontrare nel nostro stile cosa che ti dispiaccia, ciò debb' essere un altro motivo ad esaudire i desiderj della tua patria." Storia della Lett. Ital. tom. v. par. i. lib. i. pag. 76.

tore up the tombstone of Boccaccio, and ejected it from the holy precincts of St. Michael and St. James. The occasion, and, it may be hoped, the excuse, of this ejectment was the making of a new floor for the church; but the fact is, that the tombstone was taken up and thrown aside at the bottom of the building. Ignorance may share the sin with bigotry. It would be painful to relate such an exception to the devotion of the Italians for their great names, could it not be accompanied by a trait more honourably conformable to the general character of the nation. The principal person of the district, the last branch of the house of Medicis, afforded that protection to the memory of the insulted dead which her best ancestors had dispensed upon all contemporary merit. The Marchioness Lenzoni rescued the tombstone of Boccaccio from the neglect in which it had some time lain, and found for it an honourable elevation in her own mansion. She has done more; the house in which the poet lived has been as little respected as his tomb, and is falling to ruin over the head of one indifferent to the name of its former tenant. It consists of two or three little chambers, and a low tower, on which Cosmo II. affixed an inscription. This house she has taken measures to purchase, and proposes to devote to it that care and consideration which are attached to the cradle and to the roof of genius.

This is not the place to undertake the defence of Boccaccio; but the man who exhausted his little patrimony in the acquirement of learning; who was amongst the first, if not the first, to allure the science and the poetry of Greece to the bosom of Italy; —who not only invented a new style, but founded, or certainly fixed, a new language; who, besides the esteem of every polite court of Europe, was thought worthy of employment by the predominant republic of his own country, and, what is more, of the friendship of Petrarch, who lived the life of a philosopher and a freeman, and who died in the pursuit of knowledge,—such a man might have found more consideration than he has met with from the priest of Certaldo, and from a late English traveller, who strikes off his portrait as an odious, contemptible, licentious writer, whose impure remains should be suffered to rot without a record.* That English traveller, unfortunately for those who

* Classical Tour, chap. ix. vol. ii. p. 355, edit. 3d. "Of Boccaccio, the modern Petronius, we say nothing; the abuse of genius is more odious and more contemptible than its absence; and it imports little where the impure remains of a licentious author are consigned to their kindred dust. For the same reason

have to deplore the loss of a very amiable person, is beyond all criticism; but the mortality which did not protect Boccacio from Mr. Eustace, must not defend Mr. Eustace from the impartial judgment of his successors. Death may canonize his virtues, not his errors; and it may be modestly pronounced that he transgressed, not only as an author, but as a man, when he evoked the shade of Boccaccio in company of that of Aretine, amidst the sepulchres of Santa Croce, merely to dismiss it with indignity. As far as respects

"Il flagello de' Principi,
Il divin Pietro Aretino,"

it is of little import what censure is passed upon a coxcomb who owes his present existence to the above burlesque character given to him by the poet, whose amber has preserved many other grubs and worms: but to classify Boccaccio with such a person, and to excommunicate his very ashes, must of itself make us doubt of the qualification of the classical tourist for writing upon Italian, or, indeed, upon any other literature; for ignorance on one point may incapacitate an author merely for that particular topic, but subjection to a professional prejudice must render him an unsafe director on all occasions. Any perversion and injustice may be made what is vulgarly called "a case of conscience," and this poor excuse is all that can be offered for the priest of Certaldo, or the author of the Classical Tour. It would have answered the purpose to confine the censure to the novels of Boccaccio; and gratitude to that source which supplied the muse of Dryden with her last and most harmonious numbers might, perhaps, have restricted that censure to the objectionable qualities of the hundred tales. At any rate, the repentance of Boccaccio might have arrested his exhumation, and it should have been recollected and told, that in his old age he wrote a letter entreating his friend to discourage the reading of the Decameron, for the sake of modesty, and for the sake of the author, who would not have an apologist always at hand to state in his excuse that he wrote it when young, and at the command of his superiors.* It is neither the licen-

the traveller may pass unnoticed the tomb of the malignant Aretino." This dubious phrase is hardly enough to save the tourist from the suspicion of another blunder respecting the burial-place of Aretino, whose tomb was in the church of St. Luke at Venice, and gave rise to the famous controversy of which some notice is taken in Bayle. Now the words of Mr. Eustace would lead us to think the tomb was at Florence, or at least was to be somewhere recognised. Whether the inscription so much disputed was ever written on the tomb cannot now be decided, for all memorial of this author has disappeared from the church of St. Luke.

* "Non enim ubique est, qui in excusationem meam consurgens dicat, juvenis

iousness of the writer, nor the evil propensities of the reader, which have given to the Decameron alone, of all the works of Boccaccio, a perpetual popularity. The establishment of a new and delightful dialect conferred an immortality on the works in which it was first fixed. The sonnets of Petrarch were, for the same reason, fated to survive his self-admired Africa, the "favourite of kings." The invariable traits of nature and feeling with which the novels, as well as the verses, abound, have doubtless been the chief source of the foreign celebrity of both authors; but Boccaccio, as a man, is no more to be estimated by that work, than Petrarch is to be regarded in no other light than as the lover of Laura. Even, however, had the father of the Tuscan prose been known only as the author of the Decameron, a considerate writer would have been cautious to pronounce a sentence irreconcilable with the unerring voice of many ages and nations. An irrevocable value has never been stamped upon any work solely recommended by impurity.

The true source of the outcry against Boccaccio, which began at a very early period, was the choice of his scandalous personages in the cloisters as well as the courts; but the princes only laughed at the gallant adventures so unjustly charged upon queen Theodelinda, whilst the priesthood cried shame upon the debauches drawn from the convent and the hermitage; and most probably for the opposite reason, namely, that the picture was faithful to the life. Two of the novels are allowed to be facts usefully turned into tales to deride the canonization of rogues and laymen. Ser Ciappelletto and Marcellinus are cited with applause even by the decent Muratori.* The great Arnaud, as he is quoted in Bayle, states, that a new edition of the novels was proposed, of which the expurgation consisted in omitting the words "monk" and "nun," and tacking the immoralities to other names. The literary history of Italy particularizes no such edition; but it was not long before the whole of Europe had but one opinion of the Decameron; and the absolution of the author seems to have been a point settled at least a hundred years ago. "On se feroit siffler si l'on prétendoit convaincre Boccace de n'avoir pas été honnête homme, puis qu'il a fait le Décameron." So said one of the best men, and perhaps the best critic that ever lived—the

scripsit, et majoris coactus imperio." The letter was addressed to Maghinard of Cavalcanti, marshal of the kingdom of Sicily. See Tiraboschi, Storia, &c tom. v. par. ii. lib. iii.

* Dissertazioni sopra le Antichità Italiane, Diss. lviii.

very martyr to impartiality.* But as this information, that in the beginning of the last century, one would have been hooted at for pretending that Boccaccio was not a good man, may seem to come from one of those enemies who are to be suspected, even when they make us a present of truth, a more acceptable contrast with the proscription of the body, soul, and muse of Boccaccio may be found in a few words from the virtuous, the patriotic contemporary, who thought one of the tales of this impure writer worthy a Latin version from his own pen. "I have remarked elsewhere," says Petrarch, writing to Boccaccio, "that the book itself has been worried by certain dogs, but stoutly defended by your staff and voice. Nor was I astonished, for I have had proof of the vigour of your mind, and I know you have fallen on that unaccommodating, incapable race of mortals, who, whatever they either like not, or know not, or cannot do, are sure to reprehend in others; and on those occasions only put on a show of learning and eloquence, but otherwise are entirely dumb."*

It is satisfactory to find that all the priesthood do not resemble those of Certaldo, and that one of them who did not possess the bones of Boccaccio would not lose the opportunity of raising a cenotaph to his memory. Bevius, canon of Padua, at the beginning of the sixteenth century, erected at Arquà, opposite to the tomb of the Laureate, a tablet, in which he associated Boccaccio to the equal honours of Dante and of Petrarch.

No. XXII.—The Medici.

"*What is her pyramid of precious stones?*"—Stanza lx.

Our veneration for the Medici begins with Cosmo, and expires with his grandson; that stream is pure only at the source; and it is in search of some memorial of the virtuous republicans of the family, that we visit the church of St. Lorenzo at Florence. The tawdry, glaring, unfinished chapel in that church, designed for the mausoleum of the dukes of Tuscany, set round with crowns and coffins, gives birth to no emotions but those of contempt for the lavish vanity of a race of despots, whilst the pavement slab, simply inscribed to the father of his country, reconciles us to the name

---

* *Eclaircissement*, &c. &c. p. 638, edit. Basle, 1741, in the Supplement to Bayle's Dictionary.

† Opp. tom. i. p. 540, edit. Basil.

of Medici.* It was very natural for Corinna† to suppose that the statue raised to the Duke of Urbino in the *capella de' depositi* was intended for his great namesake; but the magnificent Lorenzo is only the sharer of a coffin half hidden in a niche of the sacristy. The decay of Tuscany dates from the sovereignty of the Medici. Of the sepulchral peace which succeeded to the establishment of the reigning families in Italy, our own Sidney has given us a glowing, but a faithful picture. "Notwithstanding all the seditions of Florence, and other cities of Tuscany, the horrid factions of Guelphs and Ghibelins, Neri and Bianchi, nobles and commons, they continued populous, strong, and exceeding rich; but in the space of less than a hundred and fifty years, the peaceable reign of the Medices is said to have destroyed nine parts in ten of the people of that province. Amongst other things, it is remarkable, that when Philip II. of Spain gave Sienna to the Duke of Florence, his ambassador then at Rome sent him word, that he had given away more than 65,000 subjects; and it is not believed there are now 20,000 souls inhabiting that city and territory. Pisa, Pistoia, Arezzo, Cortona, and other towns, that were then good and populous, are in the like proportion diminished, and Florence more than any. When that city had been long troubled with seditions, tumults, and war, for the most part unprosperous, they still retained such strength, that when Charles VIII. of France, being admitted as a friend with his whole army, which soon after conquered the kingdom of Naples, thought to master them, the people, taking arms, struck such a terror into him, that he was glad to depart upon such conditions as they thought fit to impose. Machiavel reports, that in that time Florence alone, with the Val d'Arno, a small territory belonging to that city, could, in a few hours, by the sound of a bell, bring together 135,000 well-armed men; whereas now that city, with all the others in the province, are brought to such despicable weakness, emptiness, poverty, and baseness, that they can neither resist the oppression of their own prince, nor defend him or themselves if they were assaulted by a foreign enemy. The people are dispersed or destroyed, and the best families sent to seek habitations in Venice, Genoa, Rome, Naples, and Lucca. This is not the effect of war or pestilence: they enjoy a perfect peace, and suffer no other plague than the government they are under."‡ From

* Cosmus Medices, Decreto Publico, Pater Patriæ.

† Corinne, liv. xviii. chap. iii. vol. iii. page 248.

‡ On Government, chap. ii. sect. xxvi. pag. 208, edit. 1751. Sidney is, together with Locke and Hoadley, one of Mr. Hume's "despicable" writers.

the usurper Cosmo down to the imbecile Gaston, we look in vain for any of those unmixed qualities which should raise a patriot to the command of his fellow citizens. The grand dukes, and particularly the third Cosmo, had operated so entire a change in the Tuscan character, that the candid Florentines, in excuse for some imperfections in the philanthropic system of Leopold, are obliged to confess that the sovereign was the only liberal man in his dominions. Yet that excellent prince himself had no other notion of a national assembly, than of a body to represent the wants and wishes, not the will, of the people.

No. XXIII.—Battle of Thrasimene.

"*An earthquake reel'd unheededly away.*"—Stanza lxiii.

"And such was their mutual animosity, so intent were they upon the battle, that the earthquake, which overthrew in great part many of the cities of Italy, which turned the course of rapid streams, poured back the sea upon the rivers, and tore down the very mountains, was not felt by one of the combatants."* Such is the description of Livy. It may be doubted whether modern tactics would admit of such an abstraction.

The site of the battle of Thrasimene is not to be mistaken. The traveller from the village under Cortona to Casa di Piano, the next stage on the way to Rome, has for the first two or three miles, around him, but more particularly to the right, that flat land which Hannibal laid waste in order to induce the Consul Flaminius to move from Arezzo. On his left, and in front of him, is a ridge of hills, bending down towards the lake of Thrasimene, called by Livy "montes Cortonenses," and now named the Gualandra. These hills he approaches at Ossaja, a village which the itineraries pretend to have been so denominated from the bones found there: but there have been no bones found there, and the battle was fought on the other side of the hill. From Ossaja the road begins to rise a little, but does not pass into the roots of the mountains until the sixty-seventh milestone from Florence. The ascent thence is not steep but perpetual, and continues for twenty minutes. The lake is soon seen below on the right, with Borghetto, a round tower, close upon the water; and the undu-

* Tit. Liv. lib. xxii. cap. xii.

lating hills partially covered with wood, amongst which the road winds, sink by degrees into the marshes near to this tower. Lower than the road, down to the right of these woody hillocks, Hannibal placed his horse* in the jaws of, or rather above the pass, which was between the lake and the present road, and most probably close to Borghetto, just under the lowest of the "tumuli."† On a summit to the left, above the road, is an old circular ruin, which the peasants call "the tower of Hannibal the Carthaginian." Arrived at the highest point of the road, the traveller has a partial view of the fatal plain, which opens fully upon him as he descends the Gualandra. He soon finds himself in a vale enclosed to the left, and in front, and behind, by the Gualandra hills, bending round in a segment larger than a semicircle, and running down at each end to the lake, which obliques to the right, and forms the chord of the mountain arc. The position cannot be guessed at from the plains of Cortona, nor appears to be so completely enclosed unless to one who is fairly within the hills. It then, indeed, appears "a place made as it were on purpose for a snare," *locus insidiis natus.* "Borghetto is then found to stand in a narrow marshy pass close to the hill, and to the lake, whilst there is no other outlet at the opposite turn of the mountains than through the little town of Passignano, which is pushed into the water by the foot of a high rocky acclivity." There is a woody eminence branching down from the mountains into the upper end of the plain nearer to the side of Passignano, and on this stands a white village called Torre. Polybius seems to allude to this eminence as the one on which Hannibal encamped, and drew out his heavy-armed Africans and Spaniards in a conspicuous position.‡ From this spot he despatched his Balearic and light-armed troops round through the Gualandra heights to the right, so as to arrive unseen and form an ambush amongst the broken acclivities which the road now passes, and to be ready to act upon the left flank and above the enemy, whilst the horse shut up the pass behind. Flaminius came to the lake near Borghetto at sunset; and, without sending any spies before him, marched through the pass the next morning before the day had quite broken, so that he perceived nothing of the horse and light troops above and about him, and saw only the heavy-armed

---

* Tit. Liv. lib. xxii. cap. iv. † Ibid.

‡ Hist. lib. iii. cap. 83. The account in Polybius is not so easily reconcilable with present appearances as that in Livy; he talks of hills to the right and left of the pass and valley; but when Flaminius entered he had the lake at the right of both.

Carthaginians in front on the hill of Torre. The consul began to draw out his army in the flat, and in the mean time the horse in ambush occupied the pass behind him at Borghetto. Thus the Romans were completely enclosed, having the lake on the right, the main army on the hill of Torre in front, the Gualandra hills filled with the light-armed on their left flank, and being prevented from receding by the cavalry, who, the farther they advanced, stopped up all the outlets in the rear. A fog rising from the lake now spread itself over the army of the consul, but the high lands were in the sunshine, and all the different corps in ambush looked toward the hill of Torre for the order of attack. Hannibal gave the signal, and moved down from his post on the height. At the same moment all his troops on the eminences behind and in the flank of Flaminius rushed forward as it were with one accord into the plain. The Romans, who were forming their array in the mist, suddenly heard the shouts of the enemy amongst them, on every side, and before they could fall into their ranks, or draw their swords, or see by whom they were attacked, felt at once that they were surrounded and lost.

There are two little rivulets which run from the Gualandra into the lake. The traveller crosses the first of these at about a mile after he comes into the plain, and this divides the Tuscan from the papal territories. The second, about a quarter of a mile further on, is called "the bloody rivulet;" and the peasants point out an open spot to the left, between the "Sanguinetto" and the hills, which, they say, was the principal scene of slaughter. The other part of the plain is covered with thick-set olive-trees in corn grounds, and is nowhere quite level except near the edge of the lake. It is, indeed, most probable that the battle was fought near this end of the valley, for the six thousand Romans, who, at the beginning of the action, broke through the enemy, escaped to the summit of an eminence which must have been in this quarter, otherwise they would have had to traverse the whole plain, and to pierce through the main army of Hannibal.

The Romans fought desperately for three hours; but the death of Flaminius was the signal for a general dispersion. The Carthaginian horse then burst in upon the fugitives, and the lake, the marsh about Borghetto, but chiefly the plain of the Sanguinetto and the passes of the Gualandra, were strewed with dead. Near some old walls on a bleak ridge to the left above the rivulet, many human bones have been repeatedly found, and this has confirmed the pretensions and the name of the "stream of blood."

Every district of Italy has its hero. In the north some painter is the usual genius of the place, and the foreign Julio Romano more than divides Mantua with her native Virgil.* To the south we hear of Roman names. Near Thrasimene tradition is still faithful to the fame of an enemy, and Hannibal the Carthaginian is the only ancient name remembered on the banks of the Perugian lake. Flaminius is unknown; but the postilions on that road have been taught to show the very spot where *Il Console Romano* was slain. Of all who fought and fell in the battle of Thrasimene, the historian himself has, besides the generals and Maharbal, preserved indeed only a single name. You overtake the Carthaginian again on the same road to Rome. The antiquary, that is, the hostler of the post-house at Spoleto, tells you that his town repulsed the victorious enemy, and shows you the gate still called *Porta di Annibale.* It is hardly worth while to remark that a French travel writer, well known by the name of the President Dupaty, saw Thrasimene in the lake of Bolsena, which lay conveniently on his way from Sienna to Rome.

No. XXIV.—Statue of Pompey.

"*And thou, dread statue! still existent in*
The austerest form of naked majesty."—Stanza lxxxvii.

The projected division of the Spada Pompey has already been recorded by the historian of the Decline and Fall of the Roman Empire. Mr. Gibbon found it in the memorials of Flaminius Vacca; and it may be added to his mention of it, that Pope Julius III. gave the contending owners five hundred crowns for the statue, and presented it to Cardinal Capo di Ferro, who had prevented the judgment of Solomon from being executed upon the image. In a more civilized age this statue was exposed to an actual operation: for the French, who acted the Brutus of Voltaire in the Coliseum, resolved that their Cæsar should fall at the base of that Pompey, which was supposed to have been sprinkled with the blood of the original dictator. The nine-foot hero was therefore removed to the arena of the amphitheatre, and, to facilitate its transport, suffered the temporary amputation of its

* About the middle of the twelfth century the coins of Mantua bore on one side the image and figure of Virgil. Zecca d' Italia, pl. xvii. i. 6. Voyage dans le Milanais, &c. par A. Z. Millin, tom. ii. pag. 294. Paris, 1817.

right arm. The republican tragedians had to plead that the arm was a restoration: but their accusers do not believe that the integrity of the statue would have protected it. The love of finding every coincidence has discovered the true Cæsarian ichor in a stain near the right knee; but colder criticism has rejected not only the blood, but the portrait, and assigned the globe of power rather to the first of the emperors than to the last of the republican masters of Rome. Winkelmann* is loath to allow an heroic statue of a Roman citizen, but the Grimani Agrippa, a contemporary almost, is heroic; and naked Roman figures were only very rare, not absolutely forbidden. The face accords much better with the "hominem integrum et castum et gravem,"† than with any of the busts of Augustus, and is too stern for him who was beautiful, says Suetonius, at all periods of his life. The pretended likeness to Alexander the Great cannot be discerned, but the traits resemble the medal of Pompey.‡ The objectionable globe may not have been an ill-applied flattery to him who found Asia Minor the boundary, and left it the centre of the Roman empire. It seems that Winkelmann has made a mistake in thinking that no proof of the identity of this statue with that which received the bloody sacrifice can be derived from the spot where it was discovered.§ Flaminius Vacca says *sotto una cantina*, and this cantina is known to have been in the Vicolo de' Leutari, near the Cancellaria; a position corresponding exactly to that of the Janus before the basilica of Pompey's theatre, to which Augustus transferred the statue after the *curia* was either burnt or taken down.‖ Part of the Pompeian shade, the portico, existed in the beginning of the fifteenth century, and the *atrium* was called *Satrum*. So says Blondus. At all events, so imposing is the stern majesty of the statue, and so memorable is the story, that the play of the imagination leaves no room for the exercise of the judgment; and the fiction, if a fiction it is, operates on the spectator with an effect not less powerful than truth.

---

* Storia delle Arti, &c. lib. ix. cap. 1. pag. 321, 322. tom. ii.

† Cicer. Epist. ad Atticum, xi. 6.

‡ Published by Causeus, in his Museum Romanum.

§ Storia delle Arti, &c. l. ix. c. i.

‖ Sueton. in vit. August. cap. 31. and in vit. C. J. Cæsar. cap. 88. Appian says it was burnt down. See a note of Pitiscus to Suetonius, pag. 224.

No. XXV.—The Bronze Wolf.

"*And thou, the thunder-stricken nurse of Rome!*"
Stanza lxxxviii.

Ancient Rome, like modern Sienna, abounded most probably with images of the foster-mother of her founder; but there were two she-wolves, of whom history makes particular mention. One of these, *of brass in ancient work*, was seen by Dionysius* at the temple of Romulus, under the Palatine, and is universally believed to be that mentioned by the Latin historian, as having been made from the money collected by a fine on usurers, and as standing under the Ruminal figtree.† The other was that which Cicero‡ has celebrated both in prose and verse, and which the historian Dion also records as having suffered the same accident as is alluded to by the orator.§ The question agitated by the antiquaries is, whether the wolf now in the Conservator's Palace is that of Livy and Dionysius, or that of Cicero, or whether it is neither one nor the other. The earlier writers differ as much as the moderns; Lucius Faunus‖ says, that it is the one alluded to by both, which is impossible, and also by Virgil, which may be. Fulvius Ursinus¶ calls it the wolf of Dionysius, and Marlianus** talks of it as the one mentioned by Cicero. To him Rycquius *tremblingly* assents.†† Nardini is inclined to suppose it may be one of the many wolves preserved in ancient Rome; but of the

---

* Antiq. Rom. lib. I.

† Liv. Hist. lib. x. cap. lxix.

‡ "Tum statua Nattæ, tum simulacra Deorum, Romulusque et Remus cum altrice bellua vi fulminis ictis conciderunt." De Divinat. ii. 20. "Tactus est ille etiam qui hanc urbem condidit Romulus, quem inauratum in Capitolio parvum atque lactantem, uberibus lupinis inhiantem fuisse meministis." In Catilin. iii. 8.

> "Hic silvestris erat Romani nominis altrix
> Martia, quæ parvos Mavortis semine natos
> Uberibus gravidis vitali rore rigebat
> Que tum cum pueris flammato fulminis ict
> Concidit, atque avulsa pedum vestigia liquat.
>
> De Consulatu, lib. ii. (lib. i. de Divinat. cap. ii.)

§ Dion. Hist. lib. xxxvii. p. 37. edit. Rob. Steph. 1548.

‖ Luc. Fauni de Antiq. Urb. Rom. lib. ii. cap. vii. ap. Sallengre, tom. i p. 217.

¶ Ap. Nardini, Roma Vetus, l. v. c. iv.

** Marliani Urb Rom. Topograph. lib. ii. cap. ix.

†† Just. Rycquii de Capit. Roman. Comm. cap. xxiv pag. 250. edit. Lugd Bat. 1696.

two rather bends to the Ciceronian statue.* Montfauçon† mentions it as a point without doubt.—Of the later writers the decisive Winkelmann‡ proclaims it as having been found at the church of Saint Theodore, where, or near where, was the temple of Romulus, and consequently makes it the wolf of Dionysius. His authority is Lucius Faunus, who, however, only says that it *was placed*, not *found*, at the Ficus Ruminalis, by the Comitium, by which he does not seem to allude to the church of Saint Theodore. Rycquius was the first to make the mistake, and Winkelmann followed Rycquius.

Flaminius Vacca tells quite a different story, and says he had heard the wolf with the twins was found§ near the arch of Septimius Severus. The commentator on Winkelmann is of the same opinion with that learned person, and is incensed at Nardini for not having remarked that Cicero, in speaking of the wolf struck with lightning in the capitol, makes use of the past tense. But, with the Abate's leave, Nardini does not positively assert the statue to be that mentioned by Cicero, and, if he had, the assumption would not perhaps have been so exceedingly indiscreet. The Abate is himself obliged to own that there are marks very like the scathing of lightning in the hinder legs of the present wolf; and, to get rid of this, adds, that the wolf seen by Dionysius might have been also struck by lightning, or otherwise injured.

Let us examine the subject by a reference to the words of Cicero. The orator in two places seems to particularize the Romulus and the Remus, especially the first, which his audience remembered to *have been* in the Capitol, as being struck with lightning. In his verses he records that the twins and wolf both fell, and that the latter left behind the marks of her feet. Cicero does not say that the wolf was consumed: and Dion only mentions that it fell down, without alluding, as the Abate had made him to the force of the blow, or the firmness with which it had been fixed. The whole strength, therefore, of the Abate's argument hangs upon the past tense; which, however, may be somewhat diminished by remarking that the phrase only shows that the statue was not then standing in its former position. Winkelmann

---

* Nardini, Roma Vetus, lib. v. cap. iv.

† Diarium Italic. tom. i. p. 174.

‡ Storia delle Arti, &c. lib. iii. cap. iii. s. ii. note 10. Winkelmann has made a strange blunder in the note, by saying the Ciceronian wolf was *not* in the Capitol, and that Dion was wrong in saying so.

§ Flam Vacca Memorie, num. iii. p. i. ap. Montfauçon, Diar. Ital. tom. i.

has observed that the present twins are modern; and it is equally clear that there are marks of gilding on the wolf, which might therefore be supposed to make part of the ancient group. It is known that the sacred images of the Capitol were not destroyed when injured by time or accident, but were put into certain underground depositories, called *favissæ*.* It may be thought possible that the wolf had been so deposited, and had been replaced in some conspicuous situation when the Capitol was rebuilt by Vespasian. Rycquius, without mentioning his authority, tells that it was transferred from the Comitium to the Lateran, and thence brought to the Capitol. If it was found near the arch of Severus, it may have been one of the images which Orosius† says was thrown down in the Forum by lightning when Alaric took the city That it is of very high antiquity the workmanship is a decisive proof; and that circumstance induced Winkelmann to believe it the wolf of Dionysius. The Capitoline wolf, however, may have been of the same early date as that at the temple of Romulus. Lactantius‡ asserts that in his time the Romans worshipped a wolf; and it is known that the Lupercalia held out to a very late period§ after every other observance of the ancient superstition had totally expired. This may account for the preservation of the ancient image longer than any other early symbols of Paganism.

It may be permitted, however, to remark, that the wolf was a Roman symbol, but that the worship of that symbol is an inference drawn by the zeal of Lactantius. The early Christian writers are not to be trusted in the charges which they make against the Pagans. Eusebius accused the Romans to their faces of worshipping Simon Magus, and raising a statue to him in the island of the Tyber. The Romans had probably never heard of such a person before, who came, however, to play a considerable, though scandalous part in the church history, and has left several

* Luc. Faun. ibid.

† See note to stanza lxxx. in "Historical Illustrations."

‡ "Romuli nutrix Lupa honoribus est affecta divinis, et ferrem, si animal ipsum fuisset, cujus figuram gerit." Lactant. de Falsa Religione, lib. i. cap. xx. pag. 101, edit. varior. 1660; that is to say, he would rather adore a wolf than a prostitute. His commentator has observed that the opinion of Livy concerning Laurentia being figured in this wolf was not universal. Strabo though so. Rycquius is wrong in saying that Lactantius mentions the wolf was in the Capitol.

§ To A.D. 496. "Quis credere possit," says Baronius, [Ann. Eccles. tom. viii. p. 602. in an. 496,] "viguisse adhuc Romæ ad Gelasii tempora, quæ fuere ante exordia urbis allata in Italiam Lupercalia?" Gelasius wrote a letter, which occupies four folio pages, to Andromachus the senator, and others, to show that the rites should be give.. .p.

tokens of his aerial combat with St. Peter at Rome, notwith standing that an inscription found in this very island of the Tyber showed the Simon Magus of Eusebius to be a certain indigenal god called Semo Sangus of Fidius.*

Even when the worship of the founder of Rome had been abandoned, it was thought expedient to humour the habits of the good matrons of the city, by sending them with their sick infants to the church of Saint Theodore, as they had before carried them to the temple of Romulus.† The practice is continued to this day: and the site of the above church seems to be thereby identified with that of the temple; so that if the wolf had been really found there, as Winkelmann says, there would be no doubt of the present statue being that seen by Dionysius. But Faunus, in saying that it was at the Ficus Ruminalis by the Comitium, is only talking of its ancient position as recorded by Pliny; and even if he had been remarking where it was found, would not have alluded to the church of Saint Theodore, but to a very different place, near which it was then thought the Ficus Ruminalis had been, and also the Comitium; that is, the three columns by the church of Santa Maria Liberatrice, at the corner of the Palatine looking on the Forum.

It is, in fact, a mere conjecture where the image was actually dug up; and perhaps, on the whole, the marks of the gilding, and of the lightning, are a better argument in favour of its being the Ciceronian wolf than any that can be adduced for the contrary opinion. At any rate, it is reasonably selected in the text of the poem as one of the most interesting relics of the ancient city,‡ and is certainly the figure, if not the very animal to which Virgil alludes in his beautiful verses:—

"Geminos huic ubera circum
Ludere pendentes pueros, et lambere matrem
Impavidos: illam tereti cervice reflexam
Mulcere alternos, et corpore fingere linguâ.§

* Eccles. Hist. lib. ii. cap. xiii. p. 40. Justin Martyr had told the story before; but Baronius himself was obliged to detect this fable. See Nardini, Roma Vet. lib. vii. cap. xii.

† Rione xii. Ripa, accurata e succincta Descrizione, &c. di Roma Moderna, dell' Ab. Ridolf. Venuti. 1766.

‡ Donatus, lib. xi. cap. 18, gives a medal representing on one side the wolf in the same position as that in the Capitol; and in the reverse the wolf with the head not reverted. It is of the time of Antoninus Pius.

§ Æn. viii. 631. See Dr. Middleton, in his Letter from Rome, who inclines to the Ciceronian wolf, but without examining the subject.

No. XXVI.—Julius Cæsar.

"*For the Roman's mind*
Was modell'd in a less terrestrial mould."—Stanza xc.

It is possible to be a very great man and to be still very inferior to Julius Cesar, the most complete character, so Lord Bacon thought, of all antiquity. Nature seems incapable of such extraordinary combinations as composed his versatile capacity, which was the wonder even of the Romans themselves. The first general—the only triumphant politician—inferior to none in eloquence—comparable to any in the attainments of wisdom, in an age made up of the greatest commanders, statesmen, orators, and philosophers that ever appeared in the world—an author who composed a perfect specimen of military annals in his travelling carriage—at one time in a controversy with Cato, at another writing a treatise on punning, and collecting a set of good sayings—fighting and making love at the same moment, and willing to abandon both his empire and his mistress for a sight of the Fountains of the Nile. Such did Julius Cæsar appear to his contemporaries and to those of the subsequent ages who were the most inclined to deplore and execrate his fatal genius.

But we must not be so much dazzled with his surpassing glory, or with his magnanimous, his amiable qualities, as to forget the decision of his impartial countrymen :—

HE WAS JUSTLY SLAIN.*

No. XXVII.—Egeria.

"*Egeria, sweet creation of some heart*
Which found no mortal resting-place so fair
As thine ideal breast."—Stanza cxv.

The respectable authority of Flaminius Vacca would incline us to believe in the claims of the Egerian grotto.† He assures us

* "Jure cæsus existimetur," says Suetonius, after a fair estimate of his character, and making use of a phrase which was a formula in Livy's time. "Melium jure cæsum pronuntiavit, etiam si regni crimine insons fuerit :" [lib. iv. cap. 48 :] and which was continued in the legal judgments pronounced in justifiable homicides, such as killing housebreakers. See Sueton. in vit. C. I. Cæsar, with the commentary of Pitiscus, p. 184.

† Memorie, &c ap. Nardini, pag. 13. He does not give the inscription.

that he saw an inscription in the pavement, stating that the fountain was that of Egeria, dedicated to the nymphs. The inscription is not there at this day; but Montfauçon quotes two lines* of Ovid from a stone in the Villa Giustiniani, which he seems to think had been brought from the same grotto.

This grotto and valley were formerly frequented in summer, and particularly the first Sunday in May, by the modern Romans, who attached a salubrious quality to the fountain, which trickles from an orifice at the bottom of the vault, and, overflowing the little pools, creeps down the matted grass into the brook below. The brook is the Ovidian Almo, whose name and qualities are lost in the modern Aquataccio. The valley itself is called Valle di Caffarelli, from the dukes of that name who made over their fountain to the Pallavicini, with sixty *rubbia* of adjoining land.

There can be little doubt that this long dell is the Egerian valley of Juvenal, and the pausing-place of Umbritius, notwithstanding the generality of his commentators have supposed the descent of the satirist and his friend to have been into the Arician grove, where the nymph met Hippolitus, and where she was more peculiarly worshipped.

The step from the Porta Capena to the Alban hill, fifteen miles distant, would be too considerable, unless we were to believe in the wild conjecture of Vossius, who makes that gate travel from its present station, where he pretends it was during the reign of the kings, as far as the Arician grove, and then makes it recede to its old site with the shrinking city.† The tufo, or pumice which the poet prefers to marble, is the substance composing the bank in which the grotto is sunk.

The modern topographers‡ find in the grotto the statue of the nymph, and nine niches for the Muses; and a late traveller§ has discovered that the cave is restored to that simplicity which the poet regretted had been exchanged for injudicious ornament. But the headless statue is palpably rather a male than a nymph, and

---

* "In villa Justiniana extat ingens lapis quadratus solidus, in quo sculpta hæc duo Ovidii carmina sunt :—

'Egeria est quæ præbet aquas dea grata Camœnis
Illa Numæ conjunx consiliumque fuit.'

Qui lapis videtur eodem Egeriæ fonte, aut ejus vicinia isthuc comportatus." Diarium Italic. p. 153.

† De Magnit. Vet. Rom. ap. Græv. An. Rom. tom. iv. p. 1507.

‡ Echinard, Descrizione di Roma e dell' Agro Romano, corretto dall' Abate Venuti, in Roma, 1750. They believe in the grotto and nymph. "Simulacro di questo fonte, essendovi sculpite le acque a pie di esso."

§ Classical Tour, chap. vi. p. 217. vol. ii.

has none of the attributes ascribed to it at present visible. The nine Muses could hardly have stood in six niches; and Juvenal certainly does not allude to any individual cave.* Nothing can be collected from the satirist but that somewhere near the Porta Capena was a spot in which it was supposed Numa held nightly consultations with his nymph, and where there was a grove and a sacred fountain, and fanes once consecrated to the Muses; and that from this spot there was a descent into the valley of Egeria, where were several artificial caves. It is clear that the statues of the Muses made no part of the decoration which the satirist thought misplaced in these caves; for he expressly assigns other fanes (delubra) to these divinities above the valley, and moreover tells us that they had been ejected to make room for the Jews. In fact, the little temple, now called that of Bacchus, was formerly thought to belong to the Muses, and Nardini† places them in a poplar grove, which was in his time above the valley.

It is probable, from the inscription and position, that the cave now shown may be one of the "artificial caverns," of which, indeed, there is another a little way higher up the valley, under a tuft of alder bushes: but a *single* grotto of Egeria is a mere modern invention, grafted upon the application of the epithet Egerian to these nymphea in general, and which might send us to look for the haunts of Numa upon the banks of the Thames.

Our English Juvenal was not seduced into mistranslation by his acquaintance with Pope: he carefully preserves the correct plural—

> "Thence slowly winding down the vale, we view
> The Egerian *grots*: oh, how unlike the true!"

The valley abounds with springs,‡ and over these springs which the Muses might haunt from their neighbouring groves, Egeria presided: hence she was said to supply them with water; and she was the nymph of the grottos through which the fountains were taught to flow.

The whole of the monuments in the vicinity of the Egerian valley have received names at will, which have been changed at will. Venuti§ owns he can see no traces of the temples of Jove, Saturn, Juno, Venus, and Diana, which Nardini found, or hoped to find. The mutatorium of Caracalla's circus, the temple of

---

* Sat. III.

† Lib. iii. cap. iii.

‡ "Undique e solo aquæ scaturiunt." Nardini, lib. iii. cap. iii.

§ Echinard, &c. Cic. cit. p. 297, 298.

Honour and Virtue, the temple of Bacchus, and, above all, the temple of the god Rediculus, are the antiquaries' despair.

The circus of Caracalla depends on a medal of that emperor cited by Fulvius Ursinus, of which the reverse shows a circus, supposed, however, by some to represent the Circus Maximus. It gives a very good idea of that place of exercise. The soil has been but little raised, if we may judge from the small cellular structure at the end of the Spina, which was probably the chapel of the god Consus. This cell is half beneath the soil, as it must have been in the circus itself; for Dionysius* could not be persuaded to believe that this divinity was the Roman Neptune, because his altar was under ground.

No. XXVIII.—The Roman Nemesis.

"*Great Nemesis!*
Here, where the ancient paid thee homage long."
Stanza cxxxii.

We read in Suetonius, that Augustus, from a warning received in a dream,† counterfeited, once a year, the beggar, sitting before the gate of his palace with his hand hollowed and stretched out for charity. A statue formerly in the villa Borghese, and which should be now at Paris, represents the emperor in that posture of supplication. The object of this self-degradation was the appeasement of Nemesis, the perpetual attendant on good fortune, of whose power the Roman conquerors were also reminded by certain symbols attached to their cars of triumph. The symbols were the whip and the *crotalo*, which were discovered in the Nemesis of the Vatican. The attitude of beggary made the above statue pass for that of Belisarius: and until the criticism of Winkelmann‡ had rectified the mistake, one fiction was called

* Antiq. Rom. lib. ii. cap. xxxi.

† Sueton. in vit. Augusti, cap. 91. Casaubon, in the note, refers to Plutarch's Lives of Camillus and Æmilius Paulus, and also to his apophthegms, for the character of this deity. The hollowed hand was reckoned the last degree of degradation; and when the dead body of the præfect Rufinus was borne about in triumph by the people, the indignity was increased by putting his hand in that position.

‡ Storia delle Arti, &c. lib. xii. cap. iii. tom. ii. p. 422. Visconti calls the statue, however, a Cybele. It is given in the Museo Pio-clement. tom. i. par

in to support another. It was the same fear of the sudden termination of prosperity that made Amasis king of Egypt warn his friend Polycrates of Samos, that the gods loved those whose lives were checkered with good and evil fortunes. Nemesis was supposed to lie in wait particularly for the prudent; that is, for those whose caution rendered them accessible only to mere accidents and her first altar was raised on the banks of the Phrygian Æsepus by Adrastus, probably the prince of that name who killed the son of Crœsus by mistake. Hence the goddess was called Adrastea.*

The Roman Nemesis was *sacred* and *august:* there was a temple to her in the Palatine under the name of Rhamnusia:† so great, indeed, was the propensity of the ancients to trust to the revolution of events, and to believe in the divinity of Fortune, that in the same Palatine there was a temple to the Fortune of the day.‡ This is the last superstition which retains its hold over the human heart; and, from concentrating in one object the credulity so natural to man, has always appeared strongest in those unembarrassed by other articles of belief. The antiquaries have supposed this goddess to be synonymous with Fortune and with Fate: but it was in her vindictive quality that she was worshipped under the name of Nemesis.

No. XXIX.—Gladiators.

"*He, their sire,*
Butcher'd to make a Roman holiday."—Stanza cxli.

Gladiators were of two kinds, compelled and voluntary; and were supplied from several conditions;—from slaves sold for that

---

40. The Abate Fea (Spiegazione dei Rami. Storia, &c. tom. iii. p. 513) calls it a Chrisippus.

* Dict. de Bayle, article Adrastea.

† It is enumerated by the regionary Victor.

‡ Fortunæ hujusce diei. Cicero mentions her, de Legib. lib. ii.

DEAE NEMESI
SIVE FORTUNAE
PISTORIVS
RVGIANVS
V. C. LEGAT.
LEG. XIII. G.
CORD.

See Questiones Romanæ, &c. ap. Græv. Antiq. Rom. tom. v. p. 942. See also Muratori, Nov. Thesaur. Inscrip. Vet. tom. i. p. 88, 89, where there are three Latin and one Greek inscription to Nemesis, and others to Fate.

purpose; from culprits; from barbarian captives either taken in war, and, after being led in triumph, set apart for the games, or those seized and condemned as rebels; also from free citizens, some fighting for hire, (*auctorati*,) others from a depraved ambition; at last even knights and senators were exhibited,—a disgrace of which the first tyrant was naturally the first inventor.* In the end, dwarfs, and even women fought; an enormity prohibited by Severus. Of these, the most to be pitied, undoubtedly, were the barbarian captives; and to this species a Christian writer† justly applies the epithet "innocent," to distinguish them from the professional gladiators. Aurelian and Claudius supplied great numbers of these unfortunate victims; the one after his triumph, and the other on the pretext of a rebellion.‡ No war, says Lipsius,§ was ever so destructive to the human race as these sports. In spite of the laws of Constantine and Constans, gladiatorial shows survived the old established religion more than seventy years; but they owed their final extinction to the courage of a Christian. In the year 404, on the kalends of January, they were exhibiting the shows in the Flavian amphitheatre before the usual immense concourse of people. Almachius, or Telemachus, an eastern monk, who had travelled to Rome intent on his holy purpose, rushed into the midst of the area, and endeavoured to separate the combatants. The prætor Alypius, a person incredibly attached to these games,‖ gave instant orders to the gladiators to slay him; and Telemachus gained the crown of martyrdom and the title of saint, which surely has never either before or since been awarded for a more noble exploit. Honorius immediately abolished the shows, which were never afterwards revived. The story is told by Theodoret¶ and Cassiodorus,** and seems worthy of credit notwithstanding its place in the Roman martyrology.†† Besides the torrents of blood which flowed at the funerals in the amphitheatres, the circus, the forums, and other public places, gladiators were introduced at feasts, and tore each

---

* Julius Cæsar, who rose by the fall of the aristocracy, brought Furius Leptinus and A. Calenus upon the arena.

† Tertullian, "certe quidem et innocentes gladiatores in ludum veniunt, et voluptatis publicæ hostiæ fiant." Just. Lips. Saturn. Sermon. lib. li. cap. iii.

‡ Vopiscus, in vit. Aurel. and in vit. Claud. ibid.

§ Just. Lips. ibid. lib. i. cap. xii.

‖ Augustinus (lib. vi. confess. cap. viii.) "Alypium suum gladiatorii spectaculi inhiatu incredibiliter abreptum," scribit. ib. lib. i. cap. xii.

¶ Hist. Eccles. cap. xxvi. lib. v.

** Cassiod. Tripartita, l. x. c. xi. Saturn. ib. ib.

†† Baronius, ad ann. et in notis ad Martyrol. Rom. I. Jan. See—Marangon delle memorie sacre e profane dell' Anfiteatro Flavio, p. 25, edit. 1746.

other to pieces amidst the supper tables, to the great delight and applause of the guests. Yet Lipsius permits himself to suppose the loss of courage, and the evident degeneracy of mankind, to be nearly connected with the abolition of these bloody spectacles.

No. XXX.

" *Here, where the Roman million's blame or praise*
Was death or life, the playthings of a crowd."—Stanza cxlii.

When one gladiator wounded another, he shouted, "he has it," "hoc habet," or "habet." The wounded combatant dropped his weapon, and advancing to the edge of the arena, supplicated the spectators. If he had fought well, the people saved him; if otherwise, or as they happened to be inclined, they turned down their thumbs, and he was slain. They were occasionally so savage that they were impatient if a combat lasted longer than ordinary without wounds or death. The emperor's presence generally saved the vanquished; and it is recorded as an instance of Caracalla's ferocity, that he sent those who supplicated him for life, in a spectacle, at Nicomedia, to ask the people; in other words, handed them over to be slain. A similar ceremony is observed at the Spanish bull-fights. The magistrate presides; and after the horsemen and piccadores have fought the bull, the matadore steps forward and bows to him for permission to kill the animal. If the bull has done his duty by killing two or three horses, or a man, which last is rare, the people interfere with shouts, the ladies wave their handkerchiefs, and the animal is saved. The wounds and death of the horses are accompanied with the loudest acclamations, and many gestures of delight, especially from the female portion of the audience, including those of the gentlest blood. Every thing depends on habit. The author of Childe Harold, the author of this note, and one or two other Englishmen, who have certainly in other days borne the sight of a pitched battle, were, during the summer of 1809, in the governor's box at the great amphitheatre of Santa Maria, opposite to Cadiz. The death of one or two horses completely satisfied their curiosity. A gentleman present, observing them shudder and look pale, noticed that unusual reception of so delightful a sport to some young ladies, who stared and smiled, and continued their applauses as another horse fell bleeding to the ground. One bull killed three horses *off his own horns.* He was saved by acclamations, which were redoubled when it was known he belonged to a priest.

An Englishman, who can be much pleased with seeing two men beat themselves to pieces, cannot bear to look at a horse galloping round an arena with his bowels trailing on the ground, and turns from the spectacle and the spectators with horror and disgust

---

No. XXXI.—The Alban Hill.

"*And afar*
The Tiber winds, and the broad ocean laves
The Latian coast, &c. &c. Stanza clxxiv.

The whole declivity of the Alban hill is of unrivalled beauty, and from the convent on the highest point, which has succeeded to the temple of the Latian Jupiter, the prospect embraces all the objects alluded to in the cited stanza; the Mediterranean; the whole scene of the latter half of the Æneid, and the coast from beyond the mouth of the Tiber to the headland of Circæum and the Cape of Terracina.

The site of Cicero's villa may be supposed either at the Grotto Ferrata, or at the Tusculum of Prince Lucien Bonaparte.

The former was thought some years ago the actual site, as may be seen from Myddleton's Life of Cicero. At present it has lost something of its credit, except for the Domenichinos. Nine monks of the Greek order live there, and the adjoining villa is a cardinal's summer-house. The other villa, called Rufinella, is on the summit of the hill above Frascati, and many rich remains of Tusculum have been found there, besides seventy-two statues of different merit and preservation, and seven busts.

From the same eminence are seen the Sabine hills, embosomed in which lies the long valley of Rustica. There are several circumstances which tend to establish the identity of this valley with the "*Ustica*" of Horace; and it seems possible that the mosaic pavement which the peasants uncover by throwing up the earth of a vineyard may belong to his villa. Rustica is pronounced short, not according to our stress upon—"*Usticæ cubantis.*"—It is more rational to think that we are wrong, than that the inhabitants of this secluded valley have changed their tone in this word. The addition of the consonant prefixed is nothing; yet it is necessary to be aware that Rustica may be a modern name which the peasants may have caught from the antiquaries.

The villa, or the mosaic, is in the vineyard on a knoll covered with chestnut trees. A stream runs down the valley; and although it is not true, as said in the guide books, that this stream is called Licenza, yet there is a village on a rock at the head of the valley which is so denominated, and which may have taken its name from the Digentia. Licenza contains 700 inhabitants. On a peak a little way beyond is Civitella, containing 300. On the banks of the Anio, a little before you turn up into Valle Rustica to the left, about an hour from the *villa*, is a town called Vicovaro, another favourable coincidence with the *Varia* of the poet. At the end of the valley, towards the Anio, there is a bare hill, crowned with a little town called Bardela. At the foot of this hill the rivulet Licenza flows, and is almost absorbed in a wide sandy bed before it reaches the Anio. Nothing can be more fortunate for the lines of the poet, whether in a metaphorical or direct sense:—

> "Me quotiens reficit gelidus Digentia rivus,
> Quem Mandela bibit rugosus frigore pagus.

The stream is clear high up the valley, but before it reaches th hill of Bardela looks green and yellow, like a sulphur rivulet.

Rocca Giovane, a ruined village in the hills, half an hour's walk from the vineyard where the pavement is shown, does seem to be the site of the fane of Vacuna, and an inscription found there tells that this temple of the Sabine Victory was repaired by Vespasian. With these helps, and a position corresponding exactly to every thing which the poet has told us of his retreat, we may feel tolerably secure of our site.

The hill which should be Lucretilis is called Campanile, and by following up the rivulet to the pretended Bandusia, you come to the roots of the higher mountain Gennaro. Singularly enough, the only spot of ploughed land in the whole valley is on the knoll where this Bandusia rises.

> ". . . . tu frigus amabile
> Fessis vomere tauris
> Præbes, et pecori vago."

The peasants show another spring near the mosaic pavement which they call "Oradina," and which flows down the hills into a tank, or mill-dam, and thence trickles over into the Digentia.

But we must not hope

"To trace the Muses upwards to their spring,"

by exploring the windings of the romantic valley in search of th Bandusian fountain. It seems strange that any one should have thought Bandusia a fountain of the Digentia—Horace has not let drop a word of it; and this immortal spring has in fact been discovered in possession of the holders of many good things in Italy, the monks. It was attached to the church of St. Gervais and Protais near Venusia, where it was most likely to be found.* We shall not be so lucky as a late traveller in finding the *occasional pine* still pendant on the poetic villa. There is not a pine in the whole valley, but there are two cypresses, which he evidently took, or mistook, for the tree in the ode.† The truth is, that the pine is now, as it was in the days of Virgil, a garden tree, and it was not at all likely to be found in the craggy acclivities of the valley of Rustica. Horace probably had one of them in the orchard close above his farm, immediately overshadowing his villa, not on the rocky heights at some distance from his abode. The tourist may have easily supposed himself to have seen this pine figured in the above cypresses; for the orange and lemon trees which throw such a bloom over his description of the royal gardens at Naples, unless they have been since displaced, were assuredly only acacias and other common garden shrubs.‡

No. XXXII.—Eustace's Classical Tour.

The extreme disappointment experienced by choosing the Classical Tourist as a guide in Italy must be allowed to find vent in a few observations, which, it is asserted without fear of contra-

---

See Historical Illustrations of the Fourth Canto, p. 43.

† See Classical Tour, &c. chap. vii. p. 250, vol. ii.

‡ "Under our windows, and bordering on the beach, is the royal garden, laid out in parterres, and walks shaded by rows of orange trees.' —Classical Tour, &c. chap xi. vol. ii. oct. 365.

diction, will be confirmed by every one who has selected the same conductor through the same country. This author is in fact one of the most inaccurate, unsatisfactory writers that have in our times attained a temporary reputation, and is very seldom to be trusted even when he speaks of objects which he must be presumed to have seen. His errors, from the simple exaggeration to the downright misstatement, are so frequent as to induce a suspicion that he had either never visited the spots described, or had trusted to the fidelity of former writers. Indeed, the Classical Tour has every characteristic of a mere compilation of former notices, strung together upon a very slender thread of personal observation, and swelled out by those decorations which are so easily supplied by a systematic adoption of all the commonplaces of praise, applied to every thing, and therefore signifying nothing.

The style which one person thinks cloggy and cumbrous, and unsuitable, may be to the taste of others, and such may experience some salutary excitement in ploughing through the periods of the Classical Tour. It must be said, however, that polish and weight are apt to beget an expectation of value. It is amongst the pains of the damned to toil up a climax with a huge round *stone*.

The tourist had the choice of his words, but there was no such latitude allowed to that of his sentiments. The love of virtue and of liberty, which must have distinguished the character, certainly adorns the pages of Mr. Eustace; and the gentlemanly spirit, so recommendatory either in an author or his productions, is very conspicuous throughout the Classical Tour. But these generous qualities are the foliage of such a performance, and may be spread about it so prominently and profusely, as to embarrass those who wish to see and find the fruit at hand. The unction of the divine, and the exhortations of the moralist, may have made this work something more and better than a book of travels, but they have not made it a book of travels; and this observation applies more especially to that enticing method of instruction conveyed by the perpetual introduction of the same Gallic Helo to reel and bluster before the rising generation, and terrify it into decency by the display of all the excesses of the revolution. An animosity against atheists and regicides in general, and Frenchmen specifically, may be honourable, and may be useful as a record; but that antidote should either be administered in any work rather than a tour, or, at least, should be served up apart, and not so mixed with the whole mass of information and reflec tion, as to give a bitterness to every page: for who would choose to have the antipathies of any man, however just, for his travelling companions? A tourist, unless he aspires to the credit of prophecy, is not answerable for the changes which may take place in the country which he describes; but his reader may very fairly esteem all his political portraits and deductions as so much waste paper, the moment they cease to assist, and more particularly if they obstruct, his actual survey.

Neither encomium nor accusation of any government, or governors, is meant to be here offered; but it is stated as an incontrovertible fact, that the change operated, either by the address of the late imperial system, or by the disappointment of every expectation by those who have succeeded to the Italian thrones, has been so considerable, and so apparent, as not only to put Mr. Eustace's antigallican philippics entirely out of date, but even to throw some suspicion upon the competency and candour of the author himself. A remarkable example may be found in the instance of Bologna, over whose papal attachments, and consequent desolation, the tourist pours forth such strains of condolence and revenge, made louder by the borrowed trumpet of Mr. Burke. Now Bologna is at this moment, and has been for some years, notorious amongst the states of Italy for its attachment to revolutionary principles, and was almost the only city which made any demonstrations in favour of the unfortunate Murat. This change may, however, have been made since Mr. Eustace visited this country; but the traveller whom he has thrilled with horror at the projected stripping of the copper from the cupola of St. Peter's, must be much relieved to find that sacrilege out of the power of the French, or any other plunderers, the cupola being covered with *lead*.*

If the conspiring voice of otherwise rival critics had not given considerable currency to the Classical Tour, it would have been unnecessary to warn the reader, that however it may adorn his library, it will be of little or no service to him in his carriage; and if the judgment of those critics had hitherto been suspended, no attempt would have been made to anticipate their decision. As it is, those who stand in the relation of posterity to Mr. Eustace may be permitted to appeal from contemporary praises,

---

* "What, then, will be the astonishment, or rather horror, of my reader when I inform him ········ the French Committee turned its attention to Saint Peter's, and employed a company of Jews to estimate and purchase the gold, silver, and bronze that adorn the inside of the edifice, as well as the copper that covers the vault and dome on the outside." Chap. iv. p. 130, vol. ii. The story about the Jews is positively denied at Rome.

and are perhaps more likely to be just in proportion as the cause of love and hatred are the farther removed. This appeal had, in some measure, been made before the above remarks were written; for one of the most respectable of the Florentine publishers, who had been persuaded by the repeated inquiries of those on their journey southwards, to reprint a cheap edition of the Classical Tour, was, by the concurring advice of returning travellers, induced to abandon his design, although he had already arranged his types and paper, and had struck off one or two of the first sheets.

The writer of these notes would wish to part (like Mr. Gibbon) on good terms with the Pope and the Cardinals, but he does not think it necessary to extend the same discreet silence to their humble partisans.

END OF CHILDE HAROLD.

A PARTIAL

Catalogue of Books

PUBLISHED BY

THOMAS Y. CROWELL & CO.

46 East Fourteenth Street, New York.

100 Purchase Street, Boston.

STANDARD AND MISCELLANEOUS.

AD LUCEM. By Mary Lloyd. Selections of Prose and Poetry for suffering ones. Parti-colored cloth, gilt top, 18mo $1.00
Seal leather, flexible. Gilt edge 1.75
Levant, padded. Gilt edge 2.50

AT HOME AND IN WAR. By Col. A. V. Verestchagin. 12mo . 1.50

BRAMPTON SKETCHES. New England Life Seventy Years Ago. By Mrs. Mary B. Claflin. Illustrated 1.00

BROWN'S CONCORDANCE 50

CAMBRIDGE BOOK OF POETRY AND SONG. By Charlotte Fiske Bates. *New and Revised Edition. New Cover Designs.* With 40 fac-simile poems in autograph, and 32 full-page Illustrations from original designs by Church, Dielman, Fredericks, Fenn, Gifford, Murphy, Schell, Smillie, and others. Engraved by Geo. T. Andrew. Over 900 pages, royal 8vo, cloth, gilt edges, boxed 5.00
Full Levant, gilt 10.00
Tree calf, gilt 10.00

CAPTAIN COIGNET, Soldier of the Empire, 1776-1850 (The Narrative of). An autobiographical account of one of Napoleon's Body Guard. Fully illustrated, 12mo, half leather, gilt top 2.50
Half calf 5.00

CENTURY OF AMERICAN LITERATURE (A). Selected and arranged by Huntington Smith. Cloth, 12mo 1.75
Half calf 3.50

CONVENIENT HOUSES AND HOW TO BUILD THEM. By Louis H. Gibson, architect, comprising a large variety of plans, photographic designs, and artistic interiors and exteriors of Ideal Homes, varying in cost from $1,000 to $10,000. 8vo, cloth $2.50

CONYBEARE AND HOWSON, Life of St. Paul. 12mo, cloth . 1.00

CRIME AND PUNISHMENT. By Feodor M. Dostoyevsky. 12mo. 1.50

DAILY FOOD. New Illustrated Edition. 18mo. Gilt edges. With 12 Photo Engravings, white back, fancy sides 75

Lavender and gold. Gilt edges 75

French silk and gold. Gilt edges 1.25

32mo. Plain 15

32mo. Gilt 20

32mo. Morocco, flexible, round corners, gilt edges 60

DEAD SOULS. Dy Nikolaï V. Gogol. 12mo 1.25

DOCTOR LAMAR. A Novel. By Elizabeth P. Train. 12mo 1.25

DICTIONARY OF QUOTATIONS FROM THE POETS (A). Based upon Bohn's Edition. *Revised, Corrected,* and *Enlarged.* By Anna L. Ward. Crown 8vo, cloth, bevelled boards 2.00

Half calf 4.00

DICTIONARY OF PROSE QUOTATIONS (A). By Anna L. Ward. Crown 8vo, cloth, bevelled boards 2.00

Half calf 4.00

Ely's Works:

ELEMENTS OF SOCIALISM. By Prof. Richard T. Ely 1.25

LABOR MOVEMENT IN AMERICA. By Prof. Richard T. Ely . 1.50

PROBLEMS OF TO-DAY. A discussion of Tariff, Taxation, and Monopolies. By Prof. Richard T. Ely. 12mo. Revised and enlarged edition 1.50

SOCIAL ASPECTS OF CHRISTIANITY. By Prof. Richard T. Ely, . .90

TAXATION IN AMERICAN STATES AND CITIES. 12mo . . 1.75

EMINENT AUTHORS OF THE NINETEENTH CENTURY. By Dr. Georg Brandes ("The Taine of the North"). 12mo . . . 2.00

Half calf 4.00

EQUITABLE TAXATION. Six essays on the subject, three of which received prizes from "The Public Opinion." By Walter E. Weyl, Robert Luce, Bolton Hall, J. W. Graham, J. W. Cabot, W. H. Cowles. With an introduction by the Hon. Jonathan A. Lane, biographical sketches of the authors, and portraits. 12mo, cloth 75

FIFTY YEARS, THREE MONTHS, TWO DAYS. By Julius Wolff. 1.25

FOSTER'S CYCLOPÆDIAS OF ILLUSTRATION. 8vo, cloth . 5.00

Sheep 6.00

1st Series Prose. Cloth.	1st Series Prose. Sheep.
2d " " "	2d " " "
1st " Poetical "	1st " Poetical "
2d " " "	2d " " "

FOSTER'S INDEX AND CATALOGUE FOR ANY LIBRARY. 2.25

Sheep 3.00

FOSTER'S SCRAP HOLDER 1.25

FOUNDING OF THE GERMAN EMPIRE BY WILLIAM I. By Heinrich von Sybel. Translated by Prof. Perrin of Boston University. 5 vols. 8vo. Cloth 10.00

Half morocco 20.00

FROM HEART AND NATURE. By Sarah K. Bolton and Chas. K. Bolton. 12mo, cloth, gilt top $1.00

GOLD NAILS TO HANG MEMORIES ON. A Rhyming Review, under their Christian Names, of old acquaintances in History, Literature, and Friendship. By Elizabeth A. Allen. 8vo, gilt edge . . 2.50

GOLDEN WORDS FOR DAILY COUNSEL. Selected and arranged by Anna H. Smith. Cloth, 16mo, red edges 1.00
Gilt edge 1.25
Seal leather, flexible, gilt 2.00
Levant morocco, flexible gilt 2.50
Levant morocco, padded 2.50

GOTTHOLD'S EMBLEMS. By Christian Scriver. 12mo 1.25

GREAT MASTERS OF RUSSIAN LITERATURE. By Dupuy. 1.25

HAPPY FIND (A). From the French of Mme. Gagnebin. 12mo . 1.25

HER MAJESTY'S TOWER. By W. H. Dixon. With 47 illustrations. Complete in 1 volume. Royal 12mo, cloth 2.00
Half calf 4.00

HER ONLY BROTHER. From the German of W. Heimburg. 12mo, 1.25

HISTORY OF FRANCE. By Victor Duruy. Translated by Mrs. M. Carey, under the supervision of J. F. Jameson, Professor of History in Brown University 2.00
Half calf 4.00

HUBBELL'S S. S. TREASURER'S CASH ACCOUNT 75

HUBBELL'S S. S. LIBRARY RECORD 1.25

IMPRESSIONS OF RUSSIA. By Dr. Georg Brandes. 12mo . . 1.25

INITIALS AND PSEUDONYMS. A Dictionary of Literary Disguises. By Wm. Cushing and Albert R. Frey. **First Series.** Royal 8vo, cloth 5.00
Half morocco 7.50
Half morocco, interleaved 10.00

INITIALS AND PSEUDONYMS. **Second Series.** Royal 8vo,
Cloth, ... 3.00
Half morocco 6.00
Half morocco, interleaved 8.00

JANE EYRE. By Charlotte Brontë. With 48 illustrations. Engraved by Andrew. 2 vols. 12mo. Cloth, gilt top 5.00
Half calf 9.00
Edition de Luxe, limited to 250 numbered copies, large paper; Japan proofs, mounted; cloth box and slip jackets 10.00

LES MISERABLES. By Victor Hugo. Translated by Isabel F. Hapgood. New edition. Complete in two volumes, with 32 full-page illustrations. 12mo. Cloth, gilt top, boxed 3.00
White back, fancy paper sides, gilt top 3.00

MARQUIS OF PENALTA (Marta y Maria). 12mo. By Valdés . . 1.50

MAXIMINA. By Don Armando Palacio Valdés. 12mo $1.50

MEDITATIONS OF A PARISH PRIEST. Thoughts by Joseph Roux. 12mo, gilt top 1.25

MEMOIRS OF NAPOLEON BONAPARTE. By Bourrienne. 34 portraits engraved on wood. 4 vols. 12mo, cloth, plain . . . 5.00
Cloth, gilt top, uncut edges, paper label 6.00
Half calf 10.00
Half levant morocco 15.00
Limited edition with over 100 illustrations, gilt top, half leather . . 10.00

METZEROTT, SHOEMAKER. A powerful novel, by Katharine Pearson Woods, treating of modern socialism. 12mo 1.50

Miller's Works:

MAKING THE MOST OF LIFE. By Rev. J. R. Miller, D.D. 16mo. White back, gilt top, boxed 1.00
Levant morocco, flexible, gilt edge 2.50

SILENT TIMES. By Rev. J. R. Miller, D.D. 16mo. White back, gilt top, boxed 1.00
Levant morocco, padded, gilt edge 2.50

THE EVERY DAY OF LIFE. By Rev. J. R. Miller, D.D. 16mo. White back, gilt top, boxed 1.00
Levant morocco, flexible gilt edges 2.50

MULLER'S LIFE OF TRUST. 12mo 1.50

PAYING THE PENALTY. By Gibbon, Fenn, and others. 12mo . 1.00

PELOUBET'S NOTES. 8vo 1.25

PLEA FOR THE GOSPEL, A. By the Rev. George D. Herron, author of "The Larger Christ," "The Message of Jesus to Men of Wealth." 12mo 75

POLISHED STONES AND SHARPENED ARROWS. By C. W. Bibb. A manual for Christian Workers. Cloth, 12mo 1.25

POLLY BUTTON'S NEW YEAR. By Mrs. C. F. Wilder, author of "Sister Rednour's Sacrifice," "Land of the Rising Sun," etc. 18mo, unique ornamental binding 75

PORTABLE COMMENTARY. By Jamieson, Fausset, and Brown. 2 vols. Crown 8vo 3.50

RECOLLECTIONS OF A PRIVATE. A Story of the Army of the Potomac. By Warren Lee Goss, author of "Jed; a Boy's Adventures in the Army of '61-'65," "The Soldier's Story of his Captivity at Andersonville and other Prisons." Illustrated with over 80 spirited engravings by Chapin and Shelton. 8vo.
Cloth 3.00
Seal Russia. Marbled edges 4.00
Half morocco. Marbled edges 5.00

ROGET'S THESAURUS OF ENGLISH WORDS AND PHRASES. New edition, revised and enlarged by the author's son, J. L. Roget.
Crown 8vo, cloth 2.00
" " " indexed 2.50
" " half calf, indexed 4.00

ROBBER COUNT, THE. By Julius Wolff 1.25

SALTMASTER (THE) OF LUNEBURG. By Julius Wolff. 12mo, 1.50

SHILLABER'S (Mrs.) COOK BOOK. 12mo, cloth 1.25
Kitchen edition in oilcloth 1.25

SISTER SAINT SULPICE. By Valdés. With portrait. 12mo. . $1.50

SHIPTON'S (Anna) WORKS. 11 vols. 16mo, cloth 6.60

Asked of God.
Lost Blessing.
Sure Mercies of David.
"Tell Jesus."
Waiting Hours.
Promise and Promiser.
Secret of the Lord.
Wayside Service.
The Watch-Tower.
Precious Gems.
The Lord was There.

SIGRID. An Icelandic Love Story 1.25

SOUL'S INQUIRIES ANSWERED. 18mo 50
Interleaved, red edges 75
" gilt edges 1.00
" seal leather, flexible 1.50

ST. JOHN'S EVE. By Nikolaï V. Gogol. 12mo 1.25

SUMMER LEGENDS. By Rudolph Baumbach. Translated by Helen B. Dole. 16mo, gilt top, laid paper, parti-color binding . . . 1.00

SURE MERCIES OF DAVID. Presentation edition, cloth, 18mo, boxed 1.00

TARAS BULBA. By Nikolaï V. Gogol. 12mo 1.00

TELL JESUS. Presentation edition. Cloth, 18mo, boxed 1.00

TENNYSON'S POEMS. New edition. Complete in two volumes. Illustrated with two photogravures and numerous wood engravings by the best artists. 2 vols. 12mo. Gilt top 3.00
White back, fancy paper sides, gilt top 3.00

TENNYSON'S POEMS. A new and complete edition. Illustrated by Church, Dielman, Schell, Harry Fenn, and other artists. With portrait, 24 full-page illustrations, and vignette titles, engraved by Andrew. The finest edition of Tennyson ever published in this country. Royal 8vo, full morocco, gilt edge 6.00

TENNYSON'S WORKS. Handy volume edition. 8 vols. Cloth, gilt top, neat cloth case 6.00
Half Russia, gilt edges, leather box uniform with binding . . . 12.00
Half calf, gilt edges, fancy leatherette case 12.00
American seal Russia, gilt edges, round corners, fancy leatherette case, 15.00
Tree calf, gilt edges, in calf box 30.00

THREE TIMES TRIED. By Farjeon, Allen, and others. 12mo . $1.00

TOLSTOI'S WORKS. 9 vols. 12mo, cloth	13.00
Half calf, extra	25.00
Anna Karénina	1.25
Childhood, Boyhood, and Youth **What to do**	1.50
Ivan Ilyitch **Family Happiness**	1.50
My Confession **My Religion** **Life**	1.50
Napoleon's Russian Campaign **Power and Liberty** **The Long Exile**	1.50
The Invaders **A Russian Proprietor**	1.50
Sevastopol **The Cossacks**	1.50
War and Peace, 2 vols.	3.00
War and Peace, 4 vols. Gilt top	5.00
Gospel Stories. 12mo	1.25

TOM BROWN'S SCHOOL DAYS. By Thomas Hughes. With 53 illustrations. Engraved by Andrew. 12mo, cloth 2.00

Full gilt edges 2.50

Edition de Luxe, limited to 250 numbered copies, large paper, Japan proofs mounted; cloth box and slip jackets 5.00

VAGRANT, THE, AND OTHER TALES. By Vladimir Korolenko. 1.25

WALTON'S COMPLETE ANGLER. New edition. Complete in two volumes. With all the original 86 illustrations of Major's edition, and two additional photogravures. 2 vols. 16mo. Gilt top 2.50

WEB OF GOLD, A. By the author of "Metzerott, Shoemaker." 12mo, 1.25

WORDSWORTH'S POEMS. Selected by Matthew Arnold, and illustrated in photogravure by Edmund H. Garrett. Printed from new plates on fine dekle edge laid paper. 12mo. *Cloth*, ornamental design, gilt top. Cloth box 2.50

Full leather, gilt top, boxed 3.50

MONICA, THE MESA MAIDEN. By Mrs. Evelyn H. Raymond, author of "Mixed Pickles." Illustrated. 12mo 1.25

STANDARD WORKS IN SETS.

FINE ILLUSTRATED EDITIONS.

LES MISÉRABLES. By Victor Hugo. Illustrated Edition. 160 full-page illustrations. Translated by Isabel F. Hapgood. 12mo, cloth, gilt top, 5 vols. $7.50
Half calf, extra 15.00
Half crushed morocco 17.50
Half crushed levant 20.00

HUGO'S (Victor) Works. Illustrated Edition. Over 600 illustrations. Calendered paper. *Cloth, gilt top*, 15 *vols.* 12mo 22.50
Half calf, extra 45.00
Half crushed morocco 52.50
Half crushed levant 60.00

Volumes in this set boxed and sold separately in cloth and half calf as follows:—

Les Misérables.	5 vols.	cloth 7.50	Half calf	15.00
Notre-Dame.	2 vols.	" 3.00	" "	6.00
Ninety-three.	2 vols.	" 3.00	" "	6.00
Toilers of the Sea.	2 vols.	" 3.00	" "	6.00
History of a Crime.	2 vols.	" 3.00	" "	6.00
By Order of the King.	2 vols.	" 3.00	" "	6.00

HUGO (Victor) Works. Library Edition. Illustrated. The above fifteen volumes bound in 10 *volumes*, cloth, gilt top. (Sold only in sets), 15.00
Half calf 30.00

POPULAR EDITIONS.

HUGO'S (Victor) Works. Popular Edition. 6 vols. 12mo, cloth . . 7.50
Half calf, 7 vols. 14.00
Half pebble calf, Roger Payne Finish, gilt top, 7 vols 13.00

Volumes in this set sold separately in cloth.

Les Misérables 1.25
Notre-Dame 1.25
Ninety-three 1.25
Toilers of the Sea 1.25
History of a Crime 1.25
By Order of the King 1.25

LES MISÉRABLES. Popular Edition. 5 vols. 12mo.
Half Russia 6.00
Half pebble calf, Roger Payne Finish, gilt top 7.50

IRVING'S (Washington), Complete Works. Popular Edition. 8 vols 8.00
Library Edition, leather titles, gilt top 10.00
Half calf 12.00
Half Russia 10.00
Half pebble calf, Roger Payne Finish, gilt top 11.00

COUNT TOLSTOI'S MASTERPIECES. 6 vols. 12mo. Half Persian levant 12.00
War and Peace. 4 vols.
Anna Karénina. 2 vols.

CHARLES DICKENS'S COMPLETE WORKS.

A NEW EDITION IN 15 AND 30 VOLUMES.

Printed from new electrotype plates made from new, large-faced type, well leaded. All the mechanical details — paper, press-work, illustrations, and binding — are first class in every respect.

15 VOLUME EDITION. Carefully printed on fine machine-finish paper, with 240 full-page illustrations. Large 12mo.

Popular Edition.	15 vols., cloth	Per set	$18.75
" "	15 vols., half calf, marbled edges	"	37.50
Library Edition.	15 vols., cloth, gilt top	"	22.50
" "	15 vols., half calf, gilt top	"	45.00

Volumes sold separately in cloth styles as follows: —

Pickwick Papers,	16	illus., popular,	cloth,	$1.25	Library,	cloth,	1.50
Nicholas Nickleby,	16	"	"	1.25	"	"	1.50
Martin Chuzzlewit,	16	"	"	1.25	"	"	1.50
Old Curiosity Shop and Reprinted Pieces,	16	"	"	1.25	"	"	1.50
Barnaby Rudge, and Hard Times,	16	"	"	1.25	"	"	1.50
Dombey and Son,	16	"	"	1.25	"	"	1.50
David Copperfield,	16	"	"	1.25	"	"	1.50
Our Mutual Friend,	16	"	"	1.25	"	"	1.50
Bleak House,	16	"	"	1.25	"	"	1.50
Little Dorrit,	16	"	"	1.25	"	"	1.50
Uncommercial Traveller and Christmas Stories,	16	"	"	1.25	"	"	1.50
Oliver Twist, Pictures from Italy, and American Notes,	16	"	"	1.25	"	"	1.50
Christmas Books and Great Expectations,	16	"	"	1.25	"	"	1.50
Tale of Two Cities and Sketches by Boz,	16	"	"	1.25	"	"	1.50
Child's History of England and Edwin Drood, etc.	16	"	"	1.25	"	"	1.50

DICKENS'S WORKS — Continued.

30 VOLUME EDITION. With all the original illustrations by Phiz, Cruikshank, etc., and many later ones, to which have been added 65 new cuts from etchings by Pailthorpe, contained in no other edition, and a steel portrait, making, in all, 799 full-page illustrations. Printed on fine calendered paper, large 12mo.

30 volumes, gilt top, cloth, gilt back . . .	Per set . .	$40.00
" " gilt top, cloth, plain back	" . .	40.00
" " half calf, gilt top	" . .	80.00
" " half crushed levant	" . .	110.00

Volumes sold separately in the plain back, cloth binding, as follows:—

Pickwick Papers	2 vols.,	66 illustrations . .	3.00
Nicholas Nickleby	2 "	39 " . .	3.00
Martin Chuzzlewit	2 "	40 " . .	3.00
Old Curiosity Shop	2 "	79 " . .	3.00
Barnaby Rudge	2 "	82 " . .	3.00
Dombey and Son	2 "	40 " . .	3.00
David Copperfield	2 "	40 " . .	3.00
Our Mutual Friend	2 "	40 " . .	3.00
Bleak House	2 "	40 " . .	3.00
Little Dorrit	2 "	40 " . .	3.00
Uncommercial Traveller		8 " . .	1.50
Christmas Stories		14 " . .	1.50
Oliver Twist		45 " . .	1.50
Pictures from Italy and American Notes . .		8 " . .	1.50
Christmas Books		65 " . .	1.50
Great Expectations		37 " . .	1.50
Tale of Two Cities		16 " . .	1.50
Sketches by Boz		40 " . .	1.50
Child's History of England		19 " . .	1.50
Edwin Drood and Miscellaneous		41 " . .	1.50

STANDARD BOOKS FOR YOUNG PEOPLE.

MRS. BOLTON'S BOOKS.

FAMOUS TYPES OF WOMANHOOD. By Sarah K. Bolton. With portraits of Queen Louise, Madam Recamier, Desirée, Miss Dix, Jenny Lind, Susanna Wesley, Harriet Martineau, etc. 12mo . . $1.50

FAMOUS ENGLISH STATESMEN. By Sarah K. Bolton. With Portraits of Gladstone, John Bright, Robert Peel, etc. 12mo . . $1.50

FAMOUS ENGLISH AUTHORS OF THE NINETEENTH CENTURY. By Sarah K. Bolton. With Portraits of Scott, Burns, Carlyle, Dickens, Tennyson, Robert Browning, etc. 12mo . . 1.50

FAMOUS EUROPEAN ARTISTS. By Sarah K. Bolton. With portraits of Raphael, Titian, Landseer, Reynolds, Rubens, Turner, and others. 12mo 1.50

FAMOUS AMERICAN AUTHORS. By Sarah K. Bolton. With Portraits of Longfellow, Holmes, Emerson, Lowell, Aldrich, and other noted writers. 12mo, ... 1.50

FAMOUS AMERICAN STATESMEN. By Sarah K. Bolton, with portraits of Sumner, Clay, Jackson, Webster, etc. 12mo . . . 1.50

FAMOUS MEN OF SCIENCE. By Sarah K. Bolton. With Portraits of Agassiz, Darwin, Linnæus, etc. 1.50

GIRLS WHO BECAME FAMOUS. By Sarah K. Bolton. With 20 Portraits. Companion book to "Poor Boys Who Became Famous." 12mo 1.50

POOR BOYS WHO BECAME FAMOUS. By Sarah K. Bolton. With 24 portraits. 12mo 1.50

STORIES FROM LIFE. By Sarah K. Bolton. 12mo 1.25

MRS. FARMER'S BOOKS.

BOYS' BOOK OF FAMOUS RULERS. By Lydia Hoyt Farmer. With portraits. Lives of Agamemnon, Julius Cæsar, Charlemagne, Frederick the Great, Napoleon, etc. 12mo 1.50

FRENCH REVOLUTION (THE), A short history of. By Lydia Hoyt Farmer. Fully Illustrated 1.50

GIRLS' BOOK OF FAMOUS QUEENS. By Lydia Hoyt Farmer. With portraits. Lives of Cleopatra, Queen Elizabeth, Catherine de Medicis, Josephine, etc. 12mo 1.50

LA FAYETTE. The Knight of Liberty. By Lydia Hoyt Farmer. Fully illustrated. 12mo 1.50

TOM CLIFTON; or, Western Boys with Grant and Sherman. By Warren Lee Goss, author of "Jed," etc. Fully illustrated. 12mo. 1.50

JED: A BOY'S ADVENTURES IN THE ARMY IN "61." By Warren Lee Goss. Fully illustrated. 12mo 1.50

JO-BOAT BOYS, THE. By Rev. J. F. Cowan, D.D., editor of "Our Young People." Illustrated by H. W. Peirce. 12mo 1.50

MOTHER OF THE KING'S CHILDREN, THE. By Rev. J. F. Cowan, D.D., author of "Jo-Boat Boys." Illustrated by H. W. Peirce. 12mo 1.50

FAMOUS COMPOSERS, A SCORE OF. By Nathan Haskell Dole. With portraits of Beethoven, Wagner, Liszt, Haydn, etc. 12mo . 1.50

AN ENTIRE STRANGER. By Rev. T. L. Baily. Illustrated. 12mo, $1.25
BOYHOOD OF LIVING AUTHORS. By Wm. H. Rideing. 12mo, 1.00
CAPTAIN'S DOG (The). By Louis Énault. 12mo, 18 illustrations . 1.00
CHRISTMAS COUNTRY. Translated from the Danish and German . 1.25
CECIL'S KNIGHT. By E. B. Hollis. 12mo. 1.25
CUORE. An Italian Schoolboy's Journal. By Edmondo de Amicis. 12mo 1.25
"FAIRY LEGENDS OF THE FRENCH PROVINCES" . . . 1.25
GENERAL GORDON, The Christian Hero. 12mo 1.25

Homer Greene's Books:
BLIND BROTHER (The). 12mo, illustrated 90
BURNHAM BREAKER. 12mo, illustrated 1.50
RIVERPARK REBELLION (The). 12mo, illustrated . . . 1.00

HINTS TO OUR BOYS. Square 16mo 50
HOME IN THE HOLY LAND. 12mo illustrated 1.50
IN PERILS OFT. By W. H. Davenport Adams. 12mo. Illustrated . 1.50

J A K Books:
BIRCHWOOD. By J A K. 12mo, illustrated 1.25
FITCH CLUB. By J A K. 12mo, illustrated 1.25
GIANT DWARF (The). By J A K. 12mo, illustrated 1.25
PROFESSOR JOHNNY. By J A K. 12mo, illustrated 1.25
RIVERSIDE MUSEUM. By J A K. 12mo, illustrated 1.25
ROLF AND HIS FRIENDS. By J A K. 12mo. Illustrated . . 1.25
SCOTCH CAPS. By J A K. 12mo. Illustrated 1.25
WHO SAVED THE SHIP? By J A K. 12mo. Illustrated. . . 1.25

LED IN UNKNOWN PATHS. By Anna F. Raffensperger. 12mo . 1.25
LITTLE ARTHUR'S ENGLAND. 12mo, illustrated 1.25
LITTLE ARTHUR'S FRANCE. 12mo, illustrated 1.25
LITTLE ARTHUR'S ROME. By Hezekiah Butterworth. 12mo . 1.25
MAKERS OF ENGLISH VERSE. By Mrs. Blanche W. Bellamy. 12mo, illustrated 1.25
MARTIN THE SKIPPER. By James F. Cobb. Illustrated . . 1.50
MIXED PICKLES. By Mrs. Evelyn Raymond. 12mo, illustrated . 1.25
MUSICAL JOURNEY, THE, OF DOROTHY AND DELIA. By the Rev. Bradley Gilman. Profusely illustrated. 12mo, unique binding .50
MUTINY ON THE LEANDER. By Bernard Heldmann. Illustrated. 1.50
OFF TO THE WILDS. By George Manville Fenn. 12mo. Illustrated, 1.50
PHILIP. A Story of the First Century. By Mrs. Mary C. Cutler. 12mo, 1.00
PRINCES, AUTHORS, AND STATESMEN OF OUR TIME. By Canon Farrar, James T. Fields, and other popular writers. Edited by James Parton. 60 illustrations. 1 vol. 8vo, cloth 2.50

Anna Chapin Ray's Books:
HALF A DOZEN BOYS. 12mo, illustrated 1.25
HALF A DOZEN GIRLS. 12mo, illustrated 1.25
IN BLUE CREEK CANON. 12mo, illustrated 1.25
CADETS OF FLEMMING HALL. 12mo, illustrated 1.25

RED CARL. From the German of J. J. Messmer. 12mo, illustrated 1.25
SEARCH FOR THE STAR; or, Life in Wild Woods of Maine. By Edward Willett. 9 illustrations, 12mo. 1.25

SHORT STUDIES IN BOTANY FOR CHILDREN. By Harriet C. Cooper. Fully illustrated. 12mo. 1.00

THROWN UPON HER OWN RESOURCES; or, What Girls Can Do. By Jenny June. 12mo, with portrait of the author 1.00

WALKS ABROAD OF TWO YOUNG NATURALISTS. From the French of Charles Beaugrand, by David Sharp, M.B., F.L.S., F.Z.S., President of Entomological Society, London. Fully illustrated. 8vo, $1.50

WATCHERS ON THE LONGSHIPS. By James F. Cobb. Illustrated, 1.50

WHAT FIDE REMEMBERS. By Faye Huntington. Illustrated . 1.25

WHITE CROSS AND DOVE OF PEARLS. By the author of Laura Linwood 1.50

WRECKED ON LABRADOR. By Winfrid A. Stearns. 12mo . . 1.50

CLASSIC JUVENILES, BY JACOB ABBOTT.

"The Prince of Writers for the Young."

ABBOTT'S AMERICAN HISTORIES FOR YOUTH. Illustrated By Darley, Herrick, Chapin, and others. 4 vols. (2 vols. in one) . $6.00

AUGUST STORIES. 4 vols. Illustrated. 16mo 4.50

JUNO STORIES. 4 vols. Illustrated. 16mo 4.50

JONAS BOOKS. 6 vols. bound in 3. Illustrated. 16mo . . . 3.75

LUCY BOOKS. 6 vols. bound in 3. Illustrated. 16mo 3.75

ROLLO BOOKS. 14 vols. in 7. Illustrated. 16mo 8.75

WALTER'S TOUR. 6 vols. 6.00

ADVENTURE LIBRARY. Fully illustrated. New and uniform style of binding. 5 vols. 12mo 7.50

In Perils Oft. By W. H. Davenport Adams. 12mo.
Mutiny on the Leander. By Bernard Heldmann. 12mo.
Martin the Skipper. By James F. Cobb. 12mo.
Off to the Wilds. By George Manville Fenn. 12mo.
Watchers on the Longships. By James F. Cobb. 12mo.

BIRCHWOOD SERIES. By J A K. 8 vols. 12mo 10.00

DOVE SERIES. 6 vols. Illustrated. 16mo 5.00

FARMER BOY SERIES. By Rev. Wm. M. Thayer. 16mo. 4 vols. 4.25

Farmer Boy. Good Girl and True Woman.
Poor Boy and Merchant Prince. Country Boy in the City.

GEORGEY'S MENAGERIE. Ry Madeline Leslie. 6 vols. Illustrated. 16mo 4.50

HANDY VOLUME CLASSICS.

An entirely new line of standard books in prose and poetry. Handy in size, carefully printed on good paper, and bound in faultless styles. Each volume is illustrated with a frontispiece and title-page, in photogravure, and most of the volumes have numerous additional illustrations by the best artists.

PARTI-COLORED CLOTH : white back, gilt side, gilt top, boxed, 23 vols., 18mo. Per vol., $1.00.

1. Browning (Robert) selections, 2 vols.
2. Burns's Poems. "
3. Lady of the Lake.
4. Lalla Rookh.
5. Lucile.
6. Poe's Poems.
7. Tennyson's Idylls of the King.
8. " In Memoriam.
9. " The Princess.
10. " Early Sonnets, etc.
11. " Locksley Hall, etc.
12. Wordsworth (selections).

---

13. Carlyle's Heroes and Hero Worship.
14. " Sartor Resartus.
15. Emerson's Essays, 2 vols.
16. Paul and Virginia
17. Pilgrim's Progress.
18. Ruskin's Crown of Wild Olive.
19. " Sesame and Lilies.
20. Vicar of Wakefield.

21 Cranford.

(Other volumes in preparation.)

All of the above volumes are bound uniformly in the following additional styles:

Cloth, Vellum Finish, neat gold border, full gilt edges, boxed, 18mo, per vol. $1.00
Silk, stamped in gold, full gilt edges, boxed, 18mo, per vol. 1.50
Half Calf, gilt top, boxed, 18mo, per vol. 2.00
Half Levant, gilt top, boxed, 18mo, per vol. 2.50

This attractive series is sure to be a favorite with those desiring something new and dainty for gifts or for the drawing-room table, and with the general reader or student who prefers his reading in small, companionable volumes.

For sale by all Booksellers, or sent postpaid by the publishers upon receipt of price.

CROWELL'S POETS.

HALF RUSSIA, Marbled Edges. Without Red Lines. In new and attractive style of binding. 108 vols., 12mo $1.00

1 Arnold (Edwin).
2 Arnold (Matthew).
3 Aurora Leigh.
4 Aytoun.
5 Beauties of Shakespeare.
6 British Female Poets.
7 Browning (Mrs.).
8 Browning (Robert).
9 Bryant.
10 Burns.
11 Byron.
12 Calverley.
13 Campbell.
14 Chaucer.
15 Childe Harold.
16 Christian Year.
17 Coleridge.
18 Cook (Eliza).
19 Cowper.
20 Crabbe.
21 Dante.
22 Dryden.
23 Eliot (George).
24 Familiar Quotations.
25 Famous Poems.
26 Favorite Poems.
27 Faust (Goethe's).
28 Frenau's Poems.
29 Gems, 1001.
30 Goethe's Poems.
31 Golden Treasury.
32 Goldsmith.
33 Gray, Thomas.
34 Greene, Marlowe and Jonson.
35 Half Hours with the Poets.
36 Halleck, Fitz-Greene.
37 Heber, Bishop.
38 Heine.
39 Hemans.
40 Herbert.
41 Hood.
42 Hugo (Victor).
43 Iliad.
44 Imitation of Christ.
45 Ingoldsby Legends.
46 Irish Humorous Poems.
47 Jean Ingelow.
48 Keats.
49 Kingsley.
50 Lady of the Lake.
51 Lalla Rookh.
52 Lay of the Last Minstrel.
53 Longfellow (Early Poems).
54 Lowell (James Russell) (Early Poems).

55 Lucile.
56 Macaulay.
57 Marmion.
58 Meredith (Owen).
59 Milton.
60 Moore.
61 Motherwell.
62 Mulock (Miss).
63 Odyssey.
64 Ossian.
65 Paradise Lost.
66 Percy's Reliques.
67 Petrarch.
68 Pilgrim's Progress.
69 Poe.
70 Poetry of Flowers.
71 Poetry of Love.
72 Poetry of Passion.
73 Poetry of Sentiment.
74 Poets of America.
75 Pope.
76 Praed.
77 Procter.
78 Red Letter Poems.
79 Religious Poems.
80 Rogers.
81 Rossetti.
82 Schiller.
83 Scott.
84 Shakespeare (1 vol.).
85 Shakespeare (2 vols.).
86 Shelley.
87 Smith, Alex.
88 Songs, Household.
89 Songs, Sacred and Devotional.
90 Southey.
91 Spanish Ballads.
92 Spenser.
93 Swinburne.
94 Tasso.
95 Taylor's Philip Van Artevelde.
96 Thackeray.
97 Tupper.
98 Tennyson.
99 Thomson.
100 Vers de Société.
101 Virgil.
102 War Songs.
103 Wesley.
104 White, Kirke.
105 Whittier (Early Poems).
106 Willis.
107 Wordsworth.

THE IMPERIAL EDITION OF STANDARD POETICAL WORKS.

All of the volumes in this new line of poets are printed from *our own plates* on fine paper, illustrated with 8 full-page illustrations by the best artists, and bound in a durable and tasteful style. The volumes are *complete* (with the one exception indicated), and have biographical and critical notes when essential. These volumes will, therefore, fill the need of good editions of standard poets suitable for library or holiday use at popular prices.

CLOTH, Full Gilt Edges. 20 vols. Full 12mo. Per vol. . . $1.50

1 Browning (Mrs.).
2 Browning, Robert (selections).
3 Burns.
4 Byron.
5 Dictionary of Quotations.
6 Favorite Poems.
7 Golden Treasury.
8 Goldsmith.
9 Jean Ingelow.
10 Lady of the Lake.
11 Lalla Rookh.
12 Lucile.
13 Meredith.
14 Milton.
15 Moore.
16 Red Letter Poems.
17 Scott.
18 Shakespeare.
19 Tennyson.
20 Wordsworth.